BACON, BEANS, AND GALANTINES

JOSEPH R. CONLIN

FOOD AND FOODWAYS ON THE WESTERN MINING FRONTIER

RENO & LAS VEGAS : UNIVERSITY OF NEVADA PRESS

BACON, BEANS, AND GALANTINES

The paper used in this book meets the requirements
of American National Standard for Information
Sciences—Permanence of Paper for
Printed Library Materials, ANSI Z39.48-1984.
Binding materials were chosen
for strength and durability.

Library of Congress Cataloging-in-Publication Data

Conlin, Joseph Robert.
    Bacon, beans, and galantines.

    Bibliography: p.
    Includes index.
    1. Diet—West (U.S.)—History. 2. Food habits—
West (U.S.)—History. 3. Mines and mineral resources—
West (U.S.)—History. 4. Miners—West (U.S.)—
History. I. Title.
TX360.U6C635   1986   394.1'0978   86-11365
ISBN 0-87417-105-9 (alk. paper)

University of Nevada Press,
Reno, Nevada 89557 USA
© Joseph R. Conlin 1986.
Book and jacket design by Steve Renick
Printed in the United States of America

OTHER BOOKS BY JOSEPH R. CONLIN

Glencoe Press, 1969   American Antiwar Movements

Syracuse University Press, 1969   Big Bill Haywood and the Radical Union Movement

Greenwood Press, 1970   Bread and Roses Too: Essays on the Wobblies

Greenwood Press, 1974   The American Radical Press, 1880–1960

Greenwood Press, 1982   At the Point of Production: The Local History of the I.W.W.

Franklin Watts, 1982   The Troubles: A Jaundiced Glance Back at the Movement of the 1960s

Harcourt Brace Jovanovich, 1984   The American Past

Morrow, 1984   Morrow Book of Quotations in American History

Coronado Publishers, 1984   Our Land, Our Time

Harcourt Brace Jovanovich, 1986   An American Harvest (with C. H. Peterson)

To the Memory of
A Kind and Generous Father

JOSEPH R. CONLIN

1917 – 1985

CONTENTS

INTRODUCTION

In the spring of the centennial year, very likely after a meal at one of Virginia City's numerous restaurants, a Nevada journalist reflected that "when the history of the Comstock is written, a chapter should be given to the miner's lunch can." The first historian of the great lode, who threw his legs under more than a few mining camp tables, fully agreed. In *Comstock Mining and Miners,* published in 1883, Eliot Lord paid close attention to food and what it meant in the lives of the miners and their womenfolk.[1]

Likewise, when old sourdoughs, hard rock men, engineers, speculators, and other denizens of the gold and silver frontier reminisced about the part they had played in opening the West, they remembered that they had needed "three square" a day through both borrasca and bonanza. Wistfully sometimes, they could rattle off whole menus from appetizer to dessert.

The people who ushered in that half-century-long era, the forty-niners, or at least those seven hundred-odd pilgrims who kept diaries that still survive, had plenty to say about food and the periodic lack of it. So did decidedly uncrusty pioneers like Dame Shirley and Mrs. Hugh Brown, respectively the first literary woman to write about American metal miners and the sophisticated and the charming wife of a lawyer in the last of the boomtowns, Tonopah and Goldfield, Nevada. Mrs. Brown vividly recalled the savor of strawberries rushed across the high desert at a gallop to grace a picnic of town notables. For her, that gastronomical trifle encapsulated as well as any other memory the bizarre juxtaposition of elegance and rawness that bemused so many visitors to the western mining frontier and, since, has intrigued historians.[2]

They—historians—are notoriously not negligent of their own bellies. The American Historical Association includes a restaurant guide in the packets distributed to registrants at its annual convention in late December and—not because members like to arrive early for the Sugar Bowl—New Orleans is one of the organization's favorite host cities. The Western History Association features two inevitably fine communal feeds at its annual meetings. And recently I heard of an academic historian from the Golden State who wept openly at a meeting of his institution's Faculty Senate because salaries rose only 7 percent during a year when Pacific storms caused the price of Dungeness crab to double.

And yet there is not much about food in those historians' work. I am not sure why this is so. It may simply have to do with the fact that most American historians lecture or jog during the day and write at night after a good supper has rendered aliments of no compelling urgency. Or the explanation may be buried in all sorts of obscure psychoanalysis that, in a book that is in part about good taste, shall be discussed no further. The fact remains that we seem to have forgotten that for the men and women of the past—of the metal mining frontier in this instance—eating was just as much a part of their lives as were dreaming of riches, laboring to survive and prosper, coupling and loving, and fighting one another across courtrooms, tables, bars, and impromptu breastworks of timber and tailings. It is possible to read a dozen otherwise excellent histories about the western miners and conclude that they and their neighbors never put anything into their mouths save whiskey and the fuse to be inserted directly into a stick of Alfred Nobel's powerful invention.[3] Except when their subjects were actually starving, most historians have regarded food, meals, preferences, table manners, and the like as trivial. To study food of the past meant little more than to compile amusing lists, the work of antiquarians, those amateurs who run errands for "real historians" when their duties take them to county historical societies. Indeed, the historians' traditional characterization of antiquarianism has zeroed in on the kitchen: antiquarianism is "just pots and pans."

I may be beating a dead horse here. Increasingly in recent years, impressed by the research into food history by the *Annales* school in France and John L. Yudkin's Queen Elizabeth College group in England and inspired by Daniel Boorstin's imaginative treatment of the subject in his monumental *The Americans,* historians are beginning to write serious studies in food history. The field is still in its infancy, but we are beginning to recognize that, even if it has not been by bread alone that men and women have lived, bread is a part of the story and, in the case of the western miners, beans and galantine truffles are too.

How big a part? That is a question yet to be answered. Anthropologists Peter Farb and George Armelagos surely go too far when they write that when we find out "where, when, and with whom the food is eaten, just about everything else can be inferred about the relations among the society's members."[4] Working with the most fragmentary shards of evidence as they do, anthropologists are incorrigible overreachers. Still, food is third only to air and water as a basis of life and, much more than the others, is an important element of culture and social relationships. People eat for reasons other than just to fuel up. Human beings encumber the circumstances of their dining with a complex of rituals, symbols, and explicit meanings. Surely the most cautious historian can agree with Farb and Armelagos when they write that food "is inseparable from the behavior and biology of the human species and from the adaption that humans have made to the conditions of existence on the planet. Cultural traits, social institutions, national histories, and individual attitudes cannot be entirely understood without an understanding of how these have meshed with our varied and peculiar modes of eating."[5]

And so, whatever the inadequacies of this book, it is not a mere inventory of the pots and pans in the wagon trains, gulches, and bonanza mining towns. I expect I have more likely erred in the direction of unwarranted inferences, such as I have twitted the anthropologists for, and self-indulgent digressions rather than toward antiquarianism. In any case, while presenting concrete information about nutrition on the overland trail and in the mining camps, about tastes and food habits, I have also tried to relate this material to some larger themes of the history of the American West.

J. R. C.
May 1986

ACKNOWLEDGMENTS

Although I have been interested in the social history of food for some years, and in western metal miners a good deal longer, my study of this particular subject owes more to the suggestions and encouragement of others than to any ingenuity and industry to which I might lay claim. I first began to investigate the food of the mining frontier when Professor James D. Foster of Arizona State University asked me to prepare a paper on the state of nutrition among the miners as a companion to his study of miners' vocational diseases, presented at the April 1980 meeting of the Organization of American Historians. The somewhat gimcrack result was kindly received but, as will happen when historians are in consistory, roundly and justly criticized by John C. Burnham of Ohio State University, Judith Walzer Leavitt of the University of Wisconsin, and William Graebner of the State University of New York, Fredonia. I am indebted to them, particularly to Professor Burnham, whose talent for cutting to essentials is exceeded only by his grace in wielding the scalpel. I wish I could say I have buried every one of their suggestions under definitive research and erudition. But, like the good scholars they are, they asked me questions of the sort they ask themselves, the tough kind that will not easily lie down.

Harwood P. Hinton, the distinguished editor of *Arizona and the West,* was kind enough to urge me to write down my remarks for publication. They appeared in that journal in Spring 1981 under a title slightly different from the one on the cover of this book. Acting Editor of *Arizona* at that time, Bruce J. Dinges, vastly improved the piece with his blue pencil. The piece was later honored beyond reasonable deserts, even after these ministrations, by the Western History Association's Ray Allen Billington Prize for 1981 and the publication of additional material in *Arizona Highways, California History,* and *CHISPAS,* the excellent quarterly of the Tuolumne County, California, Historical Society.

In the meantime, Robert Laxalt, then head of the University of Nevada Press, had asked me to expand the essay into a book. May his wild speculation—a well-known frailty of the Nevadan character—not prove to have pinched out in shale and scheiss or a seven on the dice. Again I benefitted from excellent editing at the Press by Nicholas Cady, who took charge of the project from the beginning, and Megan Benton, who improved my language.

Cynthia Davis, Jean Harvey, and Nancy Riley prepared typescripts of parts of one draft or another. Several small but *sine qua non* grubstakes from the University Foundation in Chico, California, enabled me to make progress on the work when, in a phrase that was common parlance in the days of forty-nine, I was scraping the bottom of the barrel. In the spring of 1982 a grant from the American Philosophical Society's Penrose Fund enabled me to carry out research in Alaska that was otherwise beyond my means. I also fudged a bit on the terms of a research fellowship from the American Council of Learned Societies, granted in 1982 and 1983 for another project, to work on this one. I am grateful to the ACLS for its generosity.

Finally, thanks to the many librarians and archivists who, when I called on them and explained my errand, bit the sides of their index fingers and regretted that they would never be able to locate anything in their files on so vague a topic as food, and then proceeded to work miracles. Thanks also to the many historians, folklorists, archaeologists, and, yes, anthropologists and antiquarians who were kind enough to answer the many questions I put to them. The list is a long one—that is the kind of help I had—so I have warded against duplication of information in these pages by listing the names along with the institutions with which they are affiliated in the "Note on Sources" that follows the text.

xii

BACON, BEANS, AND GALANTINES

I HOME COOKING

Dab, dab, peck, peck, grunt, growl, snort! The spoon strikes in every now and then, and a quick sucking-up noise announces the disappearance of a mouthful of huckleberries on the top of a bit of bacon, or a spoonful of custard pie on the heels of a radish. It is perfectly prodigious. It defies coherent description.

A European traveler on
American eating habits, circa 1849

The first reports in the papers did not stir up much fuss. People were more keenly interested in what they would be eating at their next meal than in tales of gold in California.

And this should not be surprising. If, at the end of the twentieth century, we are sometimes taken aback by the extravagance of nineteenth-century journalism, the alternately playful and cynical indifference to facts that Mark Twain liked to satirize, we should keep in mind that the people who read those newspapers crisp were not fools. They compensated for distortion in news reports just as John C. Frémont, finding paths, compensated for magnetic deviation from true north.

Moreover, California seemed about as remote as a part of the United States could be to New Yorkers and New Englanders and Missourians of 1848. And the fact is, the first news to reach the East of James Marshall's historic stroll along the American River was not all that sensational. On August 19, 1848, the *New York Herald* reported that thirty dollars' worth of gold had been dug out of "a stream of the Sacramento." Even to a people whose experience with gold mining was practically nil—a little bit came out of North Carolina in 1799 and out of Georgia in 1829—this was hardly the sort of thing for which one threw over a farm, a decent job, a pretty young wife.[1]

Then the letters came flying eastward like shingles in a Washoe Zephyr. San Francisco was deserted. The citizenry and garrison were off in the foothills making as much as a dollar a minute. "Your streams have minnows," crowed one of the earliest California boomers, Walter Colton, "and ours are paved with gold."[2]

Heady stuff. Headier yet were the first flaky specimens to reach Missouri in late September and Washington in early October. Then the hysteria cut loose when President James K. Polk, delighted at the chance to justify the booty from a war that, in John W. Caughey's nice phrase, "had been none too popular in the United States," told Congress that he had known it all along—that there was gold in California. That was one reason he had been so avid on detaching Mexico's northernmost province from her—and "recent discoveries render it probable that these mines are more extensive and valuable than was anticipated." It was Young Hickory's proclamation of an American El Dorado that really started it all.[3]

OF THE NATURE OF 1849

It is a truism of forty-niner lore that within one short year there were already too many men moiling in the dirt of California for too little gold. In that one turn of the calendar forty-two thousand traveled overland; fifteen hundred went via Panama; six thousand Mexicans trekked north; and forty-one thousand Americans and sundry foreigners sailed around Cape Horn, all hastening to the Pacific coast. The sheer numbers explain why so few got rich and why the vast majority either returned home chastened, encapsulating their comeuppance in the catch phrase, "I have seen the elephant"; took up farming or ranching in California; became wage workers or businessmen; or joined that permanently disoriented but visionary swarm of men who wafted frantically as hummingbirds from one new diggings to another for half a century.[4]

It is easy for us, in our twentieth-century smugness, to wax superior or sentimental when we think about the forty-niners, and the fifty-niners in Colorado and Nevada, and the ninety-eighters in the Klondike and Alaska. In fact, the recklessness and romance of what they did can be overstated and often is. They were excited all right, but most of those men and women knew pretty much what we know about the realities and risks of what they were doing. The very reason California was inundated so quickly by Americans, Sonorans, Chileans, Chinese, and dreamers from virtually every country in Europe, and why Colorado and the Comstock and the Klondike and hundreds

I Have Seen the Elephant

When a forty-niner gave up—"threw in the towel," we might say—he said, "I have seen the elephant." The catch phrase was adopted from a joke then making the rounds in the United States: A farmer learned that the circus was in town and featured a wondrous Indian elephant, something he had always wanted to see. Thinking to combine the experience with a marketing trip, he loaded the wagon with a month's produce in eggs, vegetables, and fruit.

As he drove into town, the elephant appeared from an alley beside the livery stable, frightened the farmer's horses so that they panicked, reared, bucked, and bolted, dumping the wagon, smashing eggs, spoiling the fruits and vegetables, and tossing the farmer to the ground, breaking his nose, an arm, and a leg. "Never mind," he told his wife when he was carried back home. "I have seen the elephant."

The forty-niners put two constructions on the tale. One has the farmer—the forty-niner—commenting wryly on his foolishness and well-deserved comeuppance. To others, however, the experience of crossing the great continent, the accomplishment of doing so, was the elephant. A man's quest for gold might indeed have been a disaster, but there was a glory in the doing.

of gold and silver camps in the West boomed so big and so suddenly, was that those who rushed there all knew that only the first on the scene had the remotest chance of striking it rich. To call the majority that failed irresponsible fools would imply the same of every loser since the first sprint at Olympus. It was the gold seekers' very haste that made sense. To head to the site of a gold strike at any speed other than a rush would be irrational.

And Americans knew it. If gold fever was a new disease in the United States, land fever was not and every American knew in his speculative heart that only the decisive plunger might go from rags to something more comfortable. Indeed, at least one argonaut was delighted to find *fewer* frenzied competitors than he expected massing in St. Louis in April 1849. "The number of persons going to California has been quadrupedly exaggerated," William Swain wrote home to New York. Among other things this meant that "the emigration has not kept pace with the supplies sent to the Missouri frontier, and the markets here are abundantly supplied."[5]

Swain's inference that overland outfits were therefore reasonably priced should be regarded skeptically, however. In the masterful edition of Swain's diary he published in 1981, J. S. Holliday quotes another wayfarer who might easily have jostled William Swain in the crowd at Independence: "You have only to let it be known you are a Californian . . . to have the price raised 100 percent higher than that charged any other person." Then again, it is difficult to imagine what destination "any other person" buying provisions in Independence in 1849 had in mind. The subjective truth about prices seems to lie, as it does with tiresome regularity, somewhere between these two assessments.[6]

William Swain's attention to the cost of provisions at the California trailhead should also dispel any illusions that the forty-niners and participants in later rushes simply and recklessly headed to the gold-fields without a thought for domestic daily needs such as meals. It is true that we shall meet wretched souls trudging back eastward through the Nebraska country, dodging the westering wagons, visions of the elephant dancing before their burning eyes. And in the diggings themselves there were plenty of poor devils reduced to living on "grass and acorns picked from the holes in trees where they had been placed by woodpeckers."[7] But these apparitions were no more emblematic of

5

the gold rush experience than the derelicts picking through garbage within sight of high-heaped markets were representative of American cities in 1849. Insofar as nutritional disease, hunger, and starvation were social problems on the trails and in the camps of the mining frontier, they were generally avoidable and suffered mainly by the extremely imprudent and the grotesquely unlucky.

The Mormon example, the Oregon migration, to some extent the experience of the military in the West, and the recently revived Santa Fe commerce provided gold-seekers with valuable solid information on what it took to make a long overland journey through the savage parts of North America. The vast majority of the trekkers seem to have taken these counsels providently to heart, and the economies of Independence and St. Joseph, Missouri, were tuned finely to the needs of westering pilgrims. As for those who went to California by sea, they drew on provisioning practices systematized since the days of Jason.

But the story begins to rush ahead of me even as I argue that the forty-niners did not rush ahead of their good sense. This story is of the food of the western miners and the role of food in the gold and silver mines up to about the second decade of the twentieth century, when the mining frontier closed down. It considers nutrition and how diet and food customs reflected life and social relationships in the camps. It is a story of adaptation and change but also of continuity. So it will be useful to outline, albeit sketchily, the diet and food customs of Americans when, at midcentury, the mining frontier was born.

AMERICAN DIET AT MIDCENTURY

They were a very well fed people, the Americans. They were far and away the best-fed people in the world in the middle of the nineteenth century. In 1849 the mean daily energy consumption of Americans was a little more than four thousand calories, a third in excess of what today's nutritionists recommend for a fair-sized and moderately active male in the prime of life.[8]

It bears emphasis that four thousand calories is an average, computed from an aggregate that includes infants, the aged, the often deprived urban poor, Negro slaves, and no doubt some of those antisocial people of the frontier whose heads were counted but probably not their food. Indeed, we believe with some confidence that slaves on the better-managed plantations of the Deep South, whose

NOME IN THE GOOD OLD SUMMER TIME DIOMAND FRUIT CO

Newspaper readers in the States thrilled to accounts of dog teams rushing serum over Arctic wastes to Nome, but that was in the winter. In summer, this Nome market laid out a panoply of fruit that would have turned the head of a marketer in New Jersey or Georgia. (Courtesy Alaska Historical Society, Juneau)

circumstances were hardly enviable, had a daily caloric ration in excess of four thousand![9]

The significance of these figures becomes clearer when we note that consumption in the United States today is about two thousand calories per capita. Not that Americans of 1849 were overfed. They did not have to exercise in order to keep their figures as trim as the angular, bony Brother Jonathan of caricatures. They could eat so much food and thrive because only a tiny proportion of them led lives as sedentary as most of us do today.

Farmers and farm laborers, half the population at midcentury, worked long and hard. Heavy farmwork burns between five and ten calories per minute as opposed to three to five calories per minute walking from house to house peddling encyclopedias; one and a half per minute sitting at a typewriter composing a book; and a little less than that reading one while nestled in a comfortable chair. Factory work and particularly construction work was considerably more arduous in the nineteenth century than today; likewise housework was done without "modern conveniences." Even the upper classes of the era, making their way about the country on horseback (eight calories per minute at a trot, ten at a gallop) rather than in automobiles (fewer than two calories per minute), could afford a longer sit at the table than the prudent American of the 1980s.[10]

While European travelers in the United States generally found the quality of American food abysmal compared to what they knew in drawing rooms back home, all conceded that the worst-fed Americans did about as well in the quantity of their meals as Europeans of the middling sort. Geographer Samuel Griswold Goodrich described a New England breakfast as "no evanescent thing. In a farmer's family it consists of little less than ham, beef, sausages, pork, bread, butter, boiled potatoes, pies, coffee, and cider." Professor John Mack Faragher describes the daily diet of a midwestern farm family of midcentury as including two kinds of meat, eggs, cheese, butter, cream (especially in gravies), corn in one or more forms, two kinds of bread, three or four different vegetables, jellies, preserves, relishes, cake or pie, milk, coffee, tea." Edgar Allen Poe, residing in a boarding house in 1844—and it is hard to imagine it was a first-class establishment— raved that "everything" should be "in the greatest profusion."[11]

By way of contrast, in urban England during the 1840s a six-shilling worker lived on "little more than oatmeal, gruel, potatoes, and salt." Midcentury was a time when the "better sort" of peasant in *la douce France* subsisted on bread once a day and, for a treat, lard once a week. A sufficiency of meat at a sitting, even when it was lowly rabbit, was a "supreme moment" to be remembered and recounted a generation later, "a memorable occurrence of . . . youth."[12] Serious famine was still to be reckoned with in eastern Europe. Large parts of France were threatened with starvation as late as 1853.

Such travails were unknown in the United States. Waverley Root and Richard de Rochemont have conjectured that the "food riots" in New York in 1837 had more to do with prices that were merely bothersome and the necessity of eating poorer food—rye bread instead of wheat—than with serious deprivation.

Americans had an inkling, often distorted, that they were well off. Mrs. Trollope's confrontation with a milkman in Cincinnati is amusing but probably quite representative of Jacksonian era attitudes:

> "I expect your little place of an island don't grow such dreadful fine corn as you sees here?"
> "It grows no corn at all, sir."
> "Possible! no wonder, then, that we reads such awful stories in the papers of your poor people being starved to death."
> "We have wheat, however."
> "Ay, for your rich folks, but I calculate the poor seldom gets a belly full."[13]

Specific nutritional deficiency diseases seem not to have existed on a problem scale. Kwashiorkor, caused by the paucity of protein in a calorically adequate diet (a plague in the undeveloped world today), was unknown in a country both renowned and defamed for its gluttonous consumption of meat. Adult slaves, who surely must be taken as some of the worst-fixed of Americans at midcentury, probably ate on average close to half a pound of pork per day, precisely the quantity of flesh food that, as a ration, was enough to entice French peasants to join the army. The lot of the Irish "wage slaves" of the North cannot be as reliably quantified. But it is fair to recall the old chestnut about illiterate Paddy, writing home to Ireland through his priest: "Why do you say you eat meat twice a week," the father asks, "when you know very well you have it twice a day?"

"Because," Paddy replies, "if I tell the truth, no one will believe me."

Half a century later, in order to explain the comparative conservatism of the American working class, the German sociologist Werner Sombart chose a dietary metaphor. "On the reefs of roast beef and apple pie," he wrote, "socialistic utopias of every sort are sent to their doom." In a 1976 paper that took this aphorism as its starting point, Peter R. Shergold found that it was between skilled workers in the United States and England—bricklayers, plasterers, stonemasons, and the like,—that the differential in standard of living, including diet, gaped most broadly. But even at the bottom ranks of the industrial workforce—unskilled factory hands—the meals were fuller in America. And the unskilled American worker's relative standard of living may have declined between 1850 and 1900, the date in which Shergold is most interested. Root and de Rochemont think that the 1830s was the decade when American meat consumption reached its pre-1970 peak.[14]

Rickets, a deformation of the joints caused by a deficiency of calcium during childhood, could be found in the United States. But it was rare, never known in the epidemic proportions reformers found in British cities. Scurvy, vitamin C deficiency, is a disease of isolation. Sailors knew it, although it was becoming less common by 1850. So did loggers in their isolated winter camps in New England and the Great Lakes states. However, Americans at home gave it no second thought unless they took to the emigrant trails.

Vitamin B-deficiency diseases seem to have been unusual, including the scourge of the turn of the twentieth century, pellagra. Almost always associated with peoples whose staple is maize, which lacks niacin, pellagra is simply not found among corn-eating Americans of the 1850s, even in the South where maize was the universal grain. Although southern whites and blacks would be sorely tried by pellagra at the turn of the century, a presumably larger consumption of pork (which carries niacin) apparently spared the southern poor circa 1849.[15]

Cachexia africanus, "dirt-eating," practiced in parts of the South in 1849, is sometimes diagnosed as a symptom of mineral deficiency. However, some experts hold that dirt-eating should also be considered a cultural artifact of American blacks' West African heritage and, for pregnant women, a desirable nutritional supplement. Peter Farb and George Armelagos point out that even today some Georgia clays are commercially mined and packaged for consumption. Pregnant women living in northern cities write home for it as a Chicano in Maine might send for a case of jalapeño peppers.[16]

THE REPUBLIC OF
PORKDOM

Then as now, most Americans probably preferred a good beefsteak on the table to any other viand. But pork was president of the republic. Americans had grown up and conquered half a continent with pork in their bellies. The hog is a most marvellous servant of man carnivore. In climates where the creatures flourish—everywhere but the arctic and torrid desertlands—they increase their weight 150 times in eight months, with minimal care.

Bottom of the Barrel

"Bottom of the barrel" is not the only catch phrase we inherit from the days when the pork barrel sat in the corner of every American kitchen. "Pork Barrel Bill" refers to those end-of-session congressional actions in which politicians of ostensibly different principle join hands and vote something for everybody's re-election campaign, a road improvement here, an agricultural station there, praise for a semiliterate local editor, and so on. The idea is the horrendous visual mess that a barrel of fat pork in brine was.

Like chickens, hogs pretty well take care of their own feeding where the human population is sparse, scavenging amid offal or rooting in woods for foods humans care little for. Unlike chickens, hogs need little protection, particularly the Americans' "bony, snake-headed, hairy wild beasts," which were more than a match for any common predator, including an unarmed man. Hogs were ideally suited to a people rich in land and scarce in labor and they thrived in North America from the beginning. Robert Beverley wrote in his esteemed *History of Virginia:* "hogs swarm like Vermine upon the Earth, and are often accounted such. . . . When an Inventory of any considerable Man's Estate is taken, the Hogs are left out." To less-than-handsomely appointed households, hogs were life itself. As the housewife in James Fenimore Cooper's *The Chainbearer* put it, "I hold a family to be in a desperate way when the mother can see the bottom of the pork barrel."[17]

By midcentury beef was replacing pork in the Northeast but pig-meat remained the cushion of southern comfort. There were nearly two hogs per capita in most of the southern states but fewer than one for every ten persons over most of New England.[18] A writer in *Godey's Lady's Book* sums it up:

> The United States of America might properly be called the great Hog-eating Confederacy, or the Republic of Porkdom. [In the] South and West . . . it is fat bacon and pork, fat bacon and pork only, and that continually morning, noon, and night, for all classes, sexes, ages and conditions; and except the boiled bacon and collards at dinner, the meat is generally fried, and thus supersaturated with grease in the form of hog's lard.[19]

Most important in explaining the reliance of the people of mid-century on pork was that, better than any other viand, it preserved well. Sowbelly—bacon steeped in brine in a barrel—accorded nicely with the demands of an overland trek that would take up to eight months.

JIMMY CRACK CORN

The Americans' staff of life in 1849 was still made from maize, or Indian corn, as they called it. Like pork, corn is a miracle food. It grows at sea level and nearly to the timberline in the mountains, from the equator to the subarctic. And corn flourishes best just where the United States was situated. An acre in Mississippi produced about thirty-seven bushels in 1849, an extraordinary production record that may even have been exceeded in parts of the Ohio Valley.[20]

Corn was indispensable on the frontier because it produced carbohydrates, sugar, and fat more quickly than any other grain and with scarcely more care than hogs required. (Keeping the free-ranging hogs out of the corn was the larger part of the task.) It was the staple of the South, eaten in mush, cooked before an open fire as "pone" or hoecake, and baked into a more or less proper bread.

Indian corn has its drawbacks, the most significant of which has already been noted as unimportant to Americans at midcentury, its deficiency in niacin. Less vital, corn's coarse crumb refuses to make a decent crust however it is cooked. This failing was to prove a serious matter for people about to set out on the trail, with the result that the more expensive wheat flour was to be the staple of the trek.

Whichever the flour, both left the vexatious problem of getting bread to rise. At home, housewives could make their own yeast, particularly from fermenting apples or the lees of home brews. (Com-

13

Even in Valdez, Alaska, a miner could sit down to a leisurely meal in a well-appointed restaurant. (Courtesy Anchorage Historical and Fine Arts Museum)

mercial yeast was available only after 1868.) Another way to raise bread was to beat the air into the batter, a tedious, interminable job—cookbooks often prescribed three hours at it. The common solution was pearlash or saleratus, as it was generally known, what we call baking soda. Potassium carbonate, saleratus was a by-product of burned wood, developed first in the United States and exported commercially as early as 1792. It was near the top of the list on every cross-country party's provisions list.[21]

BEANS AND WHISKEY

Beans! Beans were ubiquitous at home and would become virtually the escutcheon of the diet of miners in the diggings. (And of other westerners: loggers, soldiers, builders, and cowboys.) On the actual emigration, however, beans were not so conspicuous because they required so much time to prepare. There was no nook in a lurching covered wagon where they might soak. Only on the sabbath (for observant companies) and other layovers was there the time for the long, slow, subterranean baking that a decent bean dish required. And the breakable crock necessary for both soaking and cooking was an impractical piece of baggage that, when it was taken along, was among the items to be dumped trailside, often quite early. Moreover, many people believed that beans were a cause of cholera, a disease that raged in the United States in 1849 and was the chief killer on the overland road.[22]

Enjoyment of whiskey also depended in part on the religious inclinations of the forty-niner. While Americans were still a bibulous people, and raw white whiskey was their most common tipple, the temperance movement was off and flying by midcentury. Hundreds of thousands of people, whole congregations and denominations, had taken the pledge. Some transcontinental travel companies advertised themselves as temperance companies; others included whiskey among their stores but as medicine or something of a condiment, and never very much. Drunkenness was not to be a problem of the trail.[23]

FISH AND GAME

Americans still ate a lot of fish and game in 1849, not only those who lived close by the sea or near prime hunting grounds, but just about everyone. Even before commercial canning made preserved seafood

14

available at a reasonable price, Americans were inclined to eat much more seafood of every kind than do we today. Eliza Leslie, author of the era's leading cookbook, thought nothing of calling for three lobsters in the preparation of a sauce. Another of her recipes begins: "Take two hundred fat oysters . . ."

Oysters could not be carried on the overland trail, of course. But some forty-niners may have been familiar with a somehow unappetizing frontier recipe for "mock oysters" employing butter, beaten eggs, and grated green corn. In any case, it is, as we shall see, the history of the oyster in the gold rush that demonstrates as well as the story of any other foodstuff the longing of people in a strange environment for the tastes of home.[24]

Game was also common on the American table. Cookbooks intended for urban readers included diagrams for butchering deer and "receipts" for venison steak, venison pasty, venison ham, venison hash, venison sausage, venison soup, hare, wild duck, wild pigeon, pheasant, snipe, partridge, quail, grouse, woodcock, plover, and bobolinks.[25] Had the cookbooks been written for southerners in particular, they would have included "coon" and "possum" too. When a country-bred forty-niner turned to the wild for his food, he was indulging himself in no novelty.

FRUIT AND VEG, FRESH AND PRESERVED

It is a common misconception about the history of American food habits that we only recently began to eat lots of fresh fruit and vegetables. In part this error is due to the fact that it was indeed just yesterday, after the discovery of vitamins early in the present century, that professional dieticians began to tout them. During the decades just before the discovery of vitamins, as Harvey Levenstein has shown, the same professionals crusaded *against* fruit and vegetable eating, particularly among the poor, because fruit and vegetables were a relatively expensive way to fuel up in calories.[26]

But the generation of 1849 was not burdened by the counsels of professional dieticians. They made do with their mothers' judgment. Root and de Rochemont suggest that, particularly in matters of vegetables, "our pre-Civil War forebears were . . . more adventurous eaters than we are today, or at least, than our fathers and mothers were yesterday."

15

Among foods "discovered" by Americans of the post-World War I period that were common fare during the 1840s were broccoli and artichokes. Other vegetables, of which there are numerous off-handed recipes in the cookbooks and references in the market reports, were asparagus, lima beans, haricot or string beans, cucumber, eggplant, mushrooms, okra, rutabagas, salsify, and spinach, as well as tomatoes.

It is true that our forebears were inclined to cook their vegetables into a sodden mess, but eating greens and other vegetables raw seems not to have been uncommon. Indeed, whereas the typical European salad of the time was made up exclusively of greens (dressed with oil and vinegar), the common American salad was adventurous by comparison, "composed" of a variety of vegetables and dressed with a sweetish mayonnaise-based liquor much like the substance contemporary bottlers sometimes label "French Dressing." The most strident warning against eating "too many juicy vegetables, such as melons, salads, radishes, etc." found in the literature of the gold rush is in a traveler's manual written in German. More typical of the guidebooks the Americans read was the warning of Lansford Hastings, who informed emigrants that their appetites would be keener on the trail, "attributable to the fact of their being deprived of vegetables . . . and their being confined to meat and bread alone."[27]

Then there were the preserved vegetables and fruits, the supernumerary varieties of preserves, conserves, pickles, relishes, catsups, "sasses," jams, and jellies that filled so many pages of the cookbooks of the era and prompted Harriet Beecher Stowe to write "you shall find a sparkling jelly to your dessert where you sighed in vain for so simple a luxury as a well-cooked potato." In *Never Done: A History of American Housework*, Susan Strasser suggests that home-preserving was not so common in the United States until after the invention of the Mason jar in 1858. No doubt she is correct in the aggregate. Nevertheless, at least farm families appear to have been "putting up" the produce of gardens and orchards in some quantity in 1849. A secreted crock of jam or conserves came to loom larger in the minds of the emigrants than Independence Rock or, for the sailors, the rounding of the Horn.[28]

Commercially preserved foods were making their appearance in 1849. An English immigrant, Thomas Kennsett, had patented a process for making airtight tin cans in 1825 but, because they were hand soldered, the foods that came in them were too expensive for a mass market. But, as we shall see, cost rarely deterred the forty-niners. Moreover, in the years of the gold rush, a machine for mass producing tins was perfected. By 1855, the Mills B. Espy Company of Philadelphia was annually canning twenty thousand pounds of cherries, ten thousand pounds of strawberries, and four thousand bushels of pears, tomatoes, and peaches. The California market for these goods proved to be one of the most lucrative; tin can dumps made their first appearance in American landscapes in the Golden State. By 1857, at least one tin of peaches was for sale at Fort Kearny because emigrant Helen Carpenter snapped it up there on sight, price unspecified.[29]

COOKERY AT
THE RACES

Few good words about antebellum American cookery found their way into print. Its foundations were not auspicious, of course, being English. But that gastronomically impoverished nation's insistence on overcooking everything to which heat might be applied was compounded in North America by the utilitarian inclination of a people struggling over and over to find a foothold on the frontier.

The westering Americans' implements of cookery were the spit and the pan. Once settled, they added only a pot or dutch oven to the arsenal. Foreign travelers in the United States during the age of Jackson gagged in revulsion at the fact that every foodstuff seemed to be sent swimming in grease. "I have never undergone such gastronomic privations," wrote Prince Maximilian of Wied-Neuwied, who toured the United States in 1843, "as in the western parts of America."[30]

James Beard points out that things were brighter "in a few great houses in parts of the South and in New York, Boston, and Philadelphia." The new urban elite encouraged European-born or trained chefs to found fine restaurants in their cities, while southerners, particularly Louisianans, began to send talented slaves to Paris to study *haute cuisine*. Indeed, Thomas Jefferson was the peer in sophistication of any European gourmet by the end of the eighteenth century and, in 1840, "Frenchified cooking" was known to exist by enough Americans that the Whigs could successfully twit Martin Van Buren for fancying it.[31]

A prospector with his dutch oven in
front of his rock-and-sod hut. Men may
have developed a yen for fancy foods
after long periods of cooking by
primitive methods. (Courtesy
Huntington Library,
San Marino, Calif.)

HOME COOKING

But the lesson in the "log cabin and hard cider" campaign of 1840 would seem to remain that the voters opted for the simple, the native, and—surely the European critics were right—the almost inevitably horrid. Americans continued to be more gluttons than epicures whose approach to meals was "to get through—not necessarily in a hurry, *but without pause.*"[32] In that respect as well as in others, they were a people made for a rush.

How beautiful to think of lean tough Yankee settlers, tough as gutta percha with most *occult* unsubduable fire in their belly, steering over the Western Mountains to annihilate the jungle, and bring bacon and corn out of it for the Posterity of Adam!

Thomas Carlyle,
letter to
Ralph Waldo Emerson, 1849

Not food but forage and high water determined the day when the would-be gold barons left Independence, St. Joseph, or one of the other, lesser trailhead towns. Like the Oregon emigrants before them, the forty-niners bivouacked on the outskirts of those bustling mercantile centers, ready and itching to be off long before it was possible to go. They gossiped, gambled, prayed, sang, drank, and—more out of restlessness than a failure of confidence—checked and rechecked their carefully assembled outfits and larders. Then they chewed their lips, watched the spring grass closely enough to retard its growth, and descended in swarms on every wayfarer who rode in from the west to learn how the grazing and spring flood looked along the Platte. California beckoned more voluptuously with each lengthening day that passed. Everyone wanted to be early on the trail.

But in the end, only a few jumped the gun. The vast majority understood full well that it was foolish to take oxen, mules, and horses into last season's frost-charred stubble and wagons to the banks of spring's unfordable waterways. Common sense and the guidebooks told a man that.

THE GUIDEBOOKS

The fact is, most of the forty-niners had a pretty fair idea of what they were in for on the road west. The impulse to go mine gold in California was not the same thing as the impulse to jump into a canal. There was a lapse of time involved in which the steadfast gold-seekers could read about what they were going to do or listen to others who had pored over the ample body of available literature on continent-crossing.

Joseph Ware's definitive *Emigrant's Guide to California,* which charted the way mile by mile, was available to few of the first year's travelers: it was published in 1849. But there were other books, not so systematic, perhaps, but still valuable. Lansford Hastings's *Emigrants' Guide,* prolix and rambling where Ware was barebones essentials, had been in circulation four years. John C. Frémont's books on his explorations—de facto guides—were the best-selling government publications of the time, well enough known to help make Frémont in 1856 the first consciously constructed celebrity presidential candidate. Dozens of diarists mentioned their debt to them, somewhat fewer to John Bidwell's *A Trip to California in 1841* and manuals by Bryant and Sanford.[1]

In addition to the books, newspapers in every section of the country had published long and detailed "letters" by emigrants who had already made the long journey. California boosters who sometimes had no firsthand experience of the trail (having arrived there by sea) did not allow such a trifle to disqualify them from the business. For that matter, Joseph Ware published his guidebook *nonpareil* before he himself put it to use.[2]

Then there were the merchants of Independence, St. Joe, Council Bluffs, and places like Bloomington, Iowa, who opined that their town was "a very suitable point to start from because we have an abundance of the necessary supplies." They circulated their puffs as widely as resources allowed. With the journalistic practice of copying papers in its golden age, that was widely enough.[3]

Finally, trailhead printshops and New York City publishers churned out numerous travel manuals. Typically, they were shamelessly cribbed from the competition. But in the process of repeated piracy, just as repeated editing almost always improves a book, much dross was discarded. Still, the collective "Advice to Emigrants" was by no means flawless. Rare was the traveler on Sublette's Cutoff in present-day Wyoming who did not vilify the author of his guidebook in impious language for guessing at the length of the trail and falling grossly short.[4]

It may be that we are inclined to leaf through these old books to assure ourselves of how much brighter we are than the authors. But at

22

The long-handled frying pan was doubly handy when the buffalo chips were damp. (Courtesy Huntington Library, San Marino, Calif.)

least in the matter of the provisions a party of pilgrims needed on the trail, downright poor advice is hard to find. When the advisors did err, it was almost always in the direction of caution. Where larders fell short on the trail, the fault was rarely in the advice available to emigrants but in the disregard of it.

SOUND COUNSEL The guidebooks and the trailhead boomers cautioned overlanders to assemble *complete* outfits before they started on their trip. That advice was meant to help travelers forego purchases at the expensive army post stores along the way and avoid the avaricious commercial practices conventionally attributed to the Mormons (among others) and the "Parsi's Shops" that sprang up at both likely and unlikely turnings of the road—not to mention the fabulous prices found even in pre-gold rush California. Occasionally, a flash of passion illuminated an otherwise sober page of a guidebook, as in one writer's admonition to Pike's Peakers in 1859 that they ought to bypass Capioma in Kansas Territory because the town was peopled "by as scurvy a set of bipeds as ever demoralized any community."[5]

It was, of course, in the self-interest of the trailhead town boosters to pocket as many of their customers' dollars as possible before the pilgrims departed forever into the sunset. But the advice was good. Bargains on the trail were restricted to provisions purchased from trekkers who busted early and turned around with stores more or less intact. The people in the trailhead towns did not think in terms of early busts.

Moreover, the cost of foodstuffs represented a fairly small part of the emigrant's cash outlay. Forty-niners from midwestern farms often brought staples from home, and there was scant opportunity to gouge the city boys and men mustering in the trailhead towns when so many competing merchants were peddling the same commodities. The hucksters of Independence and St. Joe reserved their capacity for lying (and disservice to the emigrants) for their descriptions of the quality, serviceability, and absolutely indispensable character of this kind of wagon, that make of revolver, a certain cut of trousers, the fine bloodline of horses in their corrals, up-to-date mining tools, and the innumerable gadgets and household items the overlanders never should have taken in the first place.

There was a lot of junk in those prairie schooners. "Cheyenne," a correspondent who lived at Fort Laramie, tried to correct the traveler's eternal penchant for carrying excess baggage while emphasizing the paramount importance of adequate food after the first season of massive emigration had reaffirmed the lesson. He wrote to the *Missouri Republican* in April 1850:

By the first of June we shall again be inundated with the gold seeking gentry from the states, with their six pounders, gold rockers, saw mills, etc. If some of them would bring along a ready-made steamboat it might be of use to them when they reach California—at least it would be about as valuable as most of the trash which was brought on the plains last year. If an emigrant has enough provisions and comfortable clothing, he cannot shave down too close in all other articles.[6]

He was quite right, of course, and just as reliably ignored. Despite the nagging of the guidebook authors, the emigrants of 1850, like the forty-niners, inclined to overdo the gewgaws. Nonessentials would litter the way west until the transcontinental railroad was built.

However, in the process of packing the kitchen sink, few overlanders made room for it by shorting their larders. Foodstuff surpluses were more common than shortages until the last leg of the journey, and even then sides of bacon and barrels of flour among the discarded "freight by the wayside" provided other trekkers, canny scavengers like J. W. Cooper, with much of their provisioning. Cooper "did not suffer for the want of anything seriously." One forty-niner estimated he had seen thirty thousand pounds of provisions by the road. There was a huge dump at Fort Kearny from which a band of Shoshone Indians survived for a year. Other parties piled their bacon like cordwood, soaked it with turpentine, and set it ablaze to deny the aborigines this source of food. Mormon "collection parties" learned that many marked forty-niner graves were actually caches of expensive provisions and learned how to resurrect such persons.[7]

In part, the forty-niners were inclined to be conservative in food matters—that is, to pack abundantly—because of the impact on their imaginations of the Donner Party tragedy of 1846–1847. Although the error of that infamous expedition was not inadequate provisioning but negotiating the Sierra Nevada too late in the season, the part of the tale that stuck with a man was the starvation and cannibalism. It was quite enough to prompt the giddiest to hoist just one more barrel of pork into the wagon, or to buy that extra sack of flour. Locally known were the stories of other pre-gold rush parties that were guilty of less calamitous but nevertheless memorable mistakes. For example, an Oregon company organized in Bloomington, Iowa, in March 1843 required each member to contribute only thirty pounds of bacon to the larder. Iowans acquainted with the hardships that group faced from the letters they sent home knew to pack much more.[8]

The guidebook authors must be accorded major credit for hammering home the necessity of taking plenty of food, and for the fact that, while more than forty-two thousand people in 1849 made a trip that was new, daring, and grand, hunger was not a major problem on the way west. None of the books available in 1849 and 1850 called for less than a round hundredweight of bacon per person. Lansford Hastings called for a hundred and fifty pounds, and he recommended two hundred pounds of flour per person too, double what most of the others called for. "Children as well as adults," he admonished,

require about twice the quantity of provisions, which they would require at home, for the same length of time. This is attributable to the fact of their being deprived of vegetables, and other sauce, and their being confined to meat and bread alone; as well as the fact of their being subjected to continued and regular exercise, in the open air, which gives additional vigor and strength, which greatly improves the health, and, therefore, gives an additional demand for food.[9]

A few advisors actually upped Hastings's ante in particulars, especially salt and sugar, and added items like rice and beans, agreeing that "much more will be used on the prairie than here." One emigrant said to pack rations for four weeks more than one expected to be on the trail. Another advisor said to play safer than safe, to take a full year's supply of food: "any overplus can be disposed of at an excellent price at the different trading posts which will be passed on the route."[10] And here and there was the eccentric although perhaps not unique wagon master of the Dowdle Company, who had an additional

No doubt the opportunity to gaze at
Mary of Mary's Hotel near Bonanza,
Alaska, had more to do with this brisk
trade than the quality of her overpriced
coffee, beans, doughnuts, and pie.
(Courtesy Hegg Collection, University
of Washington, Seattle)

and peculiar but—who knows?—possibly sensible reason to pack a few extra sides of bacon. As one traveler recalled:

> Mr. Vassar said, "Boys, you have good horses and they will need great care. You want to take all the extra bacon you can carry to kill the effects of the alkali." The bacon would turn the alkali into soap and it would pass off. It would kill the poisonous effect of it. We also had five pounds of citric acid to put in the water we gave to our horses. The horses, of course, didn't know what the bacon was. We would get hold of their tongue and lay a thin slice back on top of it and when we let go of the tongue the bacon went with it. The horses found out it was a good thing for them and they would eat it as readily as sugar. We got the horses fixed so they were comparatively safe from the poison of alkali. . . . Along the route there were some teams ahead of us and they had an overload and were willing to sell and wherever we found anybody willing to sell bacon or horse feed we would take it.[11]

By 1849 most of the guides had outgrown Captain Frémont's well-intentioned but potentially mischievous implication that a party's store of provisions "did not much matter in a country where rarely one day passed without seeing some kind of game, and where it was frequently abundant." Not that the deer and the antelope—and the elk and the buffalo herds and the braces of sage hens—had been wiped out by 1849 or, for that matter, by 1859, when the rush was to Colorado. But, as one wise advisor put it, "in that wild and remote region, depending upon the buffalo for meat, would, in nine cases out of ten, result in immediate or ultimate starvation."[12]

It was one thing for The Pathfinder's motley little squadron to live off the land. It was quite another for a company of fifty or a hundred people in a train made up of dozens of troupes like it to do so. Even the infamously dull-witted bison knew enough to retreat in the face of an invasion of rumbling, rattling prairie schooners and two-legged creatures who whooped and hollered ungodly sounds when they were feeling good.

In fact, while the guidebook authors could not anticipate the enormity of the population movement of 1849, nor could the forty-niners themselves during their bivouac in Missouri, they were not to be puny specks in an enormous landscape but citizens of a very long, very narrow, moving city. "The road is literally filled with two weeks' travel," John A. Johnson would write. The difficulty was not to make do on one's own but "to get out of the way or to pass others."

Margaret Frink, from a rural background like many forty-niners, found the wilderness more crowded than the place where she had grown up. "The country was so level we could see the long trains of white-topped wagons for many miles. It seemed to me I had never seen so many human beings before in all my life." J. S. Holliday put the point very nicely: "Though the wilderness stretched off to the horizon, though they were moving each day twenty miles and more through a vastness they had imagined or read about since childhood—the very places that Frémont had described, they could not escape the sight and sound of hundreds of other emigrants. At night as they waited for sleep, in the morning as they crawled from their damp blankets, they could hear and see on all sides the great crowd of cityfolk and farmers."[13] It was a fact of trail life that bore more than casually on the matter of food supply and preparation.

All seem to have agreed with Captain Frémont's recommendation that travelers take plenty of coffee. Of the baggage swept away during an early river crossing, none was looked back upon with such remorse as the drowned coffee ration. "It was a loss which none but a traveler in a strange and inhospitable country can appreciate; and often afterward, when excessive toil and long marching had overcome us with fatigue and weariness, we remembered and mourned over our loss in the Kansas."

Fewer guidebook writers listed Frémont's second favorite bevand, brandy, even though he had found nothing "more agreeable after a hard day's march. . . . All felt it to be a reviving cordial." No doubt the authors assumed that the bibbers among their readers needed no prompting in the matter of strong waters and saw no commercial sense in offending the "cold water brigades" whose book-buying money was also green.[14]

THE RATIONS   Joseph Ware listed the following provisions as necessary to a transcontinental party consisting of four persons: 824 pounds of flour, 725 of bacon, 75 of coffee, 160 of sugar, 200 of lard and suet, 200 of beans, 135 of dried peaches and apples, and 25 of salt, pepper, and saleratus. The recommendations of other books differed only incidentally, some liberally allowing "as the tastes of people differ, so will their stores of provisions." Historian John Mack Faragher has constructed a composite ration list, also for four persons, from a number of these guides:

600 pounds flour	120 pounds dried fruit
120 pounds biscuit	60 pounds coffee
400 pounds bacon	40 pounds salt
200 pounds lard	8 pounds pepper
200 pounds beans	8 pounds saleratus
	4 pounds tea

And, there being no Sons of Temperance in Faragher's hypothetical quartet, he allotted his forty-niners one keg of whiskey.[15]

With one important exception—vitamin C, a nutrient to be examined in some detail later—diets based on either of these models were nutritionally more than adequate according to standards set in 1975 by the Food and Nutrition Board of the National Academy of Sciences (NAS).[16]

An overland trekker conscientiously and with some regularity ingesting his daily share from either Ware's or Faragher's larder would be well served in calories, protein, and the historically troublesome B vitamins—thiamine, riboflavin, and niacin. Based on a crossing of 125 days—four months—excellent time but managed by many, the Ware and Faragher stores were sufficient to maintain sound health. (See the appendix for an explanation of my methodology in making these calculations and a detailed nutritional analysis of the provisions lists.)

	NAS Daily Allowance	Ware List	Faragher Composite
Calories	3000	8982	13,516
Protein (g)	54	121	137
Thiamine (mg)	1.5	5.7	5.4
Riboflavin (mg)	1.8	1.8	1
Niacin (mg)	20	41.4	45

Based on the more common crossing time of 150 days, the allowance is not so generous but quite workable.

Calories	3000	7186	10,813
Protein (g)	54	97	110
Thiamine (mg)	1.5	4.5	4.3
Riboflavin (mg)	1.8	1.5	.8
Niacin (mg)	20	8.2	36

As with all pretensions to precision in the writing of history, these numbers are useful only in graphing an impression. The forty-niners did not methodically measure out their daily rations to the gram. Nor did they daily consume the total thirteen thousand calories the Faragher composite allowed them. Had they done so they would, despite their arduous hike, have arrived at the eastern face of the Sierra Nevada too fat to scale the first rise. Moreover, some treks took more than 150 days, rather diluting the hypothetical allowance. And tons of foodstuffs were dumped along the trail with the anvils and string basses. Tons more were sold. Yet more was spoiled by inept packaging, heat, alkali dust, or simple, relentless passage of time.

Finally, the Faragher composite owes a good deal of its glut to an extremely large lard allowance (twenty-two pounds: 6,546 calories), a quantity that appears in few of the guidebooks. Lard was also used not only as an edible but as a lubricant (axle grease) and illuminant. Indeed, like many of the calories in fire-roasted bacon, much of lard's energy value was burned off into the blue western sky. Much as Europeans of the time would have demurred, the capacity of Americans for fry was limited and at least one party, described earlier, fed bacon to its horses.

Nevertheless, if we allow imprecisely for a reduction in the Ware and Faragher allotments, the point remains that on the basis of the rations of staples alone, the forty-niners should have been adequately stocked. The Wolverine Rangers, a company of sixty-four men, took along "two tons of bacon and 4400 pounds of dried beef" along with rice, beans, flour, corn meal, and "all other things in proportion." William Swain estimated that these stores allowed one-third more provisions per day than other companies of his acquaintance. This prudence (Swain was extremely food-conscious, a bit of a hypochondriac) proved providential because the dawdling Rangers had a very slow crossing. Leaving their camp near Independence on May 16, 1849, they arrived at Lassen's Ranch in far northern California on November 8; they were in transit 176 days.

Even so, without allowing for additions made on the trail by purchase and hunting, the Ranger commissary provided over a third of a pound of bacon per man per day and about two-fifths of a pound of dried beef, in themselves 1,380 calories and 73.6 grams of protein. Allowing for other provisions "in proportion," this made for a daily caloric allowance of the more than four thousand calories that was, at midcentury, the national norm.[17]

OTHER SOURCES OF FOOD

In addition to rations enumerated and weighed, the Rangers and doubtless most parties carried foodstuffs that were not listed in their inventories nor, with the few exceptions from which I am conjecturing, in the diarists' catalogues. Frémont had made it clear how much he enjoyed a "supply of excellent preserves and rich fruitcake" after a "smoky supper on the grass." Womenfolk who were staying home, as well as the comparatively few who made the crossing in 1849, joined Virginia Ivins in "putting up such preserves, pickles and other delicacies as could be kept to become most acceptable when afterwards compelled to partake of cold meals." Such treats were a common going-away gift. Allene Taylor's mother "made a large fruitcake and it was to be a surprise to the men folks after we had gone on the journey for some time." J. Smith Briggs's aunt from Chicago baked him "a large pan of beans." Some companies took potatoes although, as a staple that carried its own water, they were not very portable and were generally eaten early on.[18]

If some forty-niners sold their "overplus," others bought it. If some abandoned sacks of flour and sides of bacon, others picked up what they needed. After 1849 the surprisingly numerous roadside retailers offered canned goods for sale as well as basic provisions they "had purchased from the emigrants at a great sacrifice and sold to others at as great a profit." Thus, at Fort Kearny Helen Carpenter bought cans of peaches and blackberries (and some cheese that "took the skin off the end of my tongue"). At Upper Mormon Ferry, where the road left the Platte and pointed for the Sweetwater, thirty or forty Latter-day

Helena, Montana, was still called Last Chance Gulch in the late 1860s. Monsieur could, however, already purchase his baguette at the French Bakery. (Courtesy Montana Historical Society, Helena)

Saints shoed horses and wheels, ran a boat, and sold whatever they had been able to purchase, including whiskey at fifty cents a pint. Often they requested payment in bacon and flour rather than cash, both for the use of their colony in the Great Salt Lake basin and for resale. At a few of the other ferries that dotted the Platte and the Green rivers, meals were available. J. P. Hamelin wrote, "They gave us a good breakfast of milk, butter, beans, coffee, mean bread & no meat—the first two mentioned articles were to us great luxuries." At Fort Kearny, a group of Mormons kept a herd of forty milkcows, furnishing milk (five cents a pint), buttermilk, butter, and cream to grateful emigrants.[19]

At Scott's Bluff stood Antoine Robidoux's blacksmith shop and gimcrack commodities exchange, a landmark mentioned in many journals, sometimes as if it were a veritable Disneyland of the plains for the variety of services offered. Robidoux was willing to part with his last barrel of pork for coin. James Barnett arrived at the post shortly after he had done just that. The Frenchman was "having a dog feast," Barnett noted with unconcealed disgust. "Near the camp fire was the head of a large mastiff; a bleeding evidence of the fact."[20]

Somewhat more decorous were the Mormons of Salt Lake City. They had a generally bad press in the guidebooks but the actual travelers disagreed. To most of the overlanders who chose the Salt Lake City road over Sublette's Cutoff (about three trains in ten), the Mormon Zion could be a giddying emporium of edibles.

> We yelled, we screamed, we cheered without end and without order. Hallelujah! The Lord reigneth! At last we are in the environs of Heaven! We sang nearly all the way to our campground in the valley. We got fine pasture for our cattle and an abundance of fresh meat, vegetables, milk and butter for ourselves. We never knew the enjoyment of eating before! Perhaps, never will again.

Others were less exuberant but universally impressed that, in a few years, the Saints had created a sprawling settlement of six to seven thousand people living in five hundred homes.[21]

Brigham Young had proclaimed that "we do not intend to have any trade or commerce with the gentile world" but circumstances made it convenient for his followers to ignore him. The grain crop of 1848 had been disastrous and spring planting in 1849 had been delayed by a harsh winter during which, for three months, the recorded high temperature was 21 degrees Fahrenheit. In late spring there was "a great outcry for bread" and the ripening of the pea crop in June was greeted as a salvation comparable to the gulls' destruction of the grasshoppers.[22]

However, by the time the overlanders began to arrive, milk, cheese, and butter were abundant, as well as every common garden vegetable except potatoes. So was hospitality. "They invariably asked us to eat," Charles Ferguson wrote, "and would hardly take no for an answer." Even Brigham Young opened his doors—a crack—for, in addition to clothing, shoes, and tools at bargain prices, the Mormons were able to secure badly needed provisions at 50 to 75 percent below wholesale rates in Missouri. Rare was the visitor to Salt Lake City who did not continue along the trail in better fettle and with a more positive image of the Latter-day Saints. In a survey of letters written home from Salt

Lake City, Dale Morgan discovered that seven emigrants wrote favorably of the Mormons for every one who remained unfriendly.[23]

The experience in Salt Lake City reminds us that the pilgrims needed money. "It was generally assumed," J. S. Shepherd wrote, "that after we left the frontier money would be of no use. It is the greatest mistake possible. I know of no part of the world where money is of more use than in crossing the plains, and where a man is more helpless without it."[24]

More intriguing is how quickly some Indians caught on to the idea of bourgeois commerce. Most of the emigrants continued to think of the natives along the highway as wretched beggars and thieves: "All wanted to eat, eat. They wanted to swap moqisins [sic] for corn or anything to eat." Another wrote that he "could not eat lunch with those poor wretches watching every mouthful like hungry dogs." But others found efficient merchants among the aborigines. Along the Wakarusa River William Swain dealt with a Shawnee named Logan, purchasing twenty pounds of sugar "for extras." Another pilgrim marvelled at the way in which Logan "makes money by the handful out of the emigrants. He is a shrewd, agreeable man and understands well how to trade."[25]

Helen Carpenter, who acknowledged to herself that she was too fastidious for life on the trail, was less generous about some Pawnee vendors of buffalo meat at Fort Kearny:

They know how to charge for it too. The meat was well sold out before we knew it was to be and so would have missed this rare opportunity of adding a much needed change in the bill of fare if we had not done some lively rustling. That Indian is most likely still wondering why we so suddenly became indifferent and refused to buy. . . . I objected to the fellow's *meat chest*, down which were trickling little rivulets of perspiration.[26]

On the northern route, plodded by all but a few thousand of the overland emigrants, the trekkers seem to have been quite successful on the hunt: game provided a nonmeasurable but apparently ample source of food. The forty-niners shot and ate deer, antelope, elk, sage hens, and prairie dogs. (Some said prairie dogs tasted like squirrel, others said like fish. Opinions as to their gastronomic potential varied.)

Overland travelers were more likely to think of Indians as merchandisers than as warriors or noble savages. Plenty of business was transacted on the Great Plains. (Courtesy The Thomas Gilcrease Museum, Tulsa)

36

Some who started out in the upper midwest enjoyed an early week or so of good fishing: "Last Sunday (our party intend to keep the Sabbath) three or four men took from a lake near which we camped, not less than fifty-five wall-eyed pike. Nothing prevents our living well." This sentiment was echoed by Henry Wax Camper: "It was very nice. We had on the plains and through Iowa plenty of birds, prairie chickens, sage hens, rabbits, would catch a deer or antelope and plenty of game all the way across."

Most important—what the bravos in the train looked forward to with the gusto of Crusaders—were the bison or buffalos, as Americans already called them. Extinct in the eastern half of the country by 1849, the dusty behemoths were plentiful on the Great Plains and absurdly easy to shoot. They proved a gastronomic delight to virtually every emigrant who kept a diary. Buffalo steak was "as tender and good as could be desired."

Carcasses were shared throughout and between companies, unlike provisions from home. After a kill the wagons were "decorated with slices of meat dangling from strings fastened to ropes that reach from front to back along the side of the wagons, looking very much like coarse red fringe." Squeamish Helen Carpenter wrote that "my string of meat is to hang inside the wagon in the day time to keep it out of the dust as much as possible." What the overlanders were doing, of course, although, oddly, few of them seem to have known the word, was making *charqui* (jerky).[27]

Perhaps buffalo meat tasted so good because it was fresh in the midst of a very monotonous diet of salt pork and jerked beef. A comparable craving for new-slaughtered flesh characterized the appetites of other groups of people who were shackled to the meat barrel for long periods of time: sailors, loggers, isolated garrisons of soldiers, and slaves—whose raids on the master's pigpens were so common a feature of plantation life as to inspire a racial stereotype.[28]

37

Meals were less often varied with wild plants in prairie, plains, mountains, and desert country. Euell Gibbons could no doubt have dined nightly on forage but the forty-niners were leery of wild plants save for the ripe berries they were lucky enough to happen upon. These they greedily collected both for pleasure and because berries were known to be antiscorbutic. There were also wild currants, wild onions, and watercress, all nutritionally valuable. Captain Frémont found *koonyah*, the Indians' "tobacco root," to be aggreeable but most did not. They agreed with Frémont's aide-de-camp who called it "the most horrid food he had ever put in his mouth."[29]

Taken all together, fresh food was generally available on the trail. As far as physical condition was concerned, most gold-seekers remembered the crossing in positive terms. They commented on their growing strength, increased endurance, sound sleep at night, and keen appetites. The afflictions they dreaded were not hunger and nutritional debility but injury and the cholera, then a pandemic disease treading the transcontinental road step by step with the forty-niners.[30]

Historian Octavius T. Howe, who may have overemphasized the nutritional privations suffered by the overland gold-seekers when compared to that of those who went by sea, nevertheless noted that it was the overlanders, not the sailors, who arrived in California fit and ready to shovel dirt.[31]

Stalking the Cebolla Cimarrona
Ironically, the forty-niners were surrounded by native wild plants that were antiscorbutic. Among those that grew in abundance around the diggings, with the names by which the *californios* knew them, were

cebolla cimarrona, wild onion

ajo, wild garlic

berro, water cress

lechuguilla, dandelion

popota, miner's lettuce

verdolaga, pig weed

chual, lamb's quarters

Ana Bégué de Packman, 1938

3 EATING ON THE RUSH

"How do you like it overland?"
His mother she will say;
"All right, except for cooking,
Then the devil is to pay.

"For some won't cook,
and others can't,
And then it's curse and damn;
The coffee pot's begun to leak,
So has the frying pan."

Forty-Niner Song[1]

The forty-niners knew how much food to carry with them from the experiences of the military, the Oregonians, and the Mormons. They also borrowed from these forerunners when they designed the management of their stores and the logistics of meal preparation. Just as most overland companies associated under "the rules of war" for the extraordinary enterprise of crossing a continent, electing captains and lieutenants in whom they invested military authority, the forty-niners also imitated the army's example in provisioning the wagon trains. As a rule, basic foodstuffs were purchased not by individuals but by the company with subscribed funds, and kept in a commissary. Once on the trail, mutually agreed-upon rations were distributed weekly, usually on Sunday, which, even in companies that did not observe the sabbath by staying put, was a day of some leisure. Companies that were particularly taken with the military trappings of the crossing solemnly commissioned the man responsible for the stores quartermaster or steward.[2]

As is well known, the experiment in military-style command proved almost universally disastrous. The sturdy Jacksonians, including the Whigs, and even the Mexican War veterans among the travelers began to grumble about the competence of the captains they had selected before they were across the Nebraska country. They took exception to the commands they were issued and deposed their commanders at regular intervals. Rare was the wagon train captain elected in Missouri who still held his rank when he arrived in California.

By contrast, the military system for marshalling provisions proved a boon and was recognized as such. It typically held firm into western Nevada when forks in the trail, shortages, fatigue, and the scent of gold resulted in the breakup of most companies and the division of what provisions remained. Until then the emigrants seem to have been determined to avoid the conflicts bound to ensue if some groups within the company ran short of food while others remained well fed.

In general, they seem to have succeeded. While there were plenty of complaints about the quality of meals and the division of labor in the wagon trains, and while more than a few companies were caught short of provisions in the Humboldt Sink and the Sierra crossing, complaints about the fairness of food distribution are hard to find. Indeed, when shortages occurred, the fact that they were company-wide acted as a cohesive force.

"THE MOST ACCESSIBLE
UNIT OF SOCIAL
ORGANIZATION"

Beyond managing the larder, the emigrants usually departed from military example. Where Frémont's and other army expeditions included professional cooks to prepare meals for the lot, such specialists were rare among the forty-niners.[3] Instead the companies followed the ten-year-old example of travelers to Oregon and divided into messes of between six and nine people, with each group responsible for its own cooking arrangements. "We have one large tent and two wagons for each mess," wrote a Wolverine Ranger. "We have nine messes in all, each with seven men."[4] The system was practically universal.

It was entirely natural that the Oregonians should have arrived at this system. The Oregon migration had been a family affair. Between 15 and 20 percent of those who struck out for the Willamette were women, and a full 43.8 percent of the overland parties between 1843 and 1845 were "conjugal" with roughly an additional 40 percent tied by blood kinship. They had bound together in a company for mutual protection and, for some of them, the purpose of purchasing land in large tracts and setting up a township once they arrived. However, the family remained the institution in which those pioneers invested first loyalty. When the wagon wheels stopped turning on the Oregon Trail, at noon and in the evening, the pilgrims broke up into familiar, culturally comfortable family blocs in which (unless there were a meeting or celebration on the agenda) they remained until the next day's call to roll. "The family was," in Professor John Mack Faragher's phrase, "the most accessible unit of social organization."[5]

By contrast, there were few women among the forty-niners. The number of adult females going west overland dropped from 20.3 percent of the total in 1846 to 5.7 percent in 1850. Recognizable family units were even more scarce; only 1.4 percent of the emigrants of 1850 were children.[6] Nevertheless, the *family-size* mess remained the norm by which the preparation and taking of meals were organized.

To understand why this should have been so, it is helpful to compare the forty-niners' circumstances with those of that equally famous and comparably masculine western subculture of the next generation, the cowboys. Each morning on the great cattle drives the men knew within a mile or so the point to where the herd would be driven that day. Cattle could walk just so many miles and, of course, there would have to be water and grass where they passed the night. To avoid a mixup and the herculean labor of cutting herds apart, each had to be kept well clear of every other herd on the trail, usually a day's travel apart.

Consequently, sour-tempered Cookie had plenty of time to clean up after breakfast, drive his chuckwagon ahead of the herd, park in the best dining area he could find upwind from where the cattle would low for the night, and take his time setting his sourdough to fermenting and beans to the long, slow bake.

He had hours to get ready. He could carve out time for a nap, which, given the length of his work day, he well deserved. In brief, a single, specialized, professional cook could and did serve a dozen and more cowboys with yeast-raised bread and dishes, like a decent crock of beans, that required hours and a deft hand to prepare.[7]

Except on the sabbath, when observant companies of emigrants enjoyed their best meals of the week, possibly including a welcome crock of baked beans, the forty-niners could not in the morning predict just where they would camp that night. Any number of factors determined where a wagon train would pull up, not the least of which was where room could be found among the other pilgrims crowding the trail. All evening work, including the preparation of a satisfying meal from scratch, had to be completed within a couple of hours after the wagons were drawn up in their famous circles. There simply was not time enough for a cook to set up and complete an operation for feeding more than a handful of people. Thus the mess of six or seven. The midday break was, of course, briefer; "barely long enough to eat a cold bite."[8]

NEVER DONE Even with only a mess to serve, the cook's job was, by universal if sometimes tacit consent, the toughest on the trail. Cooks "have to get over as many miles as the others," Oliver Goldsmith pointed out. "On coming into camp they have to procure water for coffee, let it be a long or a short distance from camp, and secure fuel and make it burn, rain or shine. And regardless of their fatigue or the distance travelled they have to go to work at once, while others having turned out their teams can rest."[9]

Fuel was a common problem. Just as the emigrants thought of the transcontinental trek in terms of legs—from the Missouri River to Fort Kearny, along the Platte to Fort Laramie, and so on—they passed through a number of distinct "fuel zones," none of them entirely congenial to people who had been accustomed to a superabundance of cordwood. First, before Fort Kearny, fires were made of green willows, which needed to "be tried but once to enable one to give an opinion on this kind of fuel."[10]

Next, to about Fort Laramie, came the zone of buffalo chips.

It is the duty of the cooks on arriving at a camping place . . . to sally forth and collect chips for cooking. . . . It would amuse friends at home to see us . . . jump from the wagons, gunny bag in hand, and make a grand rush for the largest and driest chips. The contest is spirited and always fun-provoking.[11]

Perhaps not always. It took an average of five bushels to cook supper and breakfast for a mess, a lot of gathering—a lot of buffalo chips with as many as thirty thousand people on the plains at once! Moreover, while the fuel worked well enough when dry, when damp with dew the droppings were smoky and "almost fireproof," emitting "a delicate perfume." There was, however, an alternative for companies later on the trail—the abandoned wagons of their predecessors and "thousands of fine trunks, boxes, and barrels." Franklin Langworthy

43

That this splendid figure of a *chef de cuisine* should be asked to pose—and in the middle at that—with the muckers and supervisors at the entrance of this Colorado mine must mean that his meals sparkled as brightly as his apron. (Courtesy The Denver Public Library, Western History Department)

noted that "property that cost $100 in the States is none too much to make one a comfortable fire in an evening."[12]

In the Great Basin, while the landscape was often disheartening, the fuel improved. Greasewood or creosote bush was just barely preferable to buffalo chips but sagebrush was almost pleasant. To use it effectively, the cook dug a hole about a foot wide by two feet long and two feet deep. The sage was fed in until there was a tolerable bed of hot, even-burning coals, a kind of fire endorsed by no less than Mark Twain. There was no smoke, he wrote in *Roughing It,* "and consequently no swearing. Such a fire will keep all night and with very little replenishing; and it makes a very sociable camp-fire, and one around which the most impossible reminiscences sound plausible, instructive, and profoundly entertaining."[13]

Again, perhaps not so pleasant for the forty-niners. Rather than camping out on a leisurely excursion from Virginia City to Lake Tahoe, as Mark Twain did when he savored his sagebrush fires, they were three or even four months into a transcontinental trek that had taken its toll in injury, disease, and exhaustion. So weary were they that the diarists rarely mention that, once within the Sierra Nevada, they were once again cooking over respectable firewood. They had other things on their minds.

Allow several women, within whose sphere cooking decidedly lay at midcentury, to testify in the issue. Virtually all of them who left records found cooking on the overland trail an onerous and frustrating chore. "Although there is not much to cook," Helen Carpenter wrote, "the difficulty and inconvenience of doing it amounts to a great deal. So by the time one has squatted around the fire and cooked bread and bacon, made several trips to and from the wagon, washed the dishes (with no place to drain them), and gotten things ready for an early breakfast, some of the others already have their night caps on. At any rate, it is time to go to bed. In respect to the women's work, the days are all very much the same except when we stop for a day."[14]

Mary Stuart Bailey complained about having to "sit down & eat like Indians." Lodissa Frizzel wrote that cooking on the trail "goes so much 'agin the grain' at first." She never really got over the fact that everything was so often "soaked with water and dry wood [was] so scarce that our women could scarcely make coffee or fry meat." Curt notes along the lines of "could not raise enough fire to cook breakfast" and "lay down to sleep with nothing but dry crackers & cheese & meat" punctuate the diaries. James Clyman told of "one young lady which showed herself worthy of the bravest, undaunted pioneer of the West, for after having kneaded her dough she watched and nursed the fire and held an umbrella over the fire and her skillet with the greatest composure for near 2 hours."[15]

Clyman was not the only trekker who counted it a blessing to belong to a company that included women. "It's so nice to have women folks manage the cooking," wrote one. "Things look so much sweeter." Another pilgrim was more utilitarian. When there were women in a party, "the meals were more regular and better cooked, thus preventing much sickness." But in at least two companies with female members, a man did the cooking. One of the women thus displaced considered it "most amusing to see some of his operations." In the other group the chef was quickly deposed in favor of one of the women.[16] But what did it mean when, as was the rule in the emigrations of 1849 and 1850, there were no women to whom to turn?

45

INAPPROPRIATE WORK

The Well-Equipped Wagon
"In ours there is a Dutch oven, a camp kettle, frying pan, and coffee pot. These, with some tin plates, tin cups, tin spoons, knives, and forks, a rolling pin, bread pan, milk can, and a smoothing iron, constitute my entire kitchen furniture."

Helen Carpenter, 1857

It often meant trouble, as Noah Brooks explained:

At the onset none knew who should drive the oxen, who should do the cooking, or whose ingenuity would be taxed to mend broken wagons or tattered clothing. . . . We saw not a little fighting in the camps . . . and these bloody fisticuffs were invariably the outcome of disputes over the divisions of labor.[17]

It is not going too far to conjecture that resistance to doing women's work was pronounced, and because everyone was responsible for his own mending, cooking was the big problem. A mid-nineteenth-century farmer or tradesman was simply unlikely to know how, whatever he felt about the inappropriateness of a man mixing dough, wielding the long handled frying pans, fending off the complaints that there was no dried apple pie or that it was atrocious.

The tragickal experience of John A. Johnson of Tennessee illustrates Brooks's observations. As did many messes, Johnson's group decided before leaving Missouri that each member would take a turn at the cook fire. On April 1, 1849—heady early day of the great adventure—Johnson wrote boastfully to his wife that "all of us seem to understand cooking as well as our wives and are anxious to try our hands." For a few weeks, the men of the mess rotated in a job they considered quite desirable. "We have, as I said before, several excellent cooks in our company. Some crack on making one thing and some another and really we get along very well in this respect. Today each mess made a pot pie; I had the honor of officiating at our mess; it was good of course."[18]

What fools these male mortals be! The novelty of tossing off woman's work with a song wore off quickly and Johnson's mess decided to name one man fulltime cook in return for—this also was common practice—exemption from all other camp responsibilities, including the sentinel duty that everyone loathed. John jumped at the chance to take the job and congratulated himself on his good luck because it "will not be as burdensome as I have a natural taste for that kind of work and they all think so."[19]

The would-be Escoffier lasted a week, whence he wrote home:

I have given up the office of chief cook and take my turn with the rest and my portion of other duties. I had rather do so as it is more slavish work than I had anticipated and by far the hardest post to occupy. I found I was working all the time during our halts while others were at least a portion of the time resting. I could not get time to write a letter or a note—as for guarding, my time will not come oftener than once in two and perhaps three nights and then only two hours at a time, with some eight or ten others.[20]

Most forty-niners were a little quicker and more gracious in acknowledging the women's contributions that they had never particularly noticed at home. "You would be amused to see us in our operations," a Kentuckian, James Lyne, wrote to his wife from a company just ahead of Johnson's.

I feel greatly the want of counsel and advice from you or others in biscuit-making and in some approved, or improved method of brewing coffee. . . . I have always been inclined to deride the vocation of ladies until now. But I must confess it is by far the most irksome I have ever tried. . . . I wish you could take supper with me, that you might judge the hardness and durability of our biscuits. I must at some time send you a recipe for making this lasting sort.[21]

The Jahabich Grill of 1910 was located in Jarbidge, Nevada. (Courtesy Idaho State Historical Society, Boise)

James Lyne may have had something more than biscuits on his mind in wishing his wife could join him. But it would be a mistake to read his letter simply as amorous Victorian code. Helen Carpenter's husband, whose wife was along on the trip, made the same discovery of his culinary deficiencies. On the Fourth of July, always a day of rest and celebration on the trail, he "wanted something special for supper" and suggested "corn starch." Helen had never heard of it as an Independence Day dish "and furthermore I did not know how to cook it." But he did, "'just as Aunt Hannah used to.' So I stood by and saw him burn his fingers and scorch the starch which when done was the consistency of very thick gravy. But we ate it, for on a trip like this one must not be particular."[22]

The perceptive Mrs. Carpenter commented several times on the way traditional sex roles were often ignored on the overland trail. She thanked the stars, for example, that her own husband was a Yankee who, if he was not much of a cook, did not disdain to play subordinate at mealtime giving her a hand with her tasks. She also noticed another family party in which

the old gentleman farmer is very good to help 'Mother' in the culinary arrangements. He makes the fires, gets out the pots and kettles and the eatables and helps generally while 'Mother' makes the bread and coffee. 'Sister' is too small to do more than be in the way. When the four sons and men are ready for a meal each for the time being becomes his own cook so there is no occasion for anyone to grumble. Willows are sharpened and slices of bacon speared and held in the fire ad lib. It looks quite amusing.

It was a little different with Missourians, the object of Mrs. Carpenter's cryptofeminist contempt. Missouri women "had very little help" from their surly husbands.[23]

The women who stayed behind also recognized their value. They punctuated their letters with wishes that they could dispatch familiar goodies—"a cherry pie to you on the plains"—as easily as anxious letters. "Every day we wonder where poor William is, and we wish we could send you pancakes, baked potatoes, beans, and beef by telegraph."[24]

GOOD EATS AND BAD

48

Not that every male trail cook was a nincompoop. Meals on the crossing varied remarkably in quality, one mess on the trail bolting greasy, gritty slops while another, perhaps twenty yards away, was confronted with the problem that faced William Swain. The food at his mess was so good that "we are warned by discretion not to injure ourselves by gratifying our appetites, as we might burst the boiler."[25]

His group ate so well, at least during the first three-quarters of the journey, that food may explain why the Wolverine Rangers were uncommonly unhurried gold rushers. Time after time Swain commented on "good suppers," "the best of wholesome food," "an excellent dinner, good enough for any hotel," "the greatest of all delicacies," "a fine venison stew," "extras" at breakfast.[26] Not only were Mr. Bailey and Dr. Wells "the finest cooks out," preparing fine-sounding and varied breakfasts of the customary "fried bacon, boiled rice, pancakes made of flour and Indian meal, pilot bread, flour gravy, apple sauce made of dried apples, sugar, and coffee," but Swain and his messmates were as adventurous gourmets as conditions permitted. They ventured a go at every sort of game that had the ill fortune to break cover when the Rangers were around: rabbits, deer, antelope, elk, squirrels, doves, sage hens, ducks, geese, and crayfish ("fresh water lobsters"). Swain did not sample rattlesnake but others did; they called the meat "bush fish." However, he commented that "prairie dogs are nice eating" and marmots "very fat and good." Like most forty-niners, he liked buffalo steak: "certainly . . . the sweetest and tenderest meat I have ever eaten."[27]

Another rather overexuberant stylist wrote: "Oh, if I could only send this great tender piece of tenderloin to my friends at home! Such delicious, juicy meat I have never put under the operations of my masticatory organs." Others appear to have taken their dietary with equal seriousness. One company celebrated the Fourth of July with ice cream flavored by wild peppermint, an extraordinary treat made possible by the high elevation of their camp. Rather a lot of forty-niners were quite pleased with their dietary.[28]

49

SHORTAGES

Salt Lake City
Salt Lake City remained an important source of food for the mining West, particularly of the fresh fruits that meant so much to the emigrants of 1849. C. N. Teeter, who prospered as an early provisioner of Silver City, Idaho, wrote on August 31, 1863: "I am here just in the nick of time to get all the fruit I can eat. There is no end to the peaches this city affords, in fact the whole city with the exception of the business portion is one vast peach orchard, and they have just begun to ripen nicely and in size and quality they cannot very well be surpassed. I ate some yesterday that measured seven and a half inches in circumference and a half dozen such was all I could get away with at one time. There is also a good many apples, plums, and grapes raised here. Upon the whole I think it is a splendid fruit, as well as grain-growing country."

"Four Years of My Life," typescript in the Idaho State Historical Society

So was it then a lark, an exhilarating adventure culminating every evening in a three-star repast?

Hardly. In fact, if one conjectures that the surviving diaries and journals overrepresent the parties that were more successful in every way, it is likely that only a tiny minority of overlanders lived "as well as at a tavern." There were also those companies, never even counted at Fort Laramie, that gave up early. They described the *first leg* of the journey as "a kind of golgotha, inhabited by savages and armed with storms, pestilence, and famine." While most still had some provisions, others begged food—usually without success—from those still headed west.[29] For every party on every section of the trail that recorded selling rations to another, it must be remembered, another party needed to buy.

Although only a few journals and recollections of emigrants who traveled by the southern route survive, those that do indicate that they had a much more difficult time than those on the main road. There was far less game for one thing, and, contrary to the rule on the road out of Independence and St. Joe, those who began their trek in Arkansas and Texas seem to have been outright cavalier about how little food they carried along.

"We were not as well provisioned for so long a trip as we should have been," Dr. Hezekiah Crumpton remembered later in life. "We expected to kill buffalo, but they were then migrating northward and except for a few old bulls, always were beyond our reach. We also expected to be able to replenish from the Mexicans, but beyond the purchase of a few sheep, they seemed to have little to spare." His company may have been one of those met by army Lieutenant Cave J. Couts, who led an expedition east out of San Diego in 1849. Couts wrote that the would-be miners on the southern crossing were "constantly" begging "sugar, flour, molasses, pork and a little fresh beef."[30]

Charles Dexter Cleveland's southern route company turned north to Salt Lake City and barely made it.

> Our teams were poor, jaded, and well-nigh exhausted, and we were pretty much in the same condition. Living upon flour-cake, beans, rice, dried apples and parched corn, walking the entire distance, in the rain and the hot sun; for days in clouds of unavoidable dust, guarding the cattle all night, hunting them up for miles, and yoking them every morning, and then driving them all day, in their enfeebled, fatigued and half-starved condition, was depressing to the spirits and exhausting to the body.[31]

But it was not just the southerners. All but the best-provisioned parties on the northern road suffered shortages on the final two legs of the journey—along the Humboldt and across the Sierra Nevada—and even the best felt the pinch. One traveler noted wryly that the price of flour rose from twenty cents a pound to thirty cents at trading posts just ten miles apart along the Humboldt. Mary Stuart Bailey's train, which had packed abundantly, needed to buy provisions in the Carson Valley. Many companies found themselves subsisting on "rancid bacon with the grease fried out by the hot sun, musty flour, a few pinoles, some sacks of pilot bread broken and crushed and well-coated with alkali, and little coffee without sugar." Even the gastronomes of the Wolverine Rangers found themselves "badly put to it to fix up our food so that we can live well. Making puddings and breadstuffs is hard business with the material we have."[32]

THE LAST DAYS

Here and there the trekkers remembered their lessons in Christian charity and shared a little. "Got a present of about eight pounds of sugar and a small piece of bacon," one hard-put emigrant wrote. Much more common, however, were wayfarers with what passed for plenty in those last days who clung to it. William S. Greever tells of a lone traveler with a milkcow who was, no doubt, thinking of the price Bossie's product would bring in the diggings. J. Goldsborough Bruff saw an Irish couple on the Lassen Cutoff "with an ox-wagon, to the rear of which was attached a large hencoop, full of chickens and roosters. And Pat swore by the 'howly mother of Moses' that he'd starve before he'd kill one of 'em, intending to make a grand speculation on them in California."[33]

How they got the birds that far defies the imagination, but they were lucky to keep them. The forty-niners were not an entirely selfless lot. Guidebook writer Joseph E. Ware was simply dumped trailside when he became too ill to travel; incidents of violence and near-violence over provisions multiplied at the end of the trek. On the southern route a Mexican muleteer refused to sell the flour he was carrying to a distressed overland party. The forty-niners simply "dispossessed" him of sixty sacks.[34]

Up north, there was nearly a similar incident as early in the journey as August 26.

A Boston mule company of about seventy is said to be broken up and destitute of provisions and . . . troubling emigrants to sell provisions to them. They say if people will not sell to them they will take by force. Yesterday we nooned near where they camped, and some of them . . . came to our wagon and pressed hard to buy bacon, but got none. There were very fortunately, about forty wagons camped nearby. . . . Such men as these are to be dreaded and must be sharply watched.[35]

By October, with an estimated eight thousand people still on the trail "dying from thirst and hunger," those already in California acted. Sacramentans, many of them just lately off the overland road, called a meeting to raise relief parties. Believing the situation to be worst on the Lassen Cutoff to the north, U.S. Army Major D. H. Rucker dispatched John H. Peoples and later E. H. Todd to drive "fat beef cattle" as far to the east as possible, distributing them among the emigrants.[36]

Undoubtedly the sight of the herd lifted many a heart. But steak, however fresh, was not what the weary travelers most likely needed on their battered tin plates. As Rucker and Peoples reported to Washington, the most "pitiable sight" on the road were the "cripples from scurvy," particularly the "children who could not move a limb" and had to be lifted on and off the mules that carried them.[37]

It is not surprising that scurvy should have been an overland traveler too. What requires some scrutiny is why the condition is mentioned so little by both the transcontinental pilgrims and the argonauts, those forty-niners who kept their diaries and wrote their letters on the pitching decks of sailing ships and steamers.

4 THE ARGONAUTS

We've forty men in Company,
A cook and steward too,
We've twenty pigs, a dog and cat,
And what is that to you.

Song of 1849[1]

About forty-two thousand people went to California overland in 1849, the large majority of them via the Platte River, South Pass, and Humboldt Sink. Although there were plenty of easterners and European immigrants in the writhing snake of a city, the overland way was, with good reason, identified with midwesterners and, to some extent, with the less affluent. Not only were midwesterners apt to think of traveling as something that was done on *terra firma,* the overland way was—or at least looked to be—the cheapest way to the diggings. Farmers could easily convert a wagon from the yard for overland travel and provide at least some of their provisions without spending cash.[2]

Easterners, not yet tied fast to the interior by trunk-line railroads, were inclined to look to the seas for their highways. Maritime New Englanders particularly thought in terms of the all-ocean route around Cape Horn. That meant traveling eighteen thousand miles to reach a point three thousand miles from Boston, and six months or more in transit. But Yankees had been doing that kind of sailing in pursuit of whales and trade goods for a long time. To them a sturdy ship seemed infinitely more sensible than an overland trek through mountain and desert wilderness inhabited by hostile savages. Of 124 gold rush companies organized in Massachusetts in 1849, 102 announced they would sail around Cape Horn or through the Strait of Magellan. It is estimated that about forty-one thousand people entered California from seaward in 1849. However, as this number includes nearly all the many foreigners in the rush, the sea route was considerably less popular with Americans than the trails out of Missouri.[3]

A third way to the goldfields involved traveling by steamship to Chagres in Panama (then a Colombian province), crossing the narrow, sweltering isthmus by canoe and on foot, and at Panama City booking passage on a steamer north to San Francisco or, when desperate, on a sailing ship. The isthmian route had been a little-used way of negotiating the American landmass before 1849, at least for citizens of the United States. Central America was an obscure part of the world to Americans. However, it was not lost on those burning with gold fever that the people who brought the obsession back to the United States with the news of Marshall's discovery, men in a hurry, had come by way of Panama.

If the most costly way to California—the fare from Panama to San Francisco alone would run from 300 to 350 dollars—the isthmian route was, even with moderate delays, the quickest way there. Moreover, despite the complaints about tropical heat and humidity, mosquitoes, and living conditions generally, it was undoubtedly the easiest way west. The chief American apprehension about Panama was, of course, the then poorly understood tropical fevers. In fact, while Americans waiting passage in Panama City died at the grisly rate of twelve a day during the summer of 1849, most of the fatalities seem to have been the handiwork of the cholera, not exclusively a tropical affliction at all, but a disease that, pandemic at the time, was exacting a frightful toll on the overland trail and in the settled parts of the United States as well.[4]

GOING VIA PANAMA

Food was rarely a problem for the forty-niners who chose the Panama route. The first leg of the trip, by steamer from an Atlantic or Gulf port to Chagres, was a four-week journey at most, no challenge to the greenest ship's provisioner. Steamers departing from Atlantic ports often called at Santiago de Cuba where additional foodstuffs were taken aboard.

When the diarists who were not so giddy over the beginning of their adventure did mention their meals, the reviews were pretty good. "This was the first time I ever saw sardines, claret wine, or olives," H. C. Bailey remembered of a lunch on his voyage to Chagres. He added,

Dinner on a steamer bound from
Panama to San Francisco. (*Century
Illustrated Monthly Magazine*,
April 1891)

"We all ate heartily." A menu from the steamship *Tennessee* survives to confirm his observation. Just four days before Christmas 1850, argonauts ate a seven-course meal from a list that included vegetable soup, pickled salmon, corned beef, ham, pork, chicken curry, baked macaroni, roast lamb, beef, and pork, potatoes, sweet potatoes, and various pastries for dessert. Celebrating Plymouth Rock Day in Tobago, the party on the *Iconium* dined on roast turkey, apple sauce, succotash, hasty pudding, and a dessert of oranges. On quite ordinary days, the steamship *Crescent City* offered even grander fare, on paper at least, including boiled bass with oyster sauce, a duck dish, and "Sicilian Pudding." Setting out from New Orleans with a large complement of gastronomically picky Orleanians aboard, perhaps the master of the *Crescent City* knew better than to skimp at table.[5]

Few forty-niners mentioned their meals during the short trip across the isthmus but apparently there was no hunger and few shortages. The typical notices were like those of Panamanian travelers Chenery— "Our company are all in good health without exception"—and Read—"we had good food aboard and little sickness." Somewhere between Chagres and Panama City members of the Massasoit Mining and Trading Company, a Massachusetts group that sailed to the isthmus on the schooner *Harriet Neal* only to find no steamer accommodations on the Pacific side, set up a shack and sold doughnuts to other Yankees passing through. They cleared twenty dollars their first day in business. As Bayard Taylor wrote, the Panama crossing could be "rough enough but had nothing that I could exactly call hardship."[6]

Indeed, the gastronomically adventurous could have quite the good time while waiting in Panama City for a berth—for a price. Although some guidebooks suggested that Americans eat no Panamanian oysters, oranges only in moderation, and no other tropical fruits, most on the scene seem to have disregarded the warning. Fruits and most kinds of food were generally plentiful in the long-decayed, sparsely populated town, although opinions as to the quality of catered meals varied. Albert C. Wells wrote home that "a man would sit down to a table with a good chicken and a half dozen eggs with bread and cooked plantain in abundance and leave it roughly cleaned of everything save the dishes." Obviously he liked it.[7]

56

H. C. Bailey is a little harder to figure. His assessment of the bread and potatoes at one repast is cryptic (although by potatoes he probably means plantains): "The bread was never baked until it reached the extreme limit of acidity and then baked until it was mostly crust, and a superior quality of crust unknown elsewhere. The potatoes were different from any I ever saw before or since." On the other hand, his opinion of Panama's hot beverages is crystal clear: "No one at the table could tell the difference between the tea and the coffee, or would have suspicioned the stuff of being either, had they not been told so."[8]

Wells and Bailey agreed that prices were extortionate. "The prevailing opinion seemed to be that the hungry Californians cared nothing about price if their appetites and desires were gratified." Bailey told of ordering steak at a restaurant in an attempt to hearten languishing friends. "When we settled the bill for one meal," he continued, "we concluded we could live on bread until we left Panama." They would see more of astronomical prices, of course, and both had the decency not to blame those in Panama on the Panamanians. In fact, most hotels and restaurants in Panama City appear to have been owned by Americans and had names like the American Hotel, the Eureka House, the Travellers Home, and the California Hotel.[9]

Once aboard a San Francisco-bound steamer (although not necessarily on a sailing ship, which adverse winds could push south as far as the equator), the journey was a short one, about four weeks long. The meals on this leg were not only ample but in some cases rather fancy. Bailey and eighty-six other passengers ate simply—the usual pork and beans, beef and split peas, and sandy duff, a doughy pudding with raisins. But another ship offered a pound of southern hemisphere ice to every passenger who purchased a bottle of wine and garnished a long menu with offerings of two different brandies, two sherries, Madeira, an 1844 port, champagnes, clarets, hock, cider, porter, whiskey, gin, and bitters. It may safely be conjectured that it was a profitable voyage.[10]

Provisions on the Panama route were generally abundant because few forty-niners traveled that way, no more than sixty-five hundred. Moreover, the voyages both originated and called at ports where provisions were comparatively inexpensive: those on the eastern sea-

57

board and Gulf coast, Santiago, sometimes Kingston, Jamaica, or Trinidad or Tobago. Even most of those sailing vessels that called at Panama after rounding the Horn had taken supplies aboard in Chilean or occasionally Peruvian ports. Where the Panama route proved to be a trial was when a Californian who had seen the elephant set out to return home.

THE PRICE OF GOING HOME

For those sailing south, provisions had to be purchased in San Francisco, where residents competed at the markets with ships' masters. Of the very first dinner out of port, with Sausalito still in clear view off larboard, Jane McDougal wrote: "had a very poor dinner of roast beef and yams about three o'clock." Meals did not improve. Despite the brevity of the trip some ships actually ran out of food before reaching Panama.[11] Dr. Isaac Lord, who made the San Francisco–Panama trip in 1851, was picturesque, not to say livid, on the subject of the galley on his vessel:

The passengers were fed like hogs. . . . Some of the hard bread was of good quality, some moldy, and much of it was infested with black bugs burrowing into it like woodchucks in a sandbank. A cold water soak would drive them out of their holes and cause them to vamoose, and you had the supreme gratification of knowing how many escaped; but you got no satisfaction as to how many remained to be eaten. It was altogether better to soak them in hot water or in your tea, as they cooked as easily as oysters, and you didn't have to eat them raw. They were not numerous enough to be full substitutes for fresh meat.

This was just as well because, as Dr. Lord continued,

The pork was worse. Not that it was wormy. No, no, it was too strong for that. Worms know what is palatable and take good care not to get into such pork barrels. . . . Many and many a savory ten pound morsel of carrion was tossed overboard that must have proved vomit for a shark. If not disposed of in some effectual way, it would appear at the next table. Another favorite dish, at least with the cooks, was Indian pudding. . . . Dark molasses would hide the mold and strangle the bugs and tangle the worms. As to the tough beef . . . , the Lord is not to be blamed because the Mexicans raise such little, tough, sinewy, cock-fighting bundles of rattan and rubber done up in calfskin for beef.[12]

Benjamin Baxter had a similar experience. He wrote that many of his returning fellow passengers, who had come to California overland, "said they would rather be on the Humboldt desert with only two days provisions than to be on board ship."[13]

With their stores inadequate, it could be fortuitous for southbound ships when they were hailed by Cape Horners on their way to San Francisco, since the Cape Horners were generally short not of food but of water, and trades were easily arranged. The Panama-bound steamer on which Jane McDougal traveled in 1849 was stopped by a sailing vessel eighty days out of Valparaiso, short on rations and desperately in need of water. The captain of McDougal's ship sent over two large casks and some fruit and melons "for which they seemed very grateful & sent in return four nice hams and a bit of champagne over which we had a very merry dinner indeed. I have not seen so much enjoyment & good feeling among the passengers since we left."[14] That there were "four nice hams" to be traded by a ship nearly six months at sea implies quite accurately the generally adequate provisioning of the Cape Horn ships—one kind of them, at any rate.

59

THE CAPE HORN COMPANIES

The all-sea route to California around Cape Horn took longer than any other. Of the sixty-five voyages originating in New England that Octavius T. Howe identified and charted, the average time at sea was 183 days—six months—about the poorest time any overland party made. Fourteen of those ships were more than 200 days at sea. (The longest voyage was that of the brig *Acadian*, 267 days; the shortest that of the schooner *Civilian*, 143 days.)

Historian Oscar Lewis describes the food on these ships as "nourishing and usually sufficient in quantity, and at least once a day the monotony was broken by the addition of a sweet," which is generally true enough. However, the sufficiency and quality of food on these long journeys seem to have been closely related to whether or not the ship had taken passengers aboard for the payment of fare, or was owned or chartered by the gold rush company that traveled on it.[15]

A good many of the argonauts of 1849, perhaps a majority of those out of New England ports, went not as individual wayfarers but as members of joint stock corporations organized much like the compa-

The Provisions Business in '49
"Bakers keep their ovens hot day and night without supplying the demand; the provision stores of all kinds are besieged with orders."

New York Herald, January 1849

nies that founded the first English colonies in North America, or, perhaps more fittingly, like the covenanted associations that, when a Massachusetts township was overpopulated, bound together for mutual benefit and moved west as a body. Yankees afflicted with gold fever joined together and capitalized companies with names like the Cochituate Mining Company, the Hampshire and Holyoke Company, the Cape Ann Pioneers, the Bay State and California Company. Before they left port, these cautious Yankees elected officers, adopted a behavior code that included such rules as the prohibition of cursing and foul language, provisioned a ship, often purchasing the ship outright, and filled the hold with goods they believed would bring high prices in California.

"At home I saw my neighbors not oftener than two or three times a week," wrote a forty-niner who sailed on the *Edward Everett*. "Now I have them about me at every hour of the day and night." Such an assemblage was unlikely to stint on provisions. Of one set of guidelines for provisioning a Cape Horn voyage, Octavius T. Howe writes, "if carried out it would have made the cost of the trip to California prohibitive." For each duly covenanted argonaut it included:

1 barrel salt pork
10 barrels salt beef
100 pounds ham
10 barrels ship's bread
10 pounds salt
40 pounds butter, cheese, tea, sugar

Shipboard Dining
"A Feat requiring a high degree of muscular coordination; if your plate and cup are to remain right side up and your well-laden spoon successfully to make the perilous trip from dish to mouth."

This was considered a suitable commissary for one year. In other companies such as the Boston and California Joint Stock Company on the *Edward Everett,* two years' sustenance was stowed aboard.[16]

The men who ran the companies knew full well (or thought they did) what they were doing. "Even if we fail to dig an ounce of gold," wrote a member of the Boston Marine Company aboard the schooner *Roanoke,* "the supplies we are bringing out with us will return each of us a sum larger than we could have earned at home." That was also the intention of the Beverley Joint Stock San Francisco Company aboard the bark *San Francisco.*[17]

Most companies hired professional cooks to see that meals were properly prepared, paying them either in cash or in shares. For the most part, members seem to have been satisfied with the services rendered. "The cook," Carolyn Hale Russ wrote, "is many men in one—very original—it is kinder so to call him than eccentric—one of his kind. . . . He is a fine cook at his post in the galley, and there is no better, nor more willing sailor among the crew."[18]

Whereas the nature of overland travel required forty-niners to break up into messes, each of which did its own cooking, the close quarters of a ship's galley and long maritime practice meant that only one cook, with assistants, would prepare meals at sea. However, as with all sailing vessels in which passengers were the principal cargo, it was necessary to serve food to messes that ate in shifts in the small dining cabin. More common when the weather was good, the passengers took their rations to different corners of the deck.

Except inasmuch as they formed one of the largest Cape Horn companies, the Yankees on the *Edward Everett* were typical. They formed fifteen messes of ten men each. A mess captain collected the meal for the rest at the galley and supervised the serving. Edward E. Chever, who sailed on the *Saltillo,* described the kind of scene that followed.

> Our dining table is a board shaped like a half-circle, which when in use is laid on top of a sea chest, which is moved out to the center of our double cabin. The table has cleats to hold the dishes, and keep them from sliding off. Our seats are sea chests on three sides, while on the fourth the cabin stairs serve the same purpose.
>
> The meat and potatoes (which were boiled together in the same kettle) are brought to the table in a tin pan; butter is placed in a broken yellow bowl; vinegar in an earthenware jug; sugar in a tin cup; and pepper in a wooden box. Each person has a quart bowl for coffee, and iron spoon of large size, with knife and fork, but the prongs of the forks, from repeated breaking, are very dull and of irregular length.[19]

There appears to have been little grievance with the system. Actually, one finds few complaints anywhere in the literature when the inconvenience or discomfort was the consequence of uncontrollable conditions. In the companies, it is difficult to find a serious complaint about the food. More likely, when the argonauts themselves were responsible for the provisions aboard, it is much easier to run across diarists who, "having partaken of an elaborate meal on some special occasion, set about with gusto composing a catalogue of the delicacies spread before the company."[20]

PLUM DUFF AND LOBSCOUSE

As on the trail, salt pork and wheaten flour were the twin mainstays of seaborne cuisine. However, because shipboard eating was limited by dining space rather than cooking facilities or time, the Cape Horn cooks generally prepared single bowl composite dishes instead of fire-roasted meat, soda biscuits, and flapjacks. Dandy funk was a heavy pudding made by boiling ship's biscuit in molasses, sometimes with raisins and cinnamon added. Apple grunt or fruit grunt consisted of dried fruits stewed and then baked in bread dough. Salt fish, pork, and beef were done up in various ways but the favorite dish of the forty-niners, lobscouse, was a hash of meat mixed well with hard bread. No doubt the easy chewability of the dish and the moderating effect of the bread in the hash made lobscouse a relief from the shoeleather that preserved meat could often be.[21]

Another favorite sailor's dish which many argonauts learned to look forward to was plum duff, the maritime name for spotted dick. It was a pudding consisting of a suet crust enclosing raisins (the "plums"), sugar, and spice—cinnamon or nutmeg—and boiled in a floured cloth. Today it might be difficult to imagine this a grand treat. But the tedium of a six-month voyage when one is not even working and the monotony of the food attributed it with the aura of Brillat-Savarin's turkey stuffed with truffles. "Our tastes are blind," explained two argonauts keeping a joint journal, even though the forty-niners' behavior when their vessel plowed through a school of fish, when they celebrated holidays, and when they called at South American ports, would imply that this was not always the case.[22]

Fresh fish was avidly consumed by forty-niners at sea. They revelled in the distraction of fishing and the chance to shoot porpoise, seals, and seabirds. Either they were not familiar with Coleridge's *Rime of the Ancient Mariner* or they were not impressed, for a number of them shot and ate albatross.

Like other mines far from towns, the Ryland of Yavapai, Arizona, provided a cook tent (described as a "dining room") for its employees. (Courtesy Sharlot Hall Museum, Prescott)

Holidays were invariably an occasion for feasts. On July 4, 1849, although then at sea six months, the company aboard the *Edward Everett* enjoyed hot biscuits and butter, beef and pork with applesauce, plum cakes, fruit (purchased in Valparaiso), and gingerbread with "fixins." One Thanksgiving Day menu, although not typical in its main course of roast fresh pork, was not unique either. In addition to the pork there was beef pot pie, plum duff, applesauce (from dried apples), cheese, oranges, lemons, figs, and nuts.[23]

It is difficult to believe that the passengers on the bark *San Francisco* and the ship *Elizabeth* were typical in taking live hogs with them but not at all hard to observe that they ate very well on their passages, which did wonders for their spirits.

Fresh pork once more,
Once more plum duff,
Take hold, take hold, sure that's enough.
Eat, eat your fill, don't look forlorn,
Here's roasted pig, and there's Cape Horn.
So don't be making such a bother,
We'll eat up one and pass the other.[24]

The hogs were gone soon enough—before reaching Cape Horn. But, like other ships controlled by the companies that sailed on them, the *Elizabeth* and the *San Francisco* put ashore when they needed more food. The most common port-of-call was Rio de Janeiro, where "everything is high except fruits." (In 1849 oranges went for a dollar per thousand.) Forty-niners with coin in their purses feasted, as Franklin Buck did, on ham, omelette, roast chicken, steak, watercress, lettuce, guava jelly, citron, green cheese, claret, Madeira, and coffee. One argonaut did not get to the city but called at an island off the coast of Brazil where "we found benaners [*sic*] growing wild in the clearing & et our fill you eat only the core first peeling of the skin which is bitter & contains little nurisshment."[25]

Once around the Horn—frequently a frustrating, even crushing test of seamanship, nerves, and larder—the most common port of call was Valparaiso, where there were "lots of Yankees . . . roaming about the city, patronizing the fruit vendors and makers of sweetmeats." The argonauts craved sweets, no doubt a function of the monotony of their meals. Unable to gain access to more than one of several barrels of sugar in the hold, the officers of the Beverley Company chose to avoid complaints about future shortages by rationing it out immediately, five pounds to the member. When there were cases of pilferage aboard—punished harshly, even by expulsion from the company with forfeiture of shares—the stolen article was most often a sweet. Fearing the loss of a sweet gift from home, and frankly admitting he did not choose to share his treasure, Joseph Kendall wrote home: "I often take a spoonfull or two of the preserved quinces on the sly. I have a bottom berth, and I have to get down on my hands and knees, and, lying nearly flat, open my little box, and take the quinces. I have to watch some time before I can get this opportunity."[26]

THE CARRYING TRADE   Kendall sailed on the *Canton*. He was not a member of a company but one fare-paying passenger among many. On voyages of this sort, shipowners and passengers were not partners but adversaries. The former's interests were to make a maximum profit while the latter's were to have as enjoyable a passage as possible at minimal expense.

On such voyages, complaints about food were common. They were especially virulent when the shipowners, competing for passengers in port, advertised the superior quality of their meals and then did not, to say the least, deliver. One in Boston actually served ticket-shopping forty-niners with a sample repast featuring all sorts of delicacies. Mysteriously, the makings of such meals proved not to be aboard once the ship was at sea. Of another ship, the *Samoset,* Charles H. Randall wrote with some prematurity, "There is not a vessel sailed for California that is better fitted out for accomodations of provisions. There is plenty of fresh beef, veal, and pork hung up on the rigging. Chicken and poultry, pigs &c. are not scarce."[27]

Maybe at dockside they were not scarce. But after only two weeks at sea the passengers elected a committee to complain to the captain about "the meanest poorest nastiest kind of fare very poorly cooked and awfully served up." The ship's officers did not console the passengers when they said they were all "living ten thousand times better than we shall before getting to the land of promise," particularly because—it was soon discovered—the captain kept separate stores for his own mess.

Nevertheless, the men on the *Samoset* reserved their chief ire for the owners of the vessel who, it appeared, had "represented things far different from what they are." In any case, there was some improvement following their remonstrances—pork with the beans, raisins in the duff, and rice twice a week.[28] When on the briny deep at the mercy of others, one was thankful for small favors.

Today, three meals were furnished, the last consisting of "mush"; the yankees call it hasty pudding. Let no-one hereafter belie this day as unlucky. Perhaps we may be charged with talking about small matters; we contend, however, it is no small matter to get a supper of mush, cheese and molasses, after having been a week without any at all, and being promised the same every night for the future—to such a one we would say with the critic upon Sancho, "There are dreams of turtle soup as well as dreams of turtle doves."[29]

The owners of the 687-ton *Capitol,* which left Boston on January 23 with two hundred paying passengers, had also boasted of providing something like the "best eats on the ocean blue." By March 1 the entire list was in near mutiny over their fare. They presented the captain with a petition that can only be described as moderate in its mealtime standards. "If we are furnished with the United States Navy rations (except ardent spirits)," they wrote, "we are satisfied, and on no other condition shall the power of two hundred voices be hushed."[30]

The *Capitol* called at Rio for eight days, where the passengers spent a goodly time "drinking fruit syrups," and at Valparaiso for four days. They were lucky for these breaks in the voyage. As courts of inquiry in San Francisco would later learn, some ship's masters refused to put into these ports because they had been ordered by the owners of their vessels not to do so under any circumstances.[31]

The chief reason for this policy was the same one that accounted for the poor meals in the first place. The gougers did not want to be pressured by their passengers into buying additional provisions at the

66

high prices Cariocans, Valparaisans, and the denizens at other ports on the gold route learned to charge in 1849. Moreover, once dockside in consular ports, which Valparaiso was, they had little choice in the matter. If passenger complaint was not enough to move a penny-pinching steward, the American consul was, and it was directly to him that angry, hungry argonauts took themselves. The ship's master who hoped to continue to practice his profession did not want a government summons waiting at home in his wife's apron pocket.

It was, of course, unlikely that he would be officially admonished for serving a sub-par lobscouse, or for running short of provisions because it took him two months to beat around the Horn. But to refuse for reasons of cost to call at a tropical port on a six-month voyage meant to risk laying crew and passengers abed with scurvy, and that was no trivial matter.

5 THE BLACK CANKER OF THE PLAINS

SACRED TO THE MEMORY
OF W. BROWN
Of the Rough and Ready co'y
of Platte, Mo.
Died with Skervy
Sep nineteenth 1849.
Aged 35 years.

Wooden grave marker in
western Nevada[1]

Scurvy is a debilitating physical condition, fatal if not arrested, that is caused by deprivation of vitamin C—ascorbic acid—for an extended period of time. The first symptoms are mental depression and lassitude, and a failure of physical strength. Not only are these symptomatic of a great many other ailments, but both are also easily shrugged off by the ignorant or the preoccupied as merely "not feeling so hot."

Within a month of the onset of the malaise, the person afflicted with scurvy feels a nagging ache in the joints, particularly in the ankles. Victims of scurvy in the California diggings often diagnosed what was beginning to ail them as "rheumatism," itself quite a common health problem profanely attributed to the rainy winters of the western slope of the Sierra Nevada and the long hours of toil hip-deep in streams that can be frigid at every season. In this phase of scurvy, however, scorbutics can be identified (by others who are looking for the disease) by their sallow complexions and sunken eyes. Close examination of a scorbutic's skin also reveals petechial and perrifollicular hemorrhages—seen as deformed body hairs and minute specks of blood at the roots of body hairs.

The unmistakable marks of scurvy, from the first of which the disease takes its name, follow within a few more weeks: blackish spots on the skin erupt into an ugly rash of skin lesions medically described as hyperkeratotic papules; and the scorbutic begins to ail with tender spongy gums, fetid breath, and urine fouled with a strong scent of ammonia.

If the condition is not promptly treated at this stage, the lesions worsen, rendering the unfortunate victim scurvy indeed. Cuts and wounds—simple scratches—begin to scab but do not heal. Gums bleed. Teeth loosen and fall out. There are vision disorders, particularly night blindness, and serious internal hemorrhages. Now, usually about two months after the appearance of the first sores, the scorbutic is bedbound. Death usually comes as a direct result of pulmonary or kidney failure or some other infection to which the weakened scorbutic has little resistance.[2]

But let a forty-niner relate his experience with the disease:

For a long time I had been feeling that something was wrong with me. I had never felt so before—sluggish, tired, lazy—the latter I had never been guilty of before. Finally, my gums got sore and began to bleed, and I became subject to excruciating pains . . . , having to be carried to and from my bed. The painful part of my affliction seemed to be in my feet and legs. The only way for a long time I could get at ease was in lying on my back on the floor and putting my feet on the table, a luxury I dearly paid for afterwards, for when I came to put them on a level with my body, the pain was still more unbearable. I would pity the meanest dog in the world that had the scurvy.[3]

Another remembered:

I noticed its first attack upon myself by swelling and bleeding of the gums, which was followed by a swelling of both legs below the knee, which rendered me unable to walk; and for 3 weeks I was laid up in my tent, obliged to feed upon the very articles that had caused the disease, and growing daily weaker, without any reasonable prospect of relief. There were, at that time, about 800 persons at work on the river, and hoping to get some medicine, I despatched one of my companions one morning with instructions to procure me, if possible a dose of salts, and to pay for it any price asked. He returned at night with the consoling news that he had failed, having found only 2 persons who had brought the article with them, and they refused to sell it at any price.

I was almost in despair: with only a blanket between myself and the damp, cold earth, and a thin canvas to protect me from the burning sun by day, and the heavy dews by night, I lay day after day enduring the most intense suffering from pain in my limbs, which were now becoming more swollen, and were turning completely black.[4]

Yet another "began to notice that when I undertook to climb a hill I was soon out of breath, and if I sat down to rest it was hard to get up

First things first. The Blankenship family ran their restaurant and bakery under a roof while they still lived in a tent at the rear. (Courtesy Western History Collections, University of Oklahoma Library, Norman)

again. One day I was at the river bank to wash a pan of dirt, and stooped down, with my knees bent, to wash it. I tried to rise when it was done, but was unable to do so. After rolling over and pushing my legs out straight I managed to stand up. In testing my legs I found that if I pressed with my thumb or finger below the knees a dent appeared in the flesh which remained a long time." Scurvy was, one forty-niner believed, "the worst disease we have to contend with" in the diggings: "it settles in the legs and ankles making the person quite lame. The skin turns purple and if not arrested soon, spots will decay and fall off, leaving a running sore. It is brought on by eating salt food and no vegetables."[5]

Historically scurvy has been identified with ocean-going seamen who, on long voyages, depended for their sustenance almost entirely on nonperishable foods such as ship biscuit and preserved meat and ate virtually none of the fruits and vegetables in which ascorbic acid is found in abundance. Not surprisingly, for nutrition is a science of the twentieth century, many people of the nineteenth and earlier centuries believed that scurvy was caused by something found *within* foods such as the seamen ate (as in the narrative quoted above), rather than by the *lack* of a nutrient. Or they attributed the disorder to the putrescence that was inevitable after long periods in even the best salted and packaged meat, or to the weevils that infested biscuit. Or—rheumatism, again—they associated scurvy with the sailor's quarters in dank, damp ships or with the famously unsanitary character of Jack Tar's personal habits.[6]

The misconceptions and confusions of our forebears in the matter should not be made too much of. Since ancient times they also understood without benefit of modern chemistry that scurvy was cured by eating fresh fruits and vegetables and many of them deduced that a dietary including these foods prevented the disease. The Crusaders knew this. The island of Curaçao off the coast of Venezuela got its name—*curaçao* means cure in Portuguese—when Christopher Columbus left several seamen wasted with scurvy there, only to return later and find them in the pink; they had whiled away what looked to be their last mortal hours gorging on tropical fruits. British sailors (and by extension all Englishmen) were nicknamed "limeys" when the Royal Navy decided at the end of the eighteenth century to include that fruit—lemons, actually—in every ship's stores. One forty-niner obviously had a wise doctor for he was treated with a foul-tasting but efficacious spruce-needle tea. Another, whose dose began with shortness of breath, resorted to the same expedient.

Nevertheless, the nature of scurvy remained a matter of considerable speculation in the United States of the gold rush era. An outbreak at Fort Laramie in 1859 was officially attributed to "want of cleanliness" and "defective cooking" even after the post surgeon cured it by concocting an elixir of cactus. Apparently he learned the formula from the Indians.

In some badly hit parts of the Mother Lode in 1848 and 1849, Hubert H. Bancroft tells us that "a remedy for scurvy was to bury the patient in earth, all but the head. Whole camps were sometimes buried at once, except a few who remained out to keep off the grizzlies and coyotes." Another physician prescribed steam baths as well as the antiscorbutic foods.

After extensive reflections during service in scurvy "epidemics" on the eastern seaboard among Irish refugees from the potato famine and later in gold rush California, Dr. Thomas M. Logan fastened on a diet deficient in fresh vegetables as a cause of the disease and rejected "cold and moisture, hitherto regarded as the most powerful predisposing causes"; but he also continued to consider as causes the putrefaction of the meat in the miners' regimen and the men's indifference to cleanliness and fatigue.

Dr. Logan was confusing symptoms with causes and the affliction itself with circumstances of it. Good scientist that he was, Logan recognized this problem. He observed of some of his patients in California that their dysentery and scurvy "were so commingled, that in many cases it was impossible to decide which predominated." For example, although the death of G. W. Evans on the Mother Lode on December 16, 1850, was attributed to scurvy (he cancelled out of a board arrangement on November 6 because "such a diet as was ordered by my Phy."—potatoes, onions, lime juice, and wild cress— "they would not provide"), it is just as likely the ailment that did him in was something else. Medical historian George W. Groh hints that many cases of scurvy on the trek westward might have actually been Rocky Mountain spotted fever or Colorado tick fever.[7]

73

Spruce Tea
Spruce tea appears to have been universally known to North American Indians over several centuries as a specific against scurvy. Jacques Cartier's expedition up the St. Lawrence in 1608 was saved by the concoction brewed by Algonkians.

But the point remains: however vague and muddled, the connection between scurvy and diet was common knowledge. If no one could prove precisely which comestibles were antiscorbutic or could state with authority just how long a person deprived of them could trundle about without being felled by scurvy, the forty-niner who ignored counsel to eat his greens was not only defying the empirical method but common wisdom. In fact, it is well for us to remember that ascorbic acid was not conclusively identified until as late as the early 1930s. Not until the 1950s would a British scientist's experiments on himself reveal with any precision scurvy's timetable.[8]

Indeed, scientists still disagree about how much vitamin C a human being requires each day. The effects of megadoses of the acid are still intensely controversial, with all sides able to marshall persuasive empirical evidence on behalf of their case.[9]

Whichever way this debate may be resolved, there exists an "official" vitamin C requirement or, more properly, a "Recommended Daily Allowance" that historians may use to generalize about scurvy in the past. According to the Nutrition Board of the National Academy of Sciences, an adult seeking to maintain basic good health is advised to ingest a daily average of forty-five milligrams of ascorbic acid.

On the face of it, on both trail and shipboard, the forty-niners were deprived of an adequate allowance of vitamin C. Neither the list of provisions recommended by Joseph Ware nor the composite overland ration figured by John Mack Faragher came close to meeting the Nutrition Board's 45 milligrams of vitamin C. On a continental crossing of 125 days, Ware's foodstuffs would provide only 14.1 milligrams of ascorbic acid per diem and the Faragher stores only 23.5 milligrams.[10]

Even at that, virtually all the vitamin C in the overland provisions lists was to be found in the dried peaches and apples. Not particularly rich in ascorbic acid when eaten raw, dried fruit is next to worthless as an antiscorbutic when cooked. To the extent that the overland migrants ate their fruit ration in pies and other confections that were exposed to high temperatures, which they surely preferred to do, they were destroying a sorely needed nutrient.

After perching the last bottle on the top of the pyramid, a proud Denver merchant called in a photographer. (Courtesy Colorado Historical Society, Denver)

And those were the overland emigrants. While it is impossible even to pretend precision in reconstructing the diet of the forty-niners who went to California via Cape Horn, in the single per person list of provisions that Octavius T. Howe found among the sea route emigrants he studied, there is no mention of dried apples. Even if we allow the argonauts a handful of raisins in their occasional bowl of plum duff, we are providing them with only a trace of ascorbic acid. In one hundred grams of raisins there is only one milligram of vitamin C. And most of that is destroyed by cooking.[11]

THE CANKER

So was the emigration plagued by scurvy? The two historians who have addressed the problem of health and disease in the gold rush think so. In a pioneering essay published in 1943, Georgia Willis Read named scurvy the third most important health hazard the overland emigrants faced (after cholera and mountain fever). She wrote that it filled "many a grave on the California route." In a long and detailed article published in 1957, scurvy specialist Anthony J. Lorenz drew a portrait of the emigration in which "the black canker of the plains" dogged the steps of the forty-niners. "No overland company, historians agree," Lorenz wrote, "arrived intact in California."[12]

There was certainly scurvy on the overland trail. One of the best known of the gold rush diarists, J. Goldsborough Bruff, an ex-army man who guided the Washington City and California Mining Association across the continent, buried a friend who died of it. He cared for the man's widow and eight children, whom he found in a "most deplorable condition—emaciated, feeble"; nursed a number of other scorbutics while wintering in the Sierra Nevada (mostly with success); and recorded the epitaph noted at the beginning of this chapter. J. T. Kerns recorded several cases of scurvy among his company of Hoosiers and wondered if, because of the disease, "we are *treading the elephant's tail*." Reuben Shaw told of meeting "grumbling travelers" and "scurvy."

The "most pitiable sight" that greeted Californian John Peoples when he led a relief expedition east along the Lassen Cutoff in the fall of 1849 has already been noticed. Scurvy may be what Charles Dexter

Cleveland was talking about when he described his party's entrance into Salt Lake City: "our teams were poor, jaded, and well-nigh exhausted and we were pretty much in the same condition [having lived] upon flour-cake, bacon, beans, rice, dried apples, and parched corn." When "M. M." wrote a series of letters from Sutter's Fort to the *Missouri Republican* he warned prospective trekkers of 1850 that "scurvy has been the poison bane of the emigration." He estimated that a third of the people entering Sacramento were sick.[13]

But that testimony is just about the sum of it. It seems to be all the evidence to be found in the huge body of forty-niner diaries, journals, and reminiscences supporting the contention of Read and Lorenz that scurvy stalked the emigration like a ravenous predator. The fact is, scurvy is mentioned in precious few of the several hundred chronicles of the crossing that have survived, and the incidence of scurvy in the journals and recollections of the gold seekers who used the all-sea route to California is only a little higher. There are no references to it in the records of those who traveled the isthmian route.[14]

The lack of evidence that scurvy was a problem in the emigration might mean one of several things. It might mean that scurvy was as common on the road and below decks as head colds and barked shins: It simply did not merit the notice of the diarists who were interested in recording the momentous and exotic, not the humdrum.

It may mean that companies that were ravaged by scurvy did not, for that excellent reason, produce many documents that survived long enough to be gathered and catalogued by historical society archivists. It is possible that the lust for gold was so pervasive and compelling that the misfortune of fellow travelers with scurvy escaped mention. At the very least we know that trekkers were often callous to the woes of others.

However, because plenty of evidence of scurvy appears in the documents left by forty-niners writing about life in the diggings— *almost all* of those notices quoted earlier—it is impossible to reject out of hand the most obvious explanation why so few mentioned it while on the trail and aboard ship: scurvy was simply not a major problem then.

It is, in fact, no mystery why this should be so. First, there is the element of time. Scurvy, like most conditions resulting from dietary deficiencies, is slow to develop. People do not keel over with it during cocktail hour if they skip orange juice at breakfast. In the definitive modern experiments the subjects' blood level of ascorbic acid fell to zero only after they had been deprived completely of vitamin C for forty-one days. The signal rash appeared only after approximately four months, and the subjects suffered their first serious hemorrhages in the sixth month of total vitamin C deprivation.

Well before this time fatigue and depression were problems, but not until six months along are scorbutics more or less completely incapacitated. By the time six months had transpired, virtually all the overland emigrants were over the spine of the Sierra Nevada.[15]

A *caveat* is in order. The subjects in the clinical experiments began their trial saturated with vitamin C. This may also have been true for some of the forty-niners when they left Missouri or the Atlantic and Gulf ports, but surely not for all. On the other hand, the induced scorbutics of the experiments were denied any ascorbic acid whatsoever. This was equally untrue of the emigrant experience and provides the chief explanation why the black canker was not a major problem on either the plains or the waves. Most forty-niners had and accepted the opportunity to ingest, if not megadoses of vitamin C, enough to keep the black canker at bay.

While few of the pre-1849 guidebooks dealt explicitly or at length with scurvy, a few levied stern warnings to their readers. For example, Edwin Bryant apprised emigrants that they would find "wild currants . . . abundant along the trail, . . . raspberries, and a small bitter cherry" and advised his readers to avail themselves of them. A number of parties reported collecting fruit, particularly at Fort Laramie, where chokeberries and currants were abundant, along with wild onions and a kind of watercress, both recognized as antiscorbutic by the army detachment there.

A captain at the post recommended "spruce tea," which "is very conducive to health as an anti-dyspeptic and is sure to cure the scurvy." Francis Galton, whose guide came out in 1867 (just in time to

78

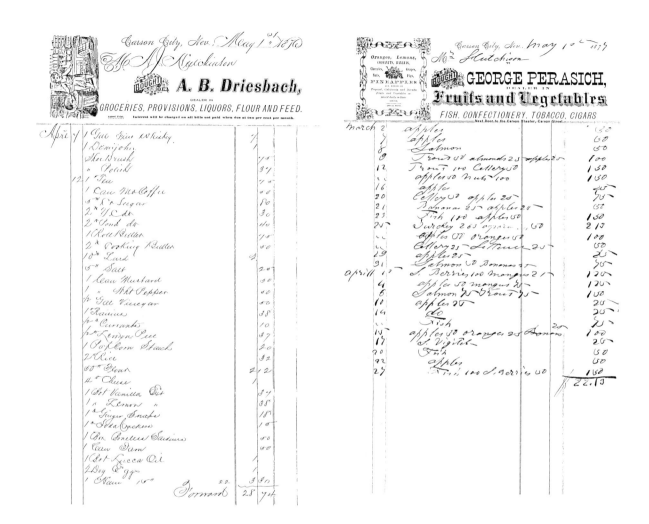

A. B. Driesbach of Carson City, Nevada, depended on the sale of staples to pay the bills, but this order also reflects the mining West's tastes for the piquant and pungent in its complement of mustard, vinegar, raisins and currants, lemon extract, ginger snaps, sardines, and the like.

The gourmet, Hutchinson, also specified that the olive oil came from Lucca, Italy, still regarded by many as the home of the world's best. Mr. Hutchinson also patronized George Perasich's store on Carson Street to obtain apples, bananas, oranges, berries,

and nuts as well as celery, lettuce, and fresh salmon and trout. The fresh fruits and vegetables were received daily during their seasons from tropical, California, and local Nevada sources. (Courtesy Special Collections, Getchell Library, University of Nevada, Reno)

be rendered obsolete by the transcontinental railroad), was very detailed: "Any vegetable diet cures it: Lime juice, treacle [not so], raw potatoes, and acid fruits are especially efficacious." Galton also named "sprouted seeds," a rather unique and quite valid insight about an acid no one had yet identified. Edward Gould Buffum was cured of his nearly fatal case thanks to an unknown forty-niner who had dropped a sack of beans nearby that burst and sprouted. A physician on the road had his party eat "lambquarter greens" and other "weeds of the prairie" in salads. From Sacramento, M. M. advised emigrants of 1850 to carry onions.[16]

The "treats" from home that overlanders took with them might have been antiscorbutics: "for luxuries we carried a gallon each of wild plum and crabapple preserves and blackberry jam." It was also possible to purchase antiscorbutics at the trailside shops. Virtually every visitor to Salt Lake City counted vegetables among the most desirable commodities to be had in Zion, particularly green peas, which they craved enough to pay ridiculous prices for.

Visited by more emigrants than Salt Lake City was Pickleville, near what is now the Utah–Idaho line. There a half-gallon jar of pickles cost eight dollars, a price that was apparently frequently paid. The emigrants, and later the miners in the diggings, craved vinegar-pickled food, believing it to be antiscorbutic—which, when the pickle itself was onion or cucumber, it was.[17]

None of this should be taken to mean that the overland emigrants arrived in California robust and vitamin C-saturated. They did not. Many were on the verge of suffering from scurvy and would drop of it in the diggings. But it did not hit many of them on the trail, an important reason why the colossal movement of population was possible.

ON THE ISTHMUS

As for the gold-seekers who took the isthmian route, scurvy never had a chance. The way to California via Panama or Nicaragua was the quickest road to the diggings; only the unluckiest trips took six months and some took as few as fifty days. Moreover, transportation to Central America was on ships, mostly steamers, that featured

THE BLACK CANKER

Exhausted miners and two ladies dine *al fresco* at Crater Lake, Alaska. (Courtesy Hegg Collection, University of Washington, Seattle)

vegetables of various sorts on their menus and over lands in which fresh fruit was among the most abundant of foodstuffs.

On a typical day's card on a steamer bound from a North American port to Nicaragua or Panama, breakfast included (in addition to midcentury's regular hearty fare) "one half a pound of preserved fruit for each ten persons," and at supper passengers received the same ration of marmalade. Once ashore on the isthmus, argonauts found that tropical fruits were so abundant they were not bought but picked. "How strange it seems," Roger S. Baldwin wrote home from Nicaragua, "to be walking under orange, and lemon, and tamarind, and palm trees, to be picking guavas and mangos. . . . You should have seen me this morning, sitting under a cocoanut tree . . . cutting the end with my machete, and drinking the rich, pulpy milk."[18]

Baldwin loved the place so avidly that one regrets for him that he continued on to California. He described mangos as "the rich fruit of which I have acquired a decided taste." While his company did suffer some shortages on the Pacific leg of their journey, he wrote from

California that although "here the most thrilling tales of sufferings hourly meet the ear . . . so far as we know with certainty, not a death nor even a dangerous attack of illness has occurred in all our company which left New York."

It is difficult to imagine vitamin C deficiency among the isthmian forty-niners. Sailing vessels from around the Horn, which did suffer shortages, called at Panama City—bottleneck and prison for those who had arrived there by land—precisely in order to reap the abundance of antiscorbutic foods. Or, if capricious winds prevented them from calling at the isthmus, they paused at other Central American ports, like Acapulco, where "fruits were easily obtained from the plaza early each morning."[19] It cannot, unhappily, be demonstrated, but it is irresistible to speculate that the mortality rate from scurvy in California—where the forty-niners ceased to think much about how they had come—was lowest among the isthmian travelers.

THE ALL-SEA ROUTE

The Cape Horners that called at Central American ports sometimes sorely needed fresh fruits in their fare. The notion of antiscorbutic foods as medicine, so common in California, was well known on the sailing ships too. Plying the all-sea route took an average of six months; the shortest passages lasted nearly five, more than enough time for scurvy to make its presence palpably known. Once again, however, the striking lesson of the documents is, given the vicissitudes of the voyage, how few argonauts seem to have had their passage ruined by the disease.

The key to a scurvy-free voyage and a healthy debarkation was calling along the way at least at one Atlantic port (usually Rio), another after rounding the Horn (usually Valparaiso), and—if the final dash north proved as it often did no dash at all but a tedious, frustrating struggle against adverse winds—at a port in Central America. Those vessels that did not make at least the Brazilian and Chilean calls because they were in too much a hurry, were poorly captained, or were abused mercilessly by the elements, arrived in San Francisco with passengers prostrate or dead.

The ship on which a German physician named Praslow sailed did not pause at Rio; everyone was in the pink of health. They discovered

THE BLACK CANKER

their error off Patagonia when several cases of scurvy appeared. For a time Dr. Praslow managed to minister successfully to the victims. But when it took seven weeks to beat around the Horn, the disease flattened twenty-five men of the two hundred aboard. At Valparaiso, there was no choice but to put in and take fruits aboard whence the victims were revived, only to be stricken again by the time Dr. Praslow's *Brooklyn* reached the Golden Gate.[20]

The story was worse on vessels that, even less provident, passed by Valparaiso. They reached the Golden Gate miserable with "a good many cases of scurvy." Even the *Edward Everett,* an extremely well provisioned ship of the company made up largely of college men, arrived with several of the baccalaureates in the "incipient stages" of the disease. There was plenty of salt pork and flour left—the *Everett* had been loaded with staples enough for two years—but few fresh fruits and vegetables had been taken aboard.[21]

Those diary-writing argonauts who visited the South American ports, on the other hand, seem all to have landed in California healthy. Their recollections of Rio and the rest are quite diverse. Some were fascinated by the exotic people and culture, others repelled. Some leapt at the chance to stretch their legs on *terra firma,* however Latin, and to eat at restaurants, however garlicky the fare. Others went ashore only briefly and then in trepidation for their Protestant souls. Some wanted to tarry, while others—visions of a California stripped clean of gold in their heads—rued every hour lying at anchor.

But virtually every one of them who recorded his feelings and doings mentioned fruit. "Everything is high except fruits," Charles H. Randall wrote of the prices in Rio. He "ate all kinds of tropical fruits growing." William DeCosta exulted when his party was permitted to go ashore "to revel in the luxury of tropical fruits." The Reverend James Wood, one of those troubled by the paganism of the place, nevertheless rushed to be the first of his number into Rio where "the first thing I did was to buy oranges."

Wood tells us as others do that, whatever the midcentury mind knew about scurvy, the midcentury body short on ascorbic acid craved just the right kind of "land food." A passenger on the ship *Pacific,* despite a ration of fresh apples aboard, not apparently a common item in the emigration, wrote of "longing for the luxuries of Rio" by which he explained in a later entry he meant "oranges, lemons and limes costing 50 cents to 75 cents per 100."[22] One group of argonauts from Maine called at the island of San Juan Fernandez, where they found "quinces and peaches . . . enough to gratify . . . the gourmandizing propensity of our earthly man." Valparaiso was the most common stop on the Pacific leg. Lewis Sanger wrote before arriving there that "the general health of our company is good" but nonetheless he and his mates stocked up on "radishes, turnips, onions and cabbage, peaches, plums, oranges, nectarines, bananas and plantains."

Charles Williams's party, in Rio in mid-March, was lucky enough to round the Horn in record time and clear Callao, Chile, on the first day of June. There they purchased fruits, cabbages, pumpkins, and potatoes. Only a few of the fruit-eaters referred to scurvy in connection with their ports-of-call but, on their minds or not, they had much to be thankful for. As one wrote of Valparaiso, "the climate is excellent, producing the finest fruits in abundance but as we were here in the early Spring, November being about the same as April with us, we could only get oranges, lemons, and strawberries. The latter were of enormous size and the best I ever tasted."[23]

So it is not surprising that some of the Cape Horn sailors arrived in San Francisco in fine health if sometimes in less than optimum physical condition for the hard work ahead. At least one, William H. Herbert, who traveled on the bark *Elvira*, gained nine pounds between Boston and Rio and another fourteen before he got to California.[24]

Still, appearances and the elation at having reached a remote destination could deceive. If the mortality from scurvy on the way to California was negligible, it soared during the two years between the spring of 1849 and the spring of 1851. It appears to have been worst among gold-seekers in their first year in the mines, that is, among those who set the scorbutogenic clock ticking while still en route. If it is reasonable to conjecture that argonauts who came via the isthmus were the least likely to suffer the disease, it is impossible to know whether overland or all-sea emigrants were the harder hit. As conditions in the diggings created a sense of community, a "sub-culture" that was to permeate western mining society for half a century, the route an "Old Californian" took to the Golden State ceased to be relevant.

However, the Cape Horners were well represented among the dead. There would have been few men actually stricken by scurvy in the mines who made it as far as San Francisco to recover or die, but scorbutics were in the city in considerable numbers. Of the 149 men who died at the State Marine Hospital between May and December 1850, 14 were victims of the black canker. The odds say they never saw a gold-bearing stream but only the sea, the Golden Gate, and the growing city of St. Francis.[25]

6 THE FOOD RUSH

Indian Valley—It came to pass that one
was sick and wanted potatoes to eat
and his brethren went and sought
potatoes until they found them at
$1.25 a pound—in time he got well.

Letter of a California miner, 1850[1]

Scurvy's most industrious historian, Anthony J. Lorenz, probably
overshot the mark when he estimated that between 1849 and 1851 ten
thousand Californians died for lack of vitamin C.[2] If, amid a population of two hundred thousand, so many forty-niners and fiftiers had
succumbed to a single disease, we should read in the diaries and
reminiscences about a great deal more aching joints, bleeding gums,
and mass burials than we do. There is no document from the rush that
resembles one of the classical chronicles of the Crusades:

The sickness began to increase in the host in such sort, and the dead flesh so to
grow upon the gums of our people, that the barber surgeons had to remove the
dead flesh in order that the people might masticate their food and swallow it.
Great pity it was to hear the cry throughout the camp of the people whose
dead flesh was being cut away; for they cried like women labouring of child.

Even the diaries from gold rush camps like Sonora, which were truly
cursed by scurvy, often treat the disease as little more than a damned
nuisance.[3]

SCURVY IN THE DIGGINGS

Nevertheless, scurvy was far more prominent in California than it was
during the emigration that was the root of its later strength. The long
months on the trail and shipboard, seemingly negotiated without
scorbutic incident for so many, left many gold-seekers in a scurvy-
prone condition. Companies that reported no cases of the disease on
the way to California suffered losses soon after arriving. This was the
fate of the men of the brig *Charlotte*, who were hit by fatalities within

three months of entering San Francisco Bay. George F. Kent, who rounded the Horn with the Shawmut and California Company—free of scurvy for seven long months at sea—reported that during the winter of 1849–1850 "nearly all of our party excepting myself were troubled" by an ailment that was almost certainly the black canker.

The reason Kent escaped the affliction probably lies in his aside about the master of his ship who became a miner and Kent's partner. "Captain Snow was very much affected with this disease, but finally drove it away by the free use of potatoes, vinegar, etc." Kent, presumably, was on a regimen similar to the cure all along. That was the remedy with which Edward Gould Buffum, an eloquent diarist of the northern diggings, combatted his scurvy. "By living principally upon a vegetable diet, which I procured by paying three dollars for a pound of potatoes, in a very short time I recovered."[4]

And in Sonora, where a scurvy epidemic inspired the residents still on their feet to incorporate a city and establish a municipal hospital, the worst was weathered by "enormous" purchases of lime juice at five dollars a bottle, potatoes at exorbitant cost, and canned fruits at "twenty-fold the usual prices."[5]

The sources reveal few forty-niners turning to the abundant native and wild antiscorbutic plants in lieu of such expensive medicines—just one example of their conservatism about unfamiliar foods. However, according to the first Methodist preacher in the state, he wrought a miracle in the San Francisco hospital with just such manna. "My friends, what are you doing here?" the Reverend William Taylor exhorted the languishing patients of the scurvy ward.

"You are cooped up in this miserable place without fresh air, without sunshine, without exercise, and without vegetable diet. You will die, the last man of you, if you don't get out of this place. You had better be turned out in the San Jose Valley to graze, like old Nebuchadnezzar, than pine away and die in such a place as this." Now, said I, "I'll tell you what will cure you. On these sand-hills back of the city there grows a kind of wild lettuce," which I described to them. "If you will go out and gather that lettuce and use it, with a little vinegar, it will cure you." I knew the open air, and sunshine, and exercise would help them and believed the prescribed salad the best thing for them within their reach.

It was an interesting thing to see those poor fellows under the inspiration of a new hope crawling out and scrambling up the hills in search of my prescribed cure. The next week, when I called again to see them, I was really surprised to see how much their condition had improved.[6]

Scurvy in the Klondike
After about 1851, scurvy did not much trouble the mining frontier until the great rush to the Klondike and the Yukon country at the end of the century. The Royal Canadian Mounted Police established demanding standards for entering the Dominion over the famous Chilkoot Pass and Dead Horse Trail, requiring just about double the provisions per person that the forty-niners had carried. And the guidebook authors were a good deal more scurvy-conscious in 1897 than their midcentury predecessors had been.

In his *Klondike Official Guide,* William Ogilvie was downright stylish: "In case of scurvy one might provide lime juice, more or less as their taste suggests, but the dried fruits . . . are antiscorbutic in their action and if we wish to make further provision in that direction we might take two or three dozen tins of good orange marmalade, and a similar quantity of strawberry or raspberry jam."

THE FOOD RUSH

Meals of beans and frozen bread in this kind of atmosphere put prospectors in the mood for a splurge at a fancy restaurant, as well as a binge and a ladyfriend, when they lit into town. (Courtesy Hegg Collection, University of Washington, Seattle)

89

Nevertheless, scurvy was a serious problem in Canada and Alaska. Jack London suffered a serious case and cured it, much as many of the forty-niners did, by buying potatoes and eating them raw. Lifelong problems with his teeth were at least in part a consequence of his affliction.

Within their reach! That, of course, was the key to the threat of scurvy and the general problem of food supply during California's first years. A country far from established trade lanes, it had been inundated with hungry people within one short year and overrun anew in 1850. Within California, transport was at first primitive and slow. (Scurvy would not again play a conspicuous part on the western mining frontier until the rush to the similarly isolated Yukon and Klondike in 1898.) Moreover, several of American California's first winters were particularly wet ones. Washed-out roads cut off wilderness camps, some of them quite sizeable, from the river port supply centers of Stockton, Sacramento, and Marysville. What is remarkable about these naturally decreed difficulties, however, is just how quickly they were overcome. Indeed, if it had not taken so long to get to California—had it required a journey of but two or three months—there would have been no scurvy and no prices so high that they form practically the symbol of the gold rush in our historical imagination. The rush of provisions to California began on the heels of the rush of men.

No characteristic of gold rush California is so well known as the astronomical prices at which everything seemed to sell. Beefs seven or eight dollars a head in February 1848, sold for twenty-five to one hundred dollars by the summer. A year later, "little of it was to be had, and then only jerked, at correspondingly high prices." Flour, eight dollars a barrel before Marshall's discovery, soared by the summer of 1849 to fifty dollars in San Francisco and eighty-five dollars at Sutter's Fort.

The year 1849 also saw bay oysters and eggs available from established *californios* going at a dollar apiece. In Sacramento potatoes and onions sold at a dollar and a half a pound, and in the mines at least a few of those changed hands for a dollar each, "entirely out of reach as an article of food." In Placerville a plain slice of bread sold for a dollar, a buttered one for two. The Sonora hospital counted out five dollars in gold dust for each six-ounce bottle of lime juice that was purchased. Canned fruits were marked up 2000 percent over retail rates on the eastern seaboard. For dinner at Sacramento on Christmas day, 1849, Catherine Haun paid two and a half dollars for a grizzly bear steak and another dollar for a side of cabbage. At a tent saloon in San Francisco, hanging out the sign "potatoes this day" meant a teeming patronage of big spenders.[7]

Almost all the forty-niners expressed bemusement that vegetables should sell by the pound rather than by the bushel. The correspondence brims with anecdotes like Charles D. Ferguson's. When potatoes "got down to $30 a hundred," Ferguson wrote, he and a partner "bought each a hundred pounds, and carried them on our backs three miles, thinking we had a great prize." One of Ferguson's earlier experiences provides the consummate experience of the California inflation of 1849.

One day, while walking through the market of Marysville, I saw some pears for sale. I had seen no fruit yet in the country. All my boyish appetite was aroused. I took one and ate it and was about to take another, when it occurred to me to ask how much they were apiece, at the same time pulling out a silver dollar to pay for the two. It somewhat jogged the intellect when in a modest and innocent way I was told that they were only $2.50 apiece. I suddenly discovered that the one I had already eaten was sufficient for me at that time. I paid for it and walked on to meet a vendor of onions, who told me that he was disposing of his vegetables for the remarkably low price of $3 a pound. I purchased of him one good large onion for $2, and ate it raw, and thought I had never before tasted anything half so delicious.[8]

As numerous as the tales of horrific prices are the accounts of those who took advantage of them. Legend has it that Mrs. Peter Wimmer, wife of a Sutter employee at Coloma who owned a few pear trees, had even more valuable fruit than the one Charles Ferguson bought. She sold her pears when they were still blossoms, tagging each flower with the name of the purchaser. Other wives of forty-niners also plunged into the giddying trade in antiscorbutics. Mary Jane Meguier purchased half a barrel of pickles, soaked the salt out of them, put them up in quart bottles, and sold each vessel for six dollars more than the price of the whole barrel—and she had plenty left for the family board. Mrs. Lewis C. Gunn, wife of a physician who built up a lucrative practice in Sonora during the scurvy scare, acquired some tomatoes, boiled them down to a "syrup," sliced in some oranges, and delighted her husband. One prostitute of legend delighted herself when, in one season, a garden she kept behind the cribs netted a fifty thousand dollar profit, enough to transform any soiled dove into a bourgeois angel.[9]

William Taylor of Sacramento recounted his wife's experience:

Our garden flourished so that in a few weeks after the commencement of the rains in October, we had turnips, greens, and lettuce in abundance, a luxury enjoyed, I believe, by but one other family in the city. A restaurant keeper, passing by our garden one day, said to Mrs. Taylor: "I would like to buy some of your greens, madam; what do you ask for them?" "We have not offered any for sale," she replied, "but as we have more than we need, you can have some at your own price." Said he, "I'll give you ten dollars for a water pail full." He took them, paid the money, and in a few days returned for more. Mrs. Taylor filled his pail again, and told him she would not take ten dollars for them, but would be well-satisfied with eight. She then asked him how he could afford to pay such prices. "Well," said he, "I boil the greens slightly, with a little bacon, and get for them, when ready for use, fifty cents a fork. I make a very good profit on them."[10]

William Dinkel of Colorado described the more complicated commerce in which his potato patch involved him. "A man named Martin gave his jack for a sack of potatos. Later he traded a pony for the jack and another sack. Still later, he gave a large horse for the pony and a third sack." Dinkel "sold the large horse for $150, thus realizing $50 a sack for the potatos."[11]

Some forty-niners spent Sunday riotously. Others attended to the Good Book. Many took the opportunity to dine in a restaurant. (Courtesy Huntington Library, San Marino, Calif.)

92

Bear Meat

"The first week in January 1850 we bought 100 lbs. of bear meat at a dollar per pound. I asked the man how many pounds he had sold and he said, 'I've sold 1300 lbs. and have 400–500 lbs. in camp yet.'"

Alvin Coffee, 1850

Somewhat farther-ranging entrepreneurs were also busy exploiting the ratio of mouths to feed with food to fill them. As early as June 1848 a San Francisco merchant wrote to an associate in Boston that "people here are perfectly crazy." He knew of two ships that were bound for Hawaii and Valparaiso after "cargos principally of eatables." On September 21, 1849, just five days after he arrived in San Francisco on a ship that had been visited by scurvy, Dr. Charles Frederick Winslow wrote to associates back East: "in sending out provisions for the men send things that will be best against the scurvy, fever and ague. Canistered provisions and vegetables and all sorts of fruit are first rate but very expensive in this country." Flour came from Oregon and Australia. Chile sent beans, China sent rice. Argentina shipped jerky, with "about as much grease in it as a strip of bark dangling in the wind from a dead tree." In July 1850 a ship arrived from Boston loaded with ice that sold for eighty cents a pound. (At that time, another ship from Mexico arrived full of cats at ten dollars each—for ratting, not for food.)[12]

Edward Austin wrote his brother that there were bushels of money to be made by the entrepreneur who could get citric acid and lemon juice to Sacramento. He also told him that "if you stop at Santiago or any place where you can buy 40# or 50# worth of onions, do so. . . . You may buy them at San Blas [too], but do not pay the Mexicans until you get them on board." An argonaut who acted himself invested the proceeds from a year in the diggings in a schooner that he set off in, bound for the "Sandwich or Society Islands after a cargo of vegetables and hogs."[13]

Tahiti proved to be the landfall and, in addition to staples, the *Columbia* took aboard four hundred barrels of sweet potatoes, two hundred squashes, two thousand limes, two thousand coconuts, fifty bunches of bananas, and forty-six thousand oranges. The purchasing agent noted that the queen of Papeete had seized a monopoly on the island's oranges, "speculating" in the California trade. But, at her price of five dollars a thousand, she was not speculating nearly so grandiosely as the California middlemen. As late as 1851, oranges sold in the Golden State at medicine rather than at food prices.[14]

In the meantime, Edward Austin was thinking about production in his new home. In September 1849 he wrote his brother to send him seeds for radishes, early cabbage and head cabbage, early white turnip, tennis ball and "curley lettuice," carrots, beets, squash, melon, spinach, peas of several varieties, celery, and other garden truck. Overly impatient, he wrote again within a few weeks to say

I am not too sanguine when I say I can get off of 10 acres of land at the present prices of vegetables 80,000$ [*sic*] in one year. I know the amount that an acre will produce of any vegetable, and I shall get five crops off of one acre in six months as I used to get at West Cambridge. So I think old Pierce's saying will come true. Said he, "This is rather hard work but you will see the time, Edward, when this digging and planting will be of use to you."[15]

Actually, Austin was a johnny-come-lately to California's second-oldest profession. The echoes of "Eureka!" had scarcely faded from the gulches before Indians were carrying in salmon, and boys who had not dumped their rifles in Nevada were shooting deer and elk and learning how to price chops and haunches. As early as January 1, 1850, well-integrated grocery companies like Warren and Co. tacked broadsides on the pines and oaks of the Sierra slope to announce the opening of such emporia as "the Excelsior tent at Mormon Island." Inside "the Large Tent on the Hill," the "Good News for Miners" included "Pork, Flour, Bread, Beef, Hams, Mackeral, Sugar, Molasses, Coffee, Teas, Butter & Cheese, Pickles, Beans, Peas, Rice, Chocolate, Spices, Salt, Soap, Vinegar, &c," as well as "Every variety of Preserved Meats and Vegetables and Fruits [more than eighty different kinds], Tongues and Sounds; Smoked Halibut; Dry Cod Fish; Eggs fresh and

There was no "Delmonico's of the West" on Colorado's San Miguel River, so the miners used humor to enhance their "dining rooms." (Courtesy The Denver Public Library, Western History Department)

THE FOOD RUSH

fine; Figs; Raisins; Almonds and Nuts; China Preserves, China Bread and Cakes; Butter Crackers, Boston Crackers, and many other very desirable and choice bits."[16]

AN UNSTABLE MARKET

No doubt the prices at the Excelsior were as fabulous as those already described. The California dream was, after all, a fortune overnight. Most of the early provisioners, as Ralph Mann points out in his valuable study of Grass Valley and Nevada City, California, seem to have been miners who wearied of aching backs and invested what capital they had in canned goods (or whiskey). Professor Mann adds that "bad luck in choosing merchandise or overextensions of credit might quickly return [the grocer] to the pick and shovel."[17]

Therein lies a clue to the nature of the retail economy of 1849 that is too little recounted in the histories. The provisions market on the California frontier—and on other metal mining frontiers to follow— was not characterized so much by dizzyingly high prices as by a crazy instability. Prices of every edible from wheaten flour and salt pork to oranges and canned caviar did not start at sky-high levels and only eventually decline to merely high levels. From the beginning they swung wildly from absurdly high to (for the merchants) dishearteningly low. The consumers of 1849 and 1859—and the western miners for half a century—were quite as apt to score incredible bargains as they were to pay prices that had easterners slapping their thighs in wonderment.

This was true of both the entrepôts of San Francisco and Sacramento and the remotest camps of leaky tents, lean-tos, and strong language. If the legendary Sam Brannan could clear thirty-six thousand dollars peddling provisions between May 1 and July 10, 1848, some ships in San Francisco Bay that very autumn had to auction their cargos at bargain rates because so many had arrived filled with the same goods at the same time. An argonaut of 1849 wrote that "every vessel was loaded with goods of all kinds and no people were here to buy them, as nine out of ten arrivals were off to the mines, and there was a glut of every thing in the market." John Henry Liening arrived with provisions that had cost him twenty-seven hundred dollars back East, "thinking such things would be needed here, and therefore salable, but the contrary proved true, as I could not

95

The Potato Rush
Some gluts actually preceded the gold rush. William Taylor tells of the "potato growing fever" that dizzied some pre-James Marshall Californians in anticipation of the flood of newcomers. He wrote that several hundred thousand dollars were invested in the crop in 1848, seed potatoes going for fifteen cents a pound and laborers hired at a hundred dollars a month to fence and cultivate them. "The result was that the markets were glutted, the price of potatoes went down to the cost value of the sacks that contained them, and hundreds of thousands of tons of the finest potatoes in the world, dug and gathered into large cribs, lay and rotted, creating such a nuisance that it was feared that they would breed a pestilence in some localities."

William Taylor, *California Life Illustrated,* 1861

get first cost on my arrival in San Francisco." Another aspiring grocery king "found provisions so abundant and cheap that we knew we would not be able to dispose of them all at wholesale. They were piled up in vacant lots and at the sides of the streets in great quantities."[18]

According to Caspar T. Hopkins,

the arrivals were so constant, every vessel bringing more or less merchandize, the Customs Service so imperfect, and no arrangements yet made for reporting manifests, or for any concert of action on the part of the dealers, that it was not uncommon to find a difference of one or two hundred percent in the price of the same article in two stores right alongside of each other.[19]

It would be difficult to overemphasize the size or economic impact of the food rush. During 1848, 47 ships called at San Francisco, itself a big jump over 1847's total. During the first three weeks of 1849, 20 ships cleared the Golden Gate. Between April 1 and November 10, there were 1,113 arrivals.

When, to the delight of the few provisioners on the scene, sides of bacon were being bid to prices as high as the buttes at auctions at Bidwell Bar or Columbia, the same commodities were being used as landfill in San Francisco and Sacramento. "The whole city is literally stuffed, crammed with provisions," Dr. Isaac Lord wrote of the River City in December 1849.

Eatables of every description [are] so exposed that almost every kind must suffer more or less damage and hundreds of thousands of dollars of damage is already done. I saw at one establishment alone over 200 boxes of herrings rotting in one pile; any amount of spoiled pork, bacon, cheese, moldy and rotten; pilot bread and most everything else. The destruction and waste here is almost or quite equal to that on the plains, with not half the necessity, and a thousand times the recklessness.[20]

Rather more striking, it could work the other way: low prices in the mines, fairly high ones in the cities. After the winter of glut in Sacramento that Lord described, merchants hastily shipped their goods up the slope. They did not resolve their problem but merely changed its venue. Now competing in the camps, the merchants had to dispose of provisions "at ruinous sacrifices" while the temporary shortage back on the river caused a modest rally in business. When Alonzo

San Francisco in 1850. Already much of
the city was built of brick. There were
also hundreds of eateries and more than
a few fine restaurants. (Courtesy
The Bancroft Library,
University of California, Berkeley)

Green walked into a bakery in Sonora and said he wanted to have fifty tons of flour brought up from Stockton, he was asked "what in the devil do you want to bring more flour into camp for we have more now than we will sell this winter." Green bought out the baker's supply and, when news of problems in the valley blew into camp, sold it back to the same man, eventually realizing a twenty-five-thousand-dollar profit.[21]

Up and down and up again was the story, not steadily exorbitant rates. When prices did stabilize in San Francisco by March 1850, it was at a rather low level. "It has astonished me," C. H. Randall wrote to his parents, "to see the change that has been effected in this place since last fall; the prices of all kinds of merchandise are cheap as they are in the states, many things lower." Alonzo Delano added: "Provisions are now obtained in the mines with much less difficulty than they were last fall and in greater variety, so that the meager diet of the miners can be replaced by that more healthful. Trading establishments keep pace with the crowds forcing their way into the mountain recesses, and competition is rapidly reducing the exorbitant prices which were common last fall."[22]

In 1851 the story was the same. In San Francisco to trade on February 16, Captain Octavius Howe wrote, "I found on my arrival the market to be extremely dull." He went to Sacramento with his stores but "the whole country is full of goods and large arrivals are expected. All kinds of trade are so very fluctuating and uncertain that for my own part I put no reliance on any predictions of great improvement." Back in San Francisco on March 22, he noted: "we find it extremely difficult to sell even a small portion of the cargo at a rate which will pay freight and charges. . . . Butter is very dull . . . preserved meat, pickles and preserves in no demand."[23] *Sic semper mercator.*

THE HUNGRY CONVENTION AND OTHER HARD TIMES

This does not mean that there was no hardship in the California diggings. William S. Greever is surely correct when he writes that "some gold seekers starved to death because they had no funds to buy food, they were too proud to ask aid, and their plight went undetected in a mining community where charity was 'emotional and demonstrative rather than reflective and organized.' " Reporters wrote that "many were driven from the mines for want of food." Charles H. Randall informed his parents that "a man in the mines must work within sight of his provisions or run the risk of them being stolen." Even in bustling Sacramento, "poor famished men were plenty . . . in November and first of December 1849." Another witness lamented that "there is a heartless unconcern in the community generally to the sufferings of the many who are dying wretched deaths in the midst of them."[24]

Nor was hunger to be a stranger to the scenes of the early days of later rushes. The Comstock was spared deprivation because of its proximity to a then-developed California. But in the Pike's Peak fields, also opened in 1859, a reporter for the *Rocky Mountain News* wrote that "every day we meet men arriving from the States . . . in a famishing condition. A few days ago a man arrived at Russelville, and reported that his companions, nine in number—had given up and lain down on the prairie some miles distant. A relief party was sent out, who found one of the number dead from actual starvation, and two others so far gone that they died soon after reaching the settlement." Colorado's Augusta Tabor "shivered every time she saw Old Phil, the Cannibal, said to have killed and eaten two Indians and one white man." Old Phil told everyone who would listen that the heads, hands, and feet were good (when thoroughly cooked) but the rest of the body was "too grisly [gristly, one presumes] and tough."[25]

In Florence, Idaho, shortages devolved into starvation for at least one person. Dr. G. A. Noble wrote:

> On an afternoon, as I was passing one of our stores, I saw a young man with emaciated frame and ghastly countenance picking up something off a pile of snow and eating it with great relish. On stepping up to him, I found that in a famishing condition he had chanced to come on a spot or bank of snow on which some kitchen slop containing a few old cooked beans had lately been thrown out from an adjoining shanty, and these he was picking up and devouring with great avidity.

On another occasion Dr. Noble was summoned to the door of his cabin and asked, "What chance can a fellow have of getting that cow's head lying on the roof?" It had been there, frozen by snow, for four months.[26]

Nevertheless, it is incorrect to refer to famine. Hunger and serious shortages were "social problems" of the mining frontier. They were as individual and localized as prices were unstable. While one diarist's

On Calamity Howlers
"Mr. H. said that in the hotels and eating houses you might see large stacks or piles of guns and pistols that had been pawned for a *single* meal of victuals, and in many instances were never redeemed.

99

situation was "critical," others writing from claims a few miles away wrote home that "our meals are good" and "you have no idea how nice Will and I are fixed up." Finding succor could amount to nothing more than a hike up the ravine and liquidation of a pouch of dust. Running out of food, a group in the northern diggings decided "we would have to take to the hills to find something with which to keep us alive. . . . We went up the divide hoping to get to Simmons' camp where the firm of Hawley, Simmons, & Co. kept a store."[27]

Nor was charity necessarily inadequate when hunger was an individual and localized problem. In Sacramento, according to one observer, "no one was denied any shelter or provision that Captain Sutter could provide, and many a life was saved by the supreme hospitality extended at Sutter Fort at that trying time." Edward Austin, who operated a hotel two miles outside the River City, celebrated dining room receipts of sixty dollars in one day but noted there "would have been much more had we not given away some 40 meals to those who had no money." In 1877 San Francisco's "Praying Abe Slocum" told a reporter about the days of 1849,

Our meals were good. To the baked beans, slap-jacks, coffee, and bacon we added a barrel of butter from Boston, potted meats, sardines, sauces, and an occasional deer as the result of a Sunday in the hills. . . . Our cabin could always accommodate a guest, our board was ever ready to welcome the stranger in our diggings with an abundant meal.[28]

The young man whom Dr. Noble found eating garbage received five dollars from the physician and later found a job, appropriately, packing bacon on his back from a supply center to Florence. He had been a stranger, Noble wrote, "without friends and wasted to a mere skeleton by want and destitution." And yet, the doctor's charity saved him.[29]

Weather was a major reason for temporary shortages in the mines. Although rainfall figures for the first winter of 1848–49 are not available, its comparative dryness (according to diarists) cruelly misrepresented what was to come. Four of the five winters between 1849 and 1854 were rainy and two were torrential. The annual rainfall, in inches, for three important gold rush locations present sobering numbers.[30]

"If Mr. H. will name *one* eating house or hotel in this country where he can see a 'pile' or a 'stack' of guns and pistols, or even a half dozen of either, or both, that have been 'pawned' for a '*single* meal of victuals,' we will enroll his name on our books as a life subscriber to the *News*. . . . He is a most egregious fool, a consummate liar, or . . . some one is lying over his name."

Editorial in Denver's *Rocky Mountain News,* 1859

100

THE FOOD RUSH

Year July 1–June 30	Nevada City	Sacramento	Marysville
1849–50	108 (est.)	34	76
1850–51	14	4	53
1851–52	54	17	65
1852–53	110	35	83
1853–54	60	19	64

Informal Charity

Generous informal charity seems to have remained a characteristic of the mining West. Of the twentieth-century mining camp of Bisbee, Arizona: "Nobody ever saw a hungry man in camp in those days. If he only said he was looking for work he had no trouble in getting fixed up in the best of shape. Otto Geisenhoffer, a German, who ran a hotel and restaurant on Main Street, just above where the Miner's & Merchant's Bank now is, was certainly a good friend to many a broke and hungry man who came into camp looking for work. It has been said that he was never known to turn a man down who wanted to stand him off for board and lodging until he could get work, and he was very good about feeding those who were just traveling through."

Frank L. Wentworth,
Bisbee with the Big B, 1938

Heavy snows caused serious shortages in Idaho's Owyhee mines. Elsewhere, after a four-day snowstorm in California's Trinity Mountains, a Weaverville shopkeeper wrote "there is a right smart chance of famine. No mule train can get through and we are reduced to beef and some of us are fortunate enough to have a few potatoes. There is no flour nor meal nor beans. I have sold everything in the shape of eatables but the pickles and the sardines are going fast." It was his difficulty during that same winter that sent William Carson hiking to the port of Eureka, where he became one of the region's richest lumbermen.[31] That winter could not have been pleasant, but neither was it catastrophic. The mule trains did get through.

The experience of the miners of Grass Valley illustrates how the victims of such a crisis could view it in more sensible proportions than their overwrought chroniclers. After severe winter rains washed out the roads from Sacramento for ten days, the price of flour soared from twenty-five cents to sixty cents a pound and "bacon was scarce at seventy-five cents." With the mock pomposity characteristic of gold rush humor, "Old Block" observed that "in times of great emergencies great men always arise. Circumstances seem to develop greatness and so in this case, the exigencies of the times brought out bold spirits." In other words, like good Jacksonians, the citizens of Grass Valley called a meeting, which overflowed with "excited and interested miners."[32]

The "Hungry Convention" briefly debated seizing "the meager supplies still left with the merchants" but abandoned that suggestion in favor of the admonition that grocers must freeze prices and temporarily offer credit—often taboo in the unstable placer camps. The Convention's real animus was reserved for San Francisco's "soul-less speculators, taking advantage of our condition" by allegedly withholding provisions until prices could rise even higher. An extravagantly worded resolution threatened the port city with an invasion.

Fortunately, a day or two later the rains ceased, the mudslides were shoveled from the roads, and several teams bearing provisions were whipped on their way toward Grass Valley. "A few days more brought them in," Old Block concluded. "San Francisco was saved and at the moment stands, next to GRASS VALLEY, the pride of the Pacific Coast."[33]

Instability in prices, not unwaveringly exorbitant costs, remained characteristic of food supply on the mining frontier throughout its history. Adequate, even abundant provisions, not deprivation or famine, were characteristic of life in the mines from California to Colorado, Montana to Arizona. If we have often thought otherwise, it is usually because the extraordinary ease of our own lives leads us to equate anything more rigorous with the woes of Job. To many Americans of the late twentieth century, an inconvenience is a usurpation of rights, an unpleasantness is unbearable.

One detects a similar overreaction in Dame Shirley's famous contemporary account of gold rush California. Amid complaints of the hardship of life on the Mother Lode, she mentions that at least some of her meals are accompanied by fresh butter and cream. In a letter to her sister conveying the impression she was surviving only because of immense inner resources, Dame Shirley adds, "Don't let this account alarm you. . . . There are two or three well-filled groceries in town."[34]

Prices were as frequently low as high and food supply was almost always plentiful because provisioning was, like mining, a highly speculative endeavor that attracted the same kind of—indeed, often the same—people that mining did, and plenty of them. Just as the massive rushes to California and later to Nevada, Colorado, and elsewhere quickly crowded the mines, turning mining into a living but only a living, massive rushes of freighters and provisioners bent on mining the miners soon transformed provisioning into a business, but only a business.

It is well known that the cost of freighting represented a substantial part of the cost of food (and other goods) on the mining frontier. For

Feeding on the Comstock
"A careful comparison shows that there is no mining district in the world where the general condition of the laboring class has been better during the past twenty years than on the Comstock Lode. Nowhere has so large a guild been their own paymasters for so long a time, and in no mining district are more varied and excellent supplies offered for sale to men who can afford to buy, not only the necessities of life, but its luxuries as well. Choice cattle, fatted on the succulent grasses of the Truckee Meadows, are slaughtered for their tables. Fresh vegetables from the valley of the Carson are brought daily in their season to the mines. Venison from the Sierran foothills, plump wild-fowl from the California estuaries, and fish, which twenty-four hours before had been swimming in sea or river, can be seen in profusion on the market stands of Virginia City. Strawberries, apricots, pears, peaches, grapes, apples, figs, and all other products of the luxuriant gardens and vineyards which are the boast of the Pacific seaboard cover the counters of the open stalls in luscious heaps. The demand of moneyed customers has made the Virginia and Truckee Railroad an unfailing cornucopia of dainties."

Eliot Lord, *Comstock Mining and Miners,* 1883

example, in 1849 freight charges between San Francisco and Sacramento ran to forty dollars a ton, more than the New York to San Francisco tariff. Wagon and pack mule charges to the mines ran to seventy-five cents a pound during the dry season and, in the winter of 1848–49, actually climbed to over a dollar. In May 1849, the rate still held firm at sixty cents. Such sensational news—that the 750-ton paddle wheeler *Senator* made sixty thousand dollars a month, or that flour selling for twenty dollars a hundredweight in Stockton sold for two hundred just sixty miles away, with freighters pocketing the dandy difference—soon crowded the carrying trade as densely as the banks of the Yuba.[35]

Generally owned by Americans but often driven by Mexicans, trains of forty or fifty mules, each carrying more than three hundred pounds, literally clogged the roads out of Stockton and Sacramento. Later, light pine wagons with a capacity of five thousand pounds (drawn by four mules) and up to ten tons (twelve mules) increased the traffic. As a result the fifty to sixty dollars a hundredweight charges of May 1849 declined to twenty-five dollars in July. The tariff rose as high as fifty dollars during the following winter, but also fell as low as fifteen dollars! It bottomed out at ten dollars from Stockton to Mokelumne Hill. Stockton shipped two hundred tons of goods a week to Calaveras, Tuolumne, Mariposa, and Tulare counties. Out of Marysville, some three thousand men and twenty-five hundred mules were involved in freighting to the northern diggings. Shasta weekly imported one hundred tons of provisions on the backs of 1,876 mules.[36]

The same thing happened on the Comstock a decade later. In 1859 a teamster who pulled a load up the grade to Virginia City could sell what he had at nearly any price. By 1861 the teamster who lost his place in the traffic along Swann and Company's toll road connecting Virginia City with Placerville found the line of his competitors so dense that he had to wait hours for a gap. With five thousand teams each making eight trips of ten to twenty days each season, the freight rate crashed from twenty-five to two cents a pound. "Food, clothing, and general merchandise of all kinds," according to Eliot Lord, "were furnished in abundance by the sierran freight trains, and the charges were not exorbitant."[37]

T. McMoore's burros supplied the
Maid Mist Mine in Wyoming.
(Courtesy Idaho State Historical Society,
Boise)

THE FOOD RUSH

The White Pine District of Nevada was opened during the winter of 1868–69. By April, about as early as commerce could begin in that rugged country's climate, there were so many mules in the camps that it required "a generalship of vaqueros to segregate them." At times as many as forty wagon teams, each drawing twenty-one thousand pounds of merchandise, clogged the streets of Hamilton and Treasure City. By the summer of 1869 freight rates to the White Pine District had dropped by two-thirds. In September a cutthroat rate war worthy of Cornelius Vanderbilt and the Erie Gang had erupted on the high desert.[38]

As he dependably did, Mark Twain saw the freighting glut through a wicked eye:

> The legislature sat sixty days and passed private toll-road franchises all the time. When they adjourned it was estimated that every citizen owned about three franchises, and it was believed that unless Congress gave the territory another degree of longitude there would not be room enough to accommodate the toll roads. The ends of them were hanging over the boundary line everywhere like a fringe.
>
> The fact is, the freighting business had grown to such important proportions that there was nearly as much excitement over suddenly acquired toll-road fortunes as over wonderful silver mines.[39]

As late as 1902, in one of the last gold rushes in the United States—to Thunder Mountain, Idaho—the now-familiar pattern held firm. The strike proved rich in 1901. In January 1902, the *Grangeville Standard* warned those who contemplated joining the rush that "there is no food for sale in the camp, though the company has a few spare meals for a handy man." Nevertheless, it was risky to count on charity. "One must carry in his food, or stay away until spring." Spring came late that year. In April the Idaho County sheriff repeated the dire warning:

> From all reports there isn't an ounce of food for sale beyond Warner. A young fellow who came out while I was there said that he divided his last biscuits among four men he met on the road. They had no other food but would not turn back despite the stories that they could buy nothing further on. Men are coming out every day as far as Warner for a few supplies.[40]

This tent restaurant in Thunder Mountain, Idaho, was serving meals within months of a hunger scare in the remote camp. (Courtesy Idaho State Historical Society, Boise)

Hardly stemming the rush, such admonitions prompted what was by then a predictable second rush of provisioners and other service occupations. On April 18 an advertisement in the *Elmore County News* proclaimed, "Fortunes will be made out of town lots" in the new camp. "A month will make you wealthy. Now is the time to invest. Get in with the first rush." Food was not in short supply during the summer nor, by early fall, was it particularly expensive. Boomers expected a bustling winter as well. In early November "various freighters" reported that six hundred men would winter at Thunder Mountain. There was work for twelve hundred, they insisted in a confession of inadequacy rare on the mining frontier, "if adequate provisions had been freighted in."[41]

By the end of December, in fact, thanks to heavy early snows, only a hundred and fifty people were living in the camp and paying astronomical prices for what food was for sale. This time, in self-exculpating language more familiar in the mines, the chief freighter in

Mining camps like Cisco, California, were as likely to be clogged with freighters bearing provisions as to be caught short. (Courtesy Huntington Library, San Marino, Calif.)

the area, General Stonebreaker, held "that class of people who condemned Thunder Mountain through ignorance or malice" to be thoroughly responsible for the situation. Thunder Mountain's critics were "quoted by many newspapers and as a result owners of property, prospective businessmen, packers, and others, all hesitated to take an adequate amount of supplies into the camp." Whatever the cause of the troubles that winter—and Stonebreaker did allow that the weather had something to do with them—the fact of the matter was that throughout northern Idaho the cost of food was unstable rather than relentlessly high.[42]

The same principle applied to the retail trade: it was quickly crowded and highly competitive. In California, grocers reached most camps before prostitutes did. There was Smith and Brannan at Sacramento, Brannan's at Coloma, Weber's at French Camp, William Knight at Knight's Ferry (now Knight's Landing), and Syree's at Mokelumne Hill. The first provisions stores around Nevada City opened within months of the first strikes. In Nevada City there was one retailer for every nine miners. In Grass Valley the ratio was one for every four. In October 1860 Virginia City was served by thirty grocers, four butchers, nine bakers, and two fruiterers as well as twenty-five saloons, seven boarding houses, and nine restaurants. The San Francisco reporter who compiled these figures did not bother to count businesses operating under canvas or off wagongates. Within another year, Virginia City boasted of "fifteen or twenty as fine [meat] markets as there are found in the United States."[43]

In Idaho, the Salmon River rush began in November 1861. By the following spring there were twenty competing provisions shops in the tiny town of Florence. Indeed, Florence provides an excellent case study of the erratic character of prices in mining camps and the fact that grocers were actually more vulnerable to the inherent instability of western metal mining than the miners were. When, in the spring of 1862, news wafted into the community that better diggings had been discovered three hundred miles to the south, many Florentians, "even many that were holding good claims," hastened off to Idaho City for a shot at the big one. Gold miners were like that.

Grocers were not so flexible. Often they were caught with large inventories when the tidings of great joy elsewhere arrived and soon

Burro trains like the "Cripple Creek Express" were the only way to haul provisions into the most isolated camps. (Courtesy Huntington Library, San Marino, Calif.)

after, with a shrunken market. Among those stunned by the exodus from Florence was Alonzo F. Brown, who had just purchased four thousand dollars' worth of staples. He observed that the largest provisioner in town went broke and estimated that the twenty remaining stores held a total of forty thousand dollars' worth of goods.

When those grocers dumped their inventories, the results were food bills that any American worker of the era might have envied. In the fall of 1862, a Florence miner spent only five percent of his income to maintain a subsistence diet. Merle W. Wells has calculated that a daily regimen of half a pound of bacon, half a pound of fresh beef, two ounces of beans, half a pound of flour, and "small amounts" of sugar, coffee, butter, and lard cost a man little more than the same foods cost a worker in Portland, Oregon, where wages were considerably lower.

THE FOOD RUSH

Over the four busiest years of the camp's life, the price of a substantial daily regimen only twice rose to about a quarter of the universal wage, and even then for less than a month at a time. Prices never recovered from their collapse in the wake of the exodus to the south in early 1862.[44]

Virginia City and Gold Hill, Nevada, both with longer histories than Florence's, never experienced such a dramatic consumer windfall. But once the Comstock camps settled into permanence, the cost of a basic diet was by no means excessive. The development of efficient transportation from California brought provisions in at prices higher than they were in Sacramento and San Francisco, but still at levels a fifth or less of prevailing miners' wages. Among other western mining towns that survived beyond two years, only Idaho City and, during Indian troubles, Central City, Colorado, experienced what may be considered exorbitant food costs, such as thirty-cent-a-pound flour, two-dollar-a-dozen eggs, and fifteen-cent-a-pound potatoes.[45]

Is, then, the conventional view that living costs in mining camps were high a fiction?

No. The cost of basic foodstuffs was by no means the whole of or even typical of the miner's expenditures. A bed in a mining town rooming house was considerably more expensive than shelter in an older city. Cabins rented at extortionary rates and construction costs were high. Virginia City's Mrs. Mathews expected to pay $125 for a lodging house she had built. Her bill for an incomplete structure, three months behind schedule, was more than $3,000.[46] When such expenses and medical, fuel, and recreational costs were added to a miner's basic food bill, he found it very easy to spend his three to four dollars or even higher daily wages.

Moreover, the forty-niners and their successors endured a diet of biscuit, beans, and bacon no longer than they had to do so. When food costs represented a substantial part of a western miner's budget, it was often because the miners had very expensive tastes and the inclination to indulge them. In this way too, the experience of California, the birthplace of the western metal mining frontier, precapitulated the ways of an entire era.

I am getting to be perfectly savage and at the same time quite domestic.

Anonymous Forty-Niner[1]

I suppose you have enjoyed yourselves at home as usual this summer grumbling if your biscuits were not light enough, your coffee sweetened too much, or not enough potatoes, rare done sweet cake, apples too sour, and so on, never thinking how glad your sister Louise has been to get a dry piece of bread and a tin cup of black coffee, thinking it was sumptuous fare if there was only enough of it. Well, I dare say I relish my meals much better than you do but if I ever get into civilized society again, won't I know how to enjoy it.

Louise Cook Walters
to her sister Emma[2]

What, how, and with whom people eat can tell us a good deal about them—*when they have a choice in the issue.* That is, we don't learn very much when told that an Irishwoman of the 1830s boiled potatoes rather than corn meal mush in her iron pot. But we are told something about her and her society when, during the blight of the 1840s when Ireland's potatoes rotted into a putrid mess, she slowly starved while a sack of corn meal from America sat untouched in a corner of the cottage. It does not surprise us that an Italian navvy sojourning in the United States would, when he was on the road, retreat to a corner of the railroad station and, in solitude, silently chew on what food was available. But it's of great interest to know that when he got home with his earnings—even when home was South Philadelphia or Waterbury, Connecticut—he gathered his family and *paesani* around him for a feast of specialties from the *paese* that had been assembled and prepared at great trouble and expense.

It does not tell us much that long-bearded, lousy forty-niners squatting in rude, isolated foothills camps made do with ship biscuit, hard beans, and scorched bacon grubbed from a tin plate with grimy fingers. It is, however, of some interest that, given the opportunity, they pursued every delicacy available to them—as soon as it was available!

It is also significant that their highfalutin' tastes developed early in the gold rush era—virtually immediately—and that a hankering for fine food remained characteristic of the metal mining west into the industrialized twentieth century. A cultivated palate has never been characteristic of the mass of the American population and it is not today. Only New Orleans and the Cajun parishes of Louisiana come immediately to mind as places where a large number of ordinary people relish exquisite meals as an important part of workaday life. But the gold and silver miners had such a palate and they exercised it at every opportunity.

A DOG'S LIFE

Could the traveler through California, wrote an English chronicler of the gold rush, "be present at each and every hostel at the same moment, he would find a stereotyped bill of fare, consisting, with little variation, of a tough beefsteak, boiled potatoes, stewed beans, a nasty compound of dried apples, and a *jug of molasses*." Dried apples seem to have disgusted everyone during the early days of any mining development. A poet (of sorts) wrote:

I loathe! Abhor! Detest! Despise!
Abominate dried apple pies;
I like good bread, I like good meat;
Or anything that's good to eat;
But of all poor grub beneath the skies
The poorest is dried apple pies.
Give me a toothache or sore eyes
In preference to such kind of pies.[3]

Another forty-niner wrote home: "Our diet consists of hard bread which we eat half-cooked, and salt pork, with occasionally a salmon which we purchase of the Indians. Vegetables are not to be procured. . . . Our drinking water comes down to us thoroughly impregnated with the mineral substances washed through the thousand cradles above us." These lines are typical of the diarists' notes on mealtime during their first days in the diggings, although there was always one with his banjo on his knee, ready to sing the tune:

In cabins rude, our daily food
Is quickly counted o'er;
Beans, bread, salt meat, is all we eat—
And the cold earth is our floor.

HOW AN ELEPHANT IS EATEN

An anonymous German miner contributed an ethnic twist with this couplet:

Der Kessel hangt in dem Kamin,
Vermutlich sind Kartoffeln drmn.
      *   *   *   *
The kettle makes a great hubub,
Cooks spuds and kraut, the miner's grub.[4]

The suddenness with which California and the sites of later strikes were inundated with miners ensured that, at first, diet would remain pretty much made of what provisions had been in the wagons on the overland trail, in the holds of the emigrant ships, and lashed to the back of the prospector's burro. The nonperishable staples, those that were familiar at home, arrived in the holds below where the argonauts fidgeted, and continued to be the men's sustenance in the hills.

One significant reintroduction from home in an established camp was baked beans. Uncommon on the trail because of the time required to prepare the dish, unusual on shipboard because of the large amounts of fuel required to prepare it and the risk of a long smoldering fire, beans were a welcome addition on the slopes of the Sierra. E. S. Holden waxed rhapsodic when he concluded a day with pick and shovel by digging a hole, lining it with stones, and building a fire within. The next morning he removed the fire, inserted his crock full of beans, molasses, and salt pork, and covered it with coals and dirt. By evening the result was "delicious, so good that half the miners here are after the Yankee beans, or the mode of cooking them." As a *chef de cuisine,* Holden was an exception. "Sometimes," Dr. James L. Cogswell remembered, "dry, hard beans found their way in 'dutch ovens' and after baking for hours, to the disgust of the miner they were harder than when placed in the oven."[5]

The forty-niners seem to have learned, or at least to have retained, few culinary skills during their pilgrimage. Some miners told of filling a pot with rice but no water, placing it on the fire, and wondering why the result was not an edible fluffy *piéce.* Another "put about two pounds of rice in a small tea kettle, and as it commenced boiling he commenced bailing out the rice, till all the vessels in the cabin were

These glum miners were not dining on
the ground by choice. They were
confined in the notorious Coeur
d'Alenes "bull pen" of 1899, a
ramshackle wooden stockade built to
contain striking members of the
Western Federation of Miners. (Courtesy Barnard-Stockbridge Collection,
University of Idaho Library,
Moscow, Idaho)

full; on that occasion he had boiled rice enough to last a week." Andrew Church explained his suspect method for making a cook fire in damp weather: "I put a light charge of powder in the gun, tore off a portion of shirt flap, rammed it down easily and the next moment we had as fine a piece of ignited tinder as one could ask for." One may guess that cooking in Church's camp was performed with comparable delicacy. It certainly was in Peter Sapp's cabin, visited by Hinton R. Helper. Neither of his two utensils, Helper noted, a frying pan and a pot, "is ever washed." Californians, he concluded, were "not very squeamish."[6]

Nor did time improve many men's skills at fire and stove. After traveling to an isolated mining camp in Arizona with her new husband in 1881, Alice Curnow

accepted his offer to prepare the meal while I lay on a couch in the kitchen and watched him, too tired to move another step. He demonstrated his method of making bread but when he had smoothed it in the pan he rubbed flour over his hands, letting the little rolls drop on the mixture where they baked very hard. When it was baked he took it out of the oven and wrapped it up in a very dirty hand-towel but even that didn't arouse me to protest. I was just tired.[7]

There were others, like E. S. Holden, who ate well in the earliest days. Horace Snow claimed his biscuits "would almost sail in the air." William Swain, food fanatic of the overland highway, did not let his standards slide once in California. "My health has been extremely good since I arrived here," he wrote home. "I am fifteen pounds heavier than when I left home. . . ." Another reported, "The boys are all uncommonly fleshy and robust. We eat a great quantity of rice and sugar which is considered very healthy here."[8]

It would be a mistake to consider Swain's and the others' mealtimes typical of miner experience in the early camps. For most the frontier meant the grub of necessity and, after months of tasteless subsistence while getting to the diggings, they were sick of it. The "forlorn, hard looking lot" of argonauts that disembarked at San Francisco with H. C. Bailey checked into a hotel and settled into a "purgatorial wait" for their first meal ashore. "I would like to eat that dinner again," Bailey remembered. "It was simply opening the floodgates to the accumulation of three months of imaginary feasting. How we enjoyed

Men at the Grey Mine in Globe, Arizona, pose with their cylindrical lunch pails. (Courtesy Arizona Historical Society, Tucson)

116

it no one can know but by experience. . . . We ate till we were partly ashamed and partly afraid to eat more, and quit as hungry as at the start. The people there understood it. Every dog of them had gone through the same experience."[9]

Allowing for a Victorian reticence about sex in the documents, apparently nothing loomed larger in the fantasies of deprived miners than food. Horace Snow wrote from the hills of Mariposa County, California, "Morning begins to dawn and . . . you are awake. You rub your eyes and look for daybreak, but the cracks in the cabin are not discernible, consequently, you know not the hour of the night. You fall into a dreamy mood and think of sirloin steak, plum puddings, mince pies, potted pigeons, warm rooms, carpeted floors, convenient stoves, fresh papers, etc., etc., and never once imagine that you will awake to disappointment."[10]

In delicious western hyperbole worth quoting at length, an anonymous wag satirized the woes of bread-bacon-beans diet and the role that fine food came to play for the miners.

One miner told another, "I've been wher' I hain't e't nothin' but a pair of rawhide Ingin moccasins for four days. How's that for a fancy menoo?" The other replied, "Good strong diet, moccasins is. How'd ye have them—boiled or broiled?" Not a man to be outdone:

"Bilt or briled?" exclaimed Bill derisively. "You're a bigger fool 'an the feller 'at braked the dry 'abayons afore he bilt 'em. The way to cook moccasins is to break 'em fresh and scramble 'em. But we didn't cook these yere'ns I'm talking about. We soaked 'em over night, an' we e't 'em trampin' all day diggin' out o' Arizona deserts. . . . An' you talk about imaginin'! A hungry man can imagine a dinner fit for a million-daollar weddin'. Why, when I was fattenin' on them moccasins—they wasn't no new moccasins from Niagerry Falls, nuther—I laid down one day on my stummick, or ruther on the awful holler place wher' my stummick hed moved away from, 'an I hed a dream. . . .

". . . Ther' was everything on the biggest table you ever saw—everything. I don't except nothin'. Ther' ain't nothin' 'at a white man ever liked to eat that wasn't on that table—nothin'—nary damned thing. And—cooked? Dished up? Why you couldn't think of anything half equal to the cookin'. All the air in the world was jist a welpin' an' rainin' down with the smells o' good cookin'. And the waiters was jist a gittin' up an' dustin', a-bringin' in more an' more. An' them waiter-girls! Talk about yer sweet sixteens, yer lovely twenties, yer alabaster shoulders, yer dimples, yer peachblooms, yer orange-blossoms, yer heavy-hooded eyes 'at broods on passion-flowers, yer grace of motion, an' yer faultless forms—why they was all ther'—every one of 'em—comin' an' goin', and flingin' kisses to me from luscious lips with lily white hands. Why, you never seen such hands an' necks as them waiter-girls hed—white an' soft, an' round an' warm, an' taperin'. An' they was all a-waitin' on me—gittin' my dinner ready; and none of 'em was jellus of one another. They hadn't no need to be jellus, fer I had appetite enough fer all that dinner in my stummick, and love enough fer all them girls in my—"

"In your what" suddenly explained Colddecker.

"In my dream."

"Oh!"

"Why, wher'd ye s'pose I had it?"

"I didn't know but you was going to play a heart on me."

"No sir. Hearts has nothin' to do with love or appetite. It's stummick. Hearts doesn't do nothin', only pump. But stummicks is boss. A empty stummick in a cast-away boat at sea will eat a Christian feller-Christian, an' the heart can't do nothin' to stop it; but a full stummick loves all good things, an' the heart only keeps on a-pumpin'."

"Well, never mind about hearts. What did you do about that dinner the pretty girls were setting out for you?"

"What 'id I do? Why I just laid ther' under that old palm-cactus an' watched 'em. One of the girls—a regular Menken—come in with her bare arms over her head, and her breasts standin' out under her white satin dress

117

shinin' like twin buttes of pearl statuwerry, an' she had a done-brown roast turkey on a chiny dish trimmed with sparegrass an' sallery, an' I couldn't wait to be called to dinner, so I jumped up a hollerin', 'Hold on my darling—don't go to no more trouble on my account'; then I rubbed my eyes an' looked at the damn cactuses standin' 'round over the desert, smacked my dry lips together till the dust flew out between 'em, an' cussed the country."

"Did that imaginary dinner do you any good?"

"Yes; done me just as much good as it does you to lay abed an' imagine what a purty girl you could marry ef ye hed a chanct. An' ye don't deny takin' comfort out o' that sort of thing, do you? An' it made me ambitious to hang on an' hold out fer better days."[11]

BETTER DAYS   Just as they arrived quickly with provisions, dealers saw to it that the stuff of gastronomic dreams made it promptly to the diggings. The ships that hove into San Francisco Bay with the earliest arrivals often carried "delicacies" among the staples. In the words of the invaluable *Annals of San Francisco,* written when the days of the gold rush were still keen within living memory, "there was an endless variety . . . in the character of the provisions furnished; for besides the common products of the country, importations were constantly arriving from all sections of the globe." For example, the brig *Tigress,* arriving early in 1850, carried tucked among its tons of salt pork, coffee, sugar, spice, tea, honey, vinegar, jams, jellies, "all sorts of fruit syrups," herring, sausages, pickles, and canned lobster, and even then was written off by one observer as having "overstayed the market."[12]

However accidental the earliest arrivals of dainties—vessels enroute elsewhere hearing of the bonanza market in California and turning a quick detour—alert food suppliers soon recognized the peculiar demand for special treats among the miners and hastened to fill it. As early as 1848 the French consul in Monterey wrote home urging exporters to step up shipments of wine and brandy. Consumption was "extraordinary and still increasing daily." His prescience made it possible for two ships racing up the coast to the Golden Gate to wager as the prize of entering first "a good Champaign dinner." Edward Austin wrote to his brother, "If you can get 3 to 600 pots of fresh oysters, good ones, hermetically sealed, and some of those that Uncle Frank had from Baltimore, but half the size, [they] will sell well and at a great profit, if they are as good as those were we used to have—say

Fitzmier and Armbrust placed an advertisement in *McKenney's Business Directory* of 1877 indicating the availability of oysters as well as ice cream at their bakery and restaurant in Virginia City. (Courtesy Special Collections, Getchell Library, University of Nevada, Reno)

Fresh oysters, prepared in every style when in season, were featured at the Grotto on South C Street in 1882. (Courtesy Special Collections, Getchell Library, University of Nevada, Reno)

200 pots, 1 or two gross of anchovies . . ." By July 1850 a ship had arrived from Boston carrying 147 tons of ice with which to chill the bivalves.[13]

The subject of oysters deserves a digression. They played a curiously large role in American gourmandise by midcentury. They had become almost an obsession in the United States and a most democratic delicacy at that. While they graced the tables of the fine restaurants in large eastern cities, they were also bolted by the ton in workingmen's saloons (for a penny apiece on the waterfront) and rushed hundreds of miles into the interior even before the railroad. In Illinois about the time of the gold rush, an ambitious former congressman named Abraham Lincoln entertained his friends and associates at buffets at which oysters—and nothing but oysters—were prepared in every conceivable way.[14]

In California and throughout the mining West, genus *Ostrea* became a mania. Along with champagne, oysters were the "symbols of wealth" with which it was customary to celebrate good fortune. So voracious were the forty-niners for them that by 1851 the oyster beds of San Francisco Bay were so critically depleted—and the demand for oysters in the mines so tenacious—that a schooner set off for the north with the explicit purpose of finding more. The best beds were found in what soon became Oysterville, Washington, a town as surely a provisioner of miners as Stockton and Sacramento. In nineteenth century atlases Oysterville was labeled in larger type than Seattle and Tacoma.[15]

Many fine meals on the mining frontier began with oysters on the half shell. Dame Shirley, the first woman at Rich Bar, ate on her arrival there a meal that included oyster soup and fried oysters. Restaurants hoping for miner patrons continued to advertise oysters. Reno's Capital Chop House was typical: "Fresh and transplanted oysters always on hand and served at all hours in any style desired."[16]

As time passed, improved transportation enabled the men and women of the mining region to enjoy (as a writer of the era might phrase it) a spectacular panoply of exquisite comestibles. The result was that curious juxtaposition of rude frontier and sparkling elegance that fascinated chroniclers and distinguished the miners' frontier from

E. A. & L. A. VORBE.   J. F. VORBE.
Austin, Nevada.   San Francisco.

VORBE BRO'S,

IMPORTERS OF

FRENCH ☙ LIQUORS,

Main Street, below Pine, North side.

FIRE PROOF BRICK BUILDING.

AUSTIN.

Wholesale and Retail Dealers in

GROCERIES, LIQUORS,

AND

GENERAL MERCHANDISE.

FRENCH CLARET by the Gallon.

Goods Delivered free of Charge.

P. BARON.   I. BARON.

BARON BRO'S.

RESTAURANT,

Main Street, bet. Virginia and 6th, North side.

AUSTIN, NEVADA.

MEALS AT ALL HOURS.

Keep Open Day and Night.

ICE CREAM SALOON ATTACHED.

CONFECTIONERY of all Kinds and of the First Quality.

Separate Apartment for Ladies.

In 1866, French claret was available by the gallon in Austin, Nevada, from the Vorbe Brothers store on Main Street. The Baron brothers kept their restaurant and ice cream saloon open all day and night. (Courtesy Special Collections, Getchell Library, University of Nevada, Reno)

120

those pioneered by trappers, loggers, soldiers, ranchers, and farmers. Women in patent leather shoes and flouncy gowns picking their way across streets a foot deep in mud; opera houses at ten thousand feet; saloons with mirrors the size of a placer claim and a rosewood bar that would have pleased Louis Napoleon—all were chronicled over and over again for eastern readers who seemed never to tire of the tales.

It was the same at table. When a large majority of San Franciscans still "lodged in mean, inhospitable tents" and in "wretched and filthy shanties, where from one to three score would occupy a single large room," many stepped down the street to eat roast duck or broiled quail at the Sutter, Irving, Jackson, or Lafayette houses. Off in the diggings, "it was no unusual thing," wrote Bayard Taylor about California in 1850, "to see a company of these men, who had never before thought of luxury beyond a good beefsteak and a glass of whiskey, drinking their champagne at ten dollars a bottle, and eating their tongue and sardines, or warming in the smoky campfire their tin canisters of turtle soup and lobster salad." He attended a raucous, foot-stomping dance in a brothel that concluded with a supper comprised of "everything within the bounds of the market and the skill of the cook."[17]

The state trademark office in Sacramento registered likenesses of dozens of labels crowing something like "these preserves are a most delicious article for Luncheons; and are put up in a convenient and portable style for picnics, excursions, etc., etc." Foothill restaurants advertised "every LUXURY the market affords. . . . Game of all kinds in season."[18]

The supplier of a grocer in the Coast Range camp of Shasta worried because "there are no abalones in town and no herrings good enough for shipment." He wondered, tentatively, if his customer would accept an inferior variety. Sent to Virginia City to regale eastern readers with tales of the wild and wooly West, a reporter for the New York *Tribune* commented on the extraordinary number of empty caviar tins in the city dump. Alice Curnow described the making of a cake in then-remote Globe, Arizona, that would have graced the table of any restaurant in the country.[19]

In OK Corral days, before the railroad snaked its way into Tombstone, iced fish and oysters were rushed into camp from the Gulf of

Oysters were a mania—nothing less!—in the nineteenth century. Associated with luxury, they were nevertheless cheap. No elegant meal was commenced in Virginia City without a dozen on the half shell. They were raced into Tombstone. The most modest eateries advertised them. Canners registered their labels with the California Bureau of Trademarks. (Courtesy California State Archives, Sacramento)

Gourmandise in Juneau

At the Juneau Hotel, according to a notice in the *Daily Alaska Dispatch* for September 15, 1913, caterer Spatz had gathered an efficient corps of cooks. "August Hermann has presided over the kitchens in such well-known Bohemian restaurants as the Waldorf, New York, St. Bartholomew, Monte Carlo, and Butler, Seattle, in the years that he has followed the cafe business." Patrons were assured of visiting "a pocket edition of any of the best hotels on the West Coast."

California. The *Epitaph* announced that at the newly opened Grand Hotel "we find the same evidence of good taste in selection and arrangement that is so marked a feature of the whole interior. Three elegant chandeliers are pendant from the handsome centerpiece; walnut tables, extension and plain, covered with cut glass, china, silver casters, and the latest style of cutlery are among the many attractions of this branch of the cuisine." The Grand also boasted a twelve-foot Montagin Range, a device which would honor a fine restaurant today.[20]

In pioneer Bisbee, Arizona, a resident might dine on oysters and imported champagne at the Copper Queen hotel "and later watch the local school children scramble up a nearby hill and take cover during an 'Apache Drill.'" When Prescott's future was still uncertain, confectioner Jules Bauman found the prospects sufficient to begin manufacturing "All Kinds of Strictly Pure Plain and Fancy Candies." Soon after the days when "the exhibition of a porterhouse steak on the mainstreet would have caused a prodigious sensation" in Goldfield, Nevada, an ice cream maker arrived, immediately followed by "a little Frenchman who makes excellent caramels." Indeed, a later-to-be-celebrated San Francisco restaurateur, M. L. Winn, got his start in food service when, arriving penniless in 1849, he made candies and peddled them on the streets from a tray, calling, "Here is your own California candy! It has neither come round the Horn, nor across the Isthmus—but is made in your own city; and none but Winn can make it. Here it is!—buy it!—taste it, and try it."[21]

The day of the Apache Drill lay in the past when this tribesman passed up the chance to refresh himself with a bowl of ice cream and a Coke in Globe, Arizona. (Courtesy Arizona Historical Society, Tucson)

LA GOURMANDISE DU WEST

It is, of course, impossible to know just how "good" the fine food of the mining West was. Neither can we know how "good" the meals of Brillat-Savarin and Carême were or judge the comparative merits of tenors who sang before the invention of the Victrola. Dealing with history's sensory experiences is not quite the same thing as dealing with history's ideas and election results.

And yet, it is not entirely different either. We know from a dozen sources that by the middle of the nineteenth century the upper classes of Europe and the United States had adopted *la cuisine française*—adequately defined here as generally well-sauced dishes described in the French language—as the kind of cooking people of wealth and quality ate. And the menus of dozens, perhaps hundreds, of banquets and restaurants of the mining frontier survive. From them it is apparent that the people of the diggings, despite being just months away from the stolid, plain all-American home cooking with which they had grown up, acquired a taste for long, multi-course dinners, preferably with dishes with fancy French names and served on fine china on white linen flanked by sterling knives and forks.

The steamer *Tennessee* arrived in San Francisco in June 1850. In 1852 its passengers held a reunion banquet. For their repast they chose from four *potages* including potage à la Reine, potage Colbert, potage Milanese, and bisque d'Ecrivisse. There were five *relevés*, five *hors d'oeuvres d'office*, five *entrées froides*, nine *entrées chaudes*, five *rôtis*, six *legumes*, eight *entremets sucres* (including a nice antiscorbutic macedoine de fruits), and several *pièces montées*.[22]

Such events were common occurrences on San Francisco's social calendar. Marking the centenary of George Washington's birth the same year, the city's Masons gorged on

123

SOUP
Green Turtle   Oyster

FISH
Boiled Codfish, Oyster Sauce
Boiled Salmon, Geraise Sauce
Boiled Rockfish, Madeira Sauce

BOILED
Ham, Ornamented with Jelly
Beef, Garnished   Mutton
Beef (Corned) Pressed

SIDE DISHES
Oyster Patties   Antelope, Cranberry Sauce
Jug Hare, English Style
Plover, Broiled with Jelly Sauce
Salmi Venison   Fried Brains, Tomato Sauce
Teal Duck, Onion Sauce   Elk Steak, Cranberry Sauce
Fillet Veal, Financier Sauce
Fillet Beef, Garnish, Madeira Sauce
All Kinds Fowl   Bear Steak

ROAST
Truffled Turkey   Larded Chicken
Stuffed Pig   Ham, Champagne Sauce

Plus there were ten game dishes, sixteen "western" vegetables, jellies, pastries, nuts, raisins, oranges, pears, and grapes.[23]

On August 18, 1853, the men who had come to California on the steamer *Panama* celebrated the fourth anniversary of their fellowship (and apparent good fortune) with such fare as "*Potage à la Reine, Destignac Bisque, Tapioca des Indes, Saumon Chambord Garni d'Atellets, Turbot Hollandaise Garni de filets d'Eperlands, Brochet au Bleu, Petit Cochon de Lait, Chivry,*" and so on, all printed in gold on a blue velveteen menu, down to the last *haut sauterne.*[24]

Of the Comstock, Louise Palmer of Virginia City wrote in 1869: "How often must I declare that Nevada is not what it was when Ross Browne visited it, and wrote those atrocious, though I doubt not truthful, tales about its mines and mills, and above all its famous Washoe Zephyrs. Those things were doubtless true then, but *nous avons change tout de celà.*" If Palmer meant that dining had improved on the Comstock, she may have been mistaken about the extent of the progress. Virginia City and Gold Hill appear to have been mining camps imported ready-made from California at their very beginnings. It cannot, however, be denied that the menu of the 1869 dedication banquet of Virginia City's DeWitt Clinton Commandery of the Knights Templar and Appendant Orders was a formidable *carte.* It offered oysters au naturel with chablis for starters; turtle soup with Madeira; Tahoe trout à la Chambord, Morue à la hollandaise, or salmon with Johannesberger; seven hors d'oeuvres; galantines truf-fées, jambon de Westphalia, pâté, and boned turkey; larded tenderloin aux truffées, poulet mayonnaise, chevreuil à la Provençale, vol-au-vent financiere, tête de veau sauce tortue, poulet à la Rochambeau; three pièces montées with Chambertin for a breather; a choice of five roasts *(aussi à la française)*; eight vegetables; nine entremets; and sixteen desserts. For Christmas 1878 the Virginia City International Hotel greeted patrons with a menu almost as grand and a wine list of twenty-four *ordinaires,* six sherries and Madeiras, three ports, five beers, and two kinds of cider.[25]

At Leadville, Masons banquetting in Tom Walsh's Grand Hotel were greeted by a startling sight. "An artistic eye had amused itself by decking the table with flowers and vegetables grotesquely carved in imitation of many emblems of the order. Tall pyramids of butter also

Printed on silk, the menu of a lodge banquet in ten-year-old Virginia City was not designed for meat-and-potatoes men. (Courtesy Nevada Historical Society, Reno)

reminded the gatherers around the festive board that to the hospitalities of the mystic order they were indebted for the pleasure they had enjoyed." The banquet was five course with four kinds of "ornamental fish," nine "Small Dishes Ornamental," and the array now becoming familiar.[26]

Where circumstances simply would not permit such affectations, the miners nevertheless had a satirical go at them. In Russell Gulch, Colorado, miners celebrated with "Brook Trout à la Catch 'em First, . . . Biscuit, handmade, full weight; Beans, mountain style warranted boiled forty-eight hours à la soda; . . . Coffee in tin cups, to be washed clean for the occasion." Nor could the rigors and remoteness of Alaska prevent a Nome restaurant from offering a seven-course dinner including stuffed ptarmigan with Eskimo gravy, Council City peas, Point Barrow bananas, and Kotzebue Sound oranges. Likewise the miners at Leotta Creek near Dawson in 1898 enjoyed a nine-course Christmas banquet started with eggs and toast with beef-moose broth and "vegetable soup alla ten percent royalty." For the "fresh Moose ragout" there was a cheese-tomato sauce and onions "alla Dawson City." The feast ended with "Xmas Pudding with Lemon and Chocolate alla Nord Pole" and "Pears Pie with Milk Sauce alla 44 above degrees."[27] In order to make effective sport of pretentious dining habits, of course, the miners had to be familiar with the real things.

WHY FOOD? Could miners afford the occasional fine meal? Some implied that they could not. "It needs no argument," wrote the editor of the *Gold Hill Daily News,* "to prove that four dollars a day is as little as a man can live comfortably upon in this land of enormous prices, and that even at that price requires health, industry and economy in the miner to make ends meet." There is no example of a miners' union declaring that prevailing wages allowed their members a comfortable sum of what the economists call "discretionary income."[28]

And yet the infamous plethora of saloons thrived. The gaming tables bustled noisily twenty-four hours a day. Richard Lingenfelter and others have shown that when a camp was in bonanza the miners gambled as recklessly in the stock exchanges as in the casinos. The stereotype of the mining frontier is of a society in which coin and paper of a dozen species changed hands in a dizzying blur. To borrow a phrase from the nineteenth-century sociologist Charles H. Shinn, miners since the days of Tubal Cain have been notoriously big spenders. "As a rule in the western country," wrote a journalist in the strong union camp of Telluride, Colorado, "we have little use for copper made into money—that is, the copper cents. Back east they can be utilized when the contribution box comes around, but out here they will buy nothing but postage stamps and many postmasters will not accept them in pay for stamps."[29] Although clearly a complaint about the cost of living, the remark also reflects a society in which people parted easily with silver and gold.

American hard-rock miners made as much as seven dollars a day in a few bonanza camps and as little as three dollars a day in borrasca and in the stable, highly industrialized, employer-dominated mines. Certainly the lower wages, while considerably higher than the national norm, put severe strains on the budget of the family man. But for the single, propertyless miner, even wages at the bottom provided extra cash, and evidence indicates that they disposed of much of it on their eats.

Why should this be so? Not every worker who can afford to dine grandly does so. In the closing decades of the twentieth century, heavy equipment operators with unionized jobs would not notice the money spent on a monthly splurge at a hundred-dollars-a-head emporium of *nouvelle cuisine*. However, they are not likely to be found there. During the 1970s Alaska pipeline workers dizzy from counting the pay in their pockets chartered planes not to New Orleans but to Las Vegas. But many western metal miners earning relatively less money quite specifically chose fancy food as a worthy expenditure. Eliot Lord pointed out that the Comstock miners took no interest in spending money on other luxuries. He noted that if they "care to walk the streets in broadcloth suits and to wear gold chains, watches, and rings, they can so bedeck themselves." He added: "Few, however, are inclined to spend their wages in costly clothes or jewelry."[30]

Perhaps the point can be better made by comparing the western miners' attitudes toward food with those of the contemporary loggers, workers who, in many particulars, were very much like the miners. Loggers too worked at dangerous jobs in an unstable extractive industry in isolated locations. They were similarly footloose, apt to

The scene is elegant, and yet the ladies
of Council City, Alaska, served
Carnation evaporated milk in cans
at their banquet for the Arctic
Brotherhood. The juxtaposition of the
elegant and the primitive was a
characteristic of the mining
frontier. (Courtesy Alaska
Historical Library, Juneau)

HOW AN ELEPHANT IS EATEN

change jobs and domiciles with little or no notice. They were a rambunctious lot, as suits the life of the young and unmarried. They were *not* well paid but food was important to them. They considered the meals their employers provided an essential part of their remuneration. A logger "would work in the mud, rain, summer heat and dust, risk life and limb a dozen times a day, do without company showers, sleep in draft bunkhouses, all with a minimum of grumbling, but start cutting back on the quality and quantity of cookhouse meals and he would quit immediately and spread bad words about that camp's food wherever he went." A lumberman summed it up: "The camp that served the best meals got the best men."[31]

By the end of the nineteenth century, loggers were—nutritionally speaking—very likely the best-fed group of workers in the United States. They needed plenty of food, demanded it, and got it, virtually as a condition of employment. Their actual daily consumption has been variously calculated at from five thousand to seventy-five hundred calories a day. But the loggers did not share the miners' yen for *haute cuisine*. On the contrary, loggers were "the most conservative of men when it comes to food. They simply do not care for exotic adventures in eating or new taste sensations. They appreciate good cooking; they can tell in a second if their beans are properly seasoned and the roast beef just rare enough. But try an unfamiliar flavor on them and they immediately become antagonistic." Off the job they gravitated to "the dark and dirty restaurant" of the skid road with its greasy ham and eggs and leathery beefsteaks.[32]

Nor did other nineteenth-century westerners working at tedious, monotonous, isolated labor—who knew deprivation as part of their jobs—choose gastronomy as an outlet for energies and money. The trappers of Astor's furs, the layers of the Union Pacific's track, the soldiers on leave from Kearny, and the boys guiding cattle to Kansas all invested their wages in a warm bath, a haircut and a shave and a splash of lilac, whiskey, a woman, and a meal that filled them up. We do not associate any of them with galantines.

The difference between these other western workers and the miners lies in the visions with which the mining frontier was instituted—visions that a man was to be as rich as Croesus (or maybe Lucullus?).

A miner's family camping in Atlanta, Idaho. (Courtesy Idaho State Historical Society, Boise)

130

The sturdy farmboys and clerks and smiths and mechanics that hied themselves to California did not think in terms of making a living. They dreamed of riches and, at least in the early years of every camp, enough of them enjoyed windfalls that they were able to indulge their illusions, even if briefly.

Dining upon fancy "frenchy" or "keskydee" food was not only then emerging as an index of wealth and status in the United States, but it was also the one item in addition to warm baths, shaves, and whiskey that was immediately available in the diggings. One searches in vain among the few surviving inventories of the earliest ships to arrive for the manifest of one crammed to the gunwhales with champagne and canned lobster salad. But one cannot resist speculating that there was such a vessel and that her master got very rich. The brig *Tigress,* noted earlier, was observed as having "overstayed the market." Certainly the Piper Heidesecks, clarets, and burgundies figure with startling prominence in the earliest diary entries. Surely the California gold rush was one of the few booms of its kind in which the hors d'oeuvres were on the scene before the whores.

Desolate as this New Mexico town may
have appeared to the visitor, there
was the inevitable restaurant.
(Courtesy Huntington Library,
San Marino, Calif.)

The prostitutes caught up. They were quick enough to get to the Comstock, to Pike's Peak, and to the boom camps that regularly erupted in the wildernesses of South Dakota, Montana, Idaho, Arizona, and southern Nevada over the last half of the nineteenth century. But in every camp the experience of California was recapitulated, more quickly with each passing year: fabulous riches enjoyed by the discoverer and perhaps a few early comers; wide-open boom during which big money, at least in the form of claim certificates and mining stock, circulated freely; and only later consolidation of mineral holdings and reduction of the majority of the population to the status of wage workers who, however, were well paid and remained imbued with the habits of the first days.[33]

Among those habits was the yen for fancy eating and the belief, perhaps made more convincing by the monotonous food on long treks, that elegant meals were one way a rich man spent his riches. "Yes, it's a whole lot different now than it used to be," the discoverer and "bronzed nester" of Thunder Mountain, Idaho, reminisced. "I've seen the day when the Caswell boys couldn't afford to smoke anything more expensive than a corncob pipe, when flap-jacks and bacon were the principal items in the bill of fare." Ben Caswell puffed on a Havana and "gazed reminiscently off into the corner and then ordered the bellboy to see if the sideboard that adorns his suite of rooms was properly equipped." The restaurants he and his sort frequented advertized "game as wild as a tornado, chicken as tender as a maiden's heart, ice cream as delicious as a day in June, dessert that would charm the soul of a South Sea Islander and smiles as bright as the morning sun."[34]

Mrs. M. M. Mathews of the Comstock was appalled that

every restaurant table groans with food of every kind gathered from every kingdom on the globe. From eight to twelve different kinds of vegetables, and nearly as many kinds of meat, are on the table three times a day. Cakes, and every kind of pastry and puddings, you will find; there are also fruits from every country and clime.

Nor was such extravagance only in restaurants. In Gold Hill, Nevada, Alice Curnow inspected a champagne cellar at the thousand-foot level of the New York mine. In Globe, Arizona, she and her husband were invited to a mine's carpenter's shop "where a sumptious banquet was served from the carpenter's bench on tin plates and champagne was drunk from tin cups." Mrs. Mathews continued her disapproval of miner sybaritism in her note that

the market of Virginia City affords everything that grows which is fit to eat, and a thousand and one things which are not fit to eat—things that I do not think were ever intended to pass human lips, and have only been brought into the food-list by epicures who could not get different dishes enough to suit their perverted tastes. I never saw people like them, as a class; they wanted so many kinds of rich dishes to eat at one meal. They are not only epicures, but gourmandizers.[35]

PERVERTED TASTES

Grocers' inventories elsewhere resembled the ones that disturbed Mrs. Mathews. W. P. Williamson's account for one month at John McGrath's store included, in addition to the staples, large quantities of lemons, nuts, ginger snaps, raspberries, mushrooms, canned cherries, ginger cakes, bottled pickles, and "strong cheese." C. M. Willey bought half a gallon of vinegar every five or six days for over a year, a large jar of mustard every month, lots of cheese, canned salmon, and sundry condiments. B. F. Dolan had a similarly demanding palate and an apparent fetish for cloves, which he purchased several times a month. Such pungent regimens are scrawled across practically every page of the many grocers' ledgers now slowly disintegrating in archives, and on the menus of ordinary eating houses. The miners consumed enormous quantities of sugar, vinegar, pickles, and salt. Butte miners were notorious for pouring "copious draughts of salt" into their beloved "stirabout," which, in turn, went into their tea and drinking water.[36]

The "copious draughts" of salt provide another key to understanding why, when mining had gone underground and miners had become wage workers, they continued to make exotic foods an important part of their lives. Ellen Rockwell, who as a girl cooked for both loggers and miners, said that "loggers would eat anything! They came in out of the cold fresh air as hungry as hogs." Miners, on the other hand, "had no appetite at all. The poison air ruined their stomachs as well as their lungs. It was hard to please miners. You had to wake them up with vinegar and lots of salty things."[37]

Joe Chisholm wrote much the same thing.

The hard-rock miners of the West notoriously were the worst cranks about grub the world over [as a result of] gophering hundreds of feet deep inside the world in ill-ventilated holes, eating powder smoke for hours every day, getting a lunch bucket of dry punk and a couple of dumb prunes to eat in the hole in the ground. . . . The rule of the hard-rock miner was to kick with both hind feet at the grub when it was bad, to improve it. And kick just about as hard when it was good.[38]

Perhaps not when it was *chevreuil à la Provençale.* But there may be a relationship between the salty strong tastes of the free lunch, the miners' "perverted tastes," and *cuisine française.* Leaving aside subjective questions of quality of ingredients and art of preparation, the signal gastronomic difference between nineteenth-century *haute cuisine* and the American fare on which the miners had been raised was the former's pungency, particularly in the heavy sauces that characterize the French dishes. It may be that the miners' fancy of such meals ought to be considered a vocational disease. In his extensive survey of coroners' and hospital records on the Comstock, Eliot Lord found only one case of death by starvation and only one "disease treated" that was clearly related to nutrition. However, the records are full of ailments associated with a gamey diet: bilious fever, constipation, cramps, dyspepsia, diarrhea (excluding cases diagnosed as dysentery), enteritis, gastritis, gastric fever, hemorrhoids, inflammation of the bladder, inflammation of the bowels, kidney and liver disease, and food poisoning.[39]

Foul air and temperatures constantly rising above a hundred degrees, with the attendant need to quaff huge quantities of water, would have been quite enough to reduce a man's digestive system to one easily allayed as well as aggravated by the salty and pickled diet. Even in the placer mines of California, according to Alexander Delmar, diet and lifestyle were closely related. Labor was "intense and unremitting," he wrote, and the men were blinded to "the frightful bodily and mental risks they ran. . . . Stimulants and medicines, purchased at extravagant prices, were employed to ward off disease and death; while shelter, repose, and moderate labor, the only true palliatives for the ills that beset them, were shunned because they interfered with gold-getting."[40]

In every gulch and ravine a town was in progress of erection. Scarcely a foot of ground upon which man or beast could find a foothold was exempt from a claim. . . . Board and lodging signs over tents not more than ten feet square were as common as huckleberries in June.

J. Ross Browne,
description of Placerville,
California, 1859

It is commonplace today to say that Americans are a people who "eat out." A good part of the nation's business, from the merging of corporations to the sale of insurance policies, is accomplished "over lunch." The dinner date is still a courtship convention, and the evening out is increasingly popular among married couples, particularly the elderly. Diners, albeit with a gloss earlier generations would not recognize, still serve as the workingman's club.

Eating out is enjoyed by all social classes in the United States. The rich savor odds and ends of their good fortune in exclusive restaurants that only they can afford. Good pay, easy credit, an obsession with convenience, and the increasing incidence of the two-income family have all encouraged the burgeoning of affordable sit-down eateries for the middle class, featuring seafood, steaks, prime rib, "gourmet cuisine," and a potpourri of ethnic dishes. For low-paid working people and even the poor, mass production methods and a labor force earning minimum wage combine to put a tolerable hamburger or box of fried chicken plus cola, excellent french fried potatoes, and even an approximation of a hot apple pie on a brushed aluminum counter for a fraction of the cost of preparing a comparable meal at home. The American townscape has been sowed with a dense growth of "fast food" eateries with brand names familiar in the remotest Appalachian hollows and the most isolated Alaskan villages.

Sometimes, it seems, the American people are on the verge of liquidating the home kitchen. For every two meals consumed at home in the United States, at least one is eaten in a "restaurant," and the food service industry hungrily foresees the day when the numbers will balance. In 1977 there was one eating establishment for every 578 Americans, and in California, still the nation's experimental laboratory in affairs of lifestyle, the ratio was one for every 483.

This transformation of American dining habits has occurred during the lifetime of many people now alive, well, and brunching in the late twentieth century. Between 1945 and 1970, when the nation's population increased by 32 percent, the number of "eating and drinking places" increased by 68 percent. Between 1972 and 1982, not a rosy decade for much of the American economy, annual restaurant receipts doubled, to $113 billion.[2] Because this revolution has been so conspicuous, we are sometimes inclined to think of our restaurant habit as unprecedented, unique in history.

It is not. The people of the mining frontier also ate out a good deal, quite possibly more often than Americans do today. Much of the population of every mining camp from Coloma to Goldfield seems to have preferred eating out to eating at home. The miners were at least as "at home" in restaurants—of a number of types—as the middle-class American family of the 1980s. They supported a large if, like so much else associated with mining, highly speculative restaurant economy.

EATING OUT

"So completely" was California "inundated with taverns, boarding houses, etc.," wrote an English lady in 1851, that the Golden State could as aptly have been named "the Hotel State." At about the same time travel writer Frank Marryat remarked of Sacramento that "every other house is a hotel or boardinghouse." A miner who arrived in 1849 remembered that "there were any number of eating houses and hotels" in Coloma, where it all began. Red Dog, a camp of only two hundred people in Nevada County, California, had a restaurant featuring "Choice Meals served up at all hours, day or night, in the best style." Indian Bar's Hotel Humboldt added dinner music: "Ned, the violin-playing mulatto cook" accompanied meals of oysters, "salmon caught in the river," roast beef, mince pie and pudding, and Madeira, claret, and champagne. In the Feather River diggings, the Batavia Hotel was "a comfortable house of canvas and logs" (with, however, no surviving reviews of either cuisine or concert).[3]

Dining in Sacramento
"Old Louis Keseberg, the Donner Party Man-Eater, has made a fortune and is now running a restaurant on K Street in Sacramento City. I would not like to board there, I wouldn't."

George M. McKinstry, Letter to Edward Kern, December 1850

A TABLE FOR THE CAMP

"Cafe" connotes a more genteel ambience than "saloon," but the sparkling white tablecloths, brilliant Arizona sun pouring through the windows, and prim and proper waitresses of the Palace Cafe in Prescott were not typical. (Courtesy Sharlot Hall Museum, Prescott)

At Placerville's Cary House, hangtown fry was invented. At its El Dorado Hotel, the fare included beef under several species, veal, peas, potatoes, sauerkraut, bacon, and "hash, low grade." In Auburn, "its future on paper, its present under canvas," a Frenchman nevertheless kept a restaurant where "the rabble gathered—old men and young—Americans, Chileans, Mexicans, and Germans; some drunk, some sober, but all more or less excited."[4]

Nevada City's Broad Street beckoned with such houses as the Antelope Restaurant, the New York Hotel, and the Miners Hotel and Restaurant, F. Stumpf, prop., "French, English and German Spoken." The Miners' Hotel offered no linguistics but featured "Good Rooms, Good Meals, Good Cooks, Good Liquors, Low Prices."[5] Late in 1849 or early in 1850, at Shasta in the foothills of the Trinity Alps, Edward P. Reed found a town of two thousand where, a few months earlier, he had met one lonely man. Despite its sudden development, Shasta was already a place where sojourners could stay in comfort, "visiting the restaurants and eating our fill of all the good things we saw."[6]

As the gateway to the goldfields, San Francisco established early on its enduring reputation as a restaurant city. Hall McAllister and Sam Ward were so disgusted with ship's food when they disembarked from the steamer *Panama* on June 4, 1849, that they foreswore digging for gold and instead opened a restaurant on Telegraph Hill. At first pork and beans were the only improvement on the *Panama*'s galley they could manage. By December, however, nearby competitors at the Ward House (proprietors Russell and Myers) had improvised an ingenious menu from available ingredients that included baked trout with anchovy sauce ($1.50), curried sausages ($1), and bread pudding ($.75).[7]

Johann Knocke ran another typical restaurant for miners. He opened at five each morning and closed at eleven at night, featuring fishballs (dried fish and boiled potatoes) and "hot cakes done brown" as his specialties. More famous was the What Cheer House, built in 1852, serving men only and offering rooms for fifty cents, with meals at moderate cost. Upon arriving, argonauts purchased as many half-dollar tickets as they reckoned they would require during their stay. Upon departing, guests were reimbursed for tickets they did not use.

The traffic in refunds does not seem to have been great. The What Cheer's hundred rooms were nearly always filled and the basement

Launching the Lick House
"Next day as we drove up to Yank's road house, he called out, 'there's a large trout in the horse trough that weighs 32 pounds.' I bought it of an Indian who had speared it in a bay at the head of Lake Bingham for $2.50, packed it in snow and ice, and gave it to Tubbs and Pullen, of the Lick House, just open, and they placed it in the bar window which increased their sales that day over $500, and they served up the fish baked whole with champagne, to all the guests."

Andrew Smith Church, Reminiscence

The What Cheer restaurant was a "must" in nineteenth-century San Francisco. (Courtesy The Bancroft Library, University of California, Berkeley)

WHAT CHEER RESTAURANT

Cor. Sacramento and Leidesdorff Streets.

THE WHAT CHEER IS ONE OF THE INSTITUTIONS OF CALIFORNIA.

For
A QUARTER OF A CENTURY
The Best and Cheapest Dining Room
IN THE CITY.

Boiled Mutton, with Oyster sauce ....10 cts
Stewed Beef, with Bread, Butter and Potatoes.............. 5 cts
Roast Mutton, with Macaroni ....10 cts
Roast Beef, with Lima Beans......................................10 cts
Fried Apples and Bacon ....10 cts
Stewed Mutton, with Bread, Butter and Potatoes ....5 cts
Beefsteak and Onions, with Fried Potatoes..................10 cts
Pig's Feet, Soused or in Batter ....10 cts
Buckwheat Cakes with Honey......................................5 cts
Oysters, fried in Crumbs ....15 cts
Fried Clams...10 cts
Clam Chowder...5 cts
Cup of Chocolate...5 cts
2 Eggs, in any style..10 cts
Porterhouse Steak ....25 cts
Chicken Pot Pie ....20 cts
Mutton Chops, with Lyonese Potatoes........................10 cts
Rice, Farina, Sago, or Apple Dumplings..................5 cts
Mince, Apple, Custard, or Turnover Pie.............5 cts
Calf's Head, with Brain Sauce...................................10 cts
Boiled Mutton, with Mint Sauce..............................10 cts
Stewed Tripe, with Bread Butter and Potatoes............5 cts
Baked Apples ....5 cts
Stewed Prunes..5 cts
White Labor Cigars..5 cts
Mammoth Glass of Mason Celebrated Beer ....5 cts

Seven 15-ct. Meal Tickets for $1

Roast Turkey and Currant Jelly ....25 cts
Hot Oatmeal Mush ....10 cts
Boiled Beef, German style...10 cts
Cracked Wheat and Milk..10 cts
Buckwheat Cakes, and Honey, with Chocolate or Coffee ..10 cts
Straiton & Storms' White Labor Cigars................5 cts

dining room was bedlam. What Cheer served four thousand meals daily. Each day diners consumed twelve hundred eggs, one hundred pounds of butter, five hundred pounds of potatoes, four hundred quarts of milk. It was a temperance house with a few other rules. There was "no bread with one fish ball," but butter was free with two ten-cent dishes. Writing of the 1860s, a provisioner from the Idaho mines on a buying trip raved about the place. "After being seated you call for whatever you please which costs you five cents a dish and generally speaking four or five dishes is all that any ordinary man can dispose of at one meal. . . . Although everything is first class, the expense of putting up at this hotel is no more than stopping at any ordinary house."[8] (During the gold rush, the tariffs were higher all around.)

Equally celebrated San Francisco restaurants were the Washoe, the Lick House, and the Fountain House and "Branch" of M. L. Winn, he of the "California candy." Founded in July 1851, his two-restaurant chain fed three thousand people a day. By 1854 Winn's monthly bill for meat was eight thousand dollars, for flour four thousand, for milk two thousand, for butter two hundred, and for "other items necessary to carry on" the two restaurants, five thousand dollars. Receipts were just under two thousand dollars per day. Mary Lou Spence has devised an intriguing way to appreciate the enduring importance of eating houses in California culture; she determined that at the turn of the century the Golden State had one person waiting table for every 320 people in the state (one for every 203 in 1910) while South Dakota had one waiter for every 1,793 people in 1900 and one for every 580 in 1910.[9]

On the Comstock, Virginia City had its Downieville Restaurant, Virginia Restaurant ("supplied with the best the market affords"), New World Restaurant ("the VERY BEST the market affords"), and scores of less assertive eateries. Jim Gray, "the Handsomest Man Living," ran the International Saloon, which avidly competed with the Black Crook Saloon to serve "every luxury obtainable in this market."

Goldfield, Nevada, the last of the western gold rush towns, was also endowed with elegant restaurants such as The Idler and the usual raft of more modest houses. A mining engineer remembered:

There were some very fine eating places in Goldfield and Tonopah, but some of us after a long evening at the games preferred a big tent where a

No alcohol, including wine, was served in Tom Tigh's place in Goldfield, Nevada; the clientele must have been attracted by the fine food. (Courtesy Nevada Historical Society, Reno)

couple of good men cooks had set up with a U-shaped counter and a big iron stove in the open end of the U.

Some of my friends and I were in having a light midnight snack of steak and French fries one night when a gambler blew in and after climbing on a stool said, "Gimme a plainer rare and play it to lose."

The cook just slapped a plain steak on top of the red hot stove, turned it as soon as it browned a bit, and "coppered" it with bacon. There's nothing like knowing the language of the dealers.

Perhaps, unless it was knowing the language of the miners: a waiter in Central City, Colorado, once apologized to a patron that "the pies played out."[10]

In Colorado in 1859, California's sudden inundation with eating houses was repeated. While some Pike's Peakers still struggled with starvation, there was not only food in Denver for those who could pay, but a bustling restaurant trade. One establishment provided meals at twelve dollars a week "in advance" for men and women who had no place to shelter but slept "on the ground in the open air." The

City Bakery on Ferry Street in Auraria accepted gold dust in payment for its "meals at all hours." As the camp developed, so did the ambitions of its cuisine. Although a mile high in elevation and over a thousand miles as the crow flies from salt water, Pell's Fish House was but one of half a dozen popular seafood restaurants in the city. Charpiot's "Delmonico's of the West" offered five-course dinners for four for seven dollars. From California Gulch, where a strike was made two years after Denver's, a correspondent wrote, "we have a couple of good hotels already opened and doing a good business." By 1880 there were thirty-nine boarding restaurants in Denver.[11]

In 1867 M. Simonin wrote home to France of Colorado, "Stage coaches run everywhere, and everywhere are relay stations, eating places, saloons." Georgetown's Hotel de Paris, run by George Dupuy, a miner who had been injured in an underground explosion, maintained its own trout farm and huge wine cellar and reveled in an international reputation. Leadville, Colorado, at its peak supported 44 boarding houses and 31 restaurants (and 120 saloons where one might also catch a bite). Telluride's National Club Restaurant and Cafe boasted the "most modern equipped restaurant in the San Juan Region" along with "domestic and imported wines." Central City's Teller House claimed to offer "the most elaborate bill of fare we venture to say that has been provided by any hotel west of the Mississippi, . . . [a dinner] incomparably greater than has ever before been witnessed in the west."[12]

Given the catalogue recorded here, that was a highly dubious claim. It was, in fact, one echoed by dozens of mining region restaurants. To get a competitive edge the proprietors of the Clipper Restaurant in Silver City, Idaho, parodied the hyperbole:

We propose to feed customers better and cheaper than any other house in the city. Fresh vegetables ranging from camas to baled hay. Fruits—all kinds including strawberries (you can go out to the stack and bury yourself all over). Meats—that's our strong suit—never killing any but the strong kind. Large and well-defined steaks and mutton chops to match. Pigs feet—unless you want to go the entire swine—most of us don't, you know. Oysters, if called for, will come with a little extra assistance. Private dishes served up upon a minute's notice—charge nothing for the notice.[13]

And so it went. Pioneer Butte had its Florence Hotel, called "the big ship," which computed its daily production of stirabout by the ton; the Clarence, dubbed the "Mad House"; and the Mullin House, which fed a hundred miners daily. Butte also boasted "the smallest restaurant in the world," Tom Harris and Billy McCarthy's Success Cafe. The Success was three feet wide and thirteen feet long. Half of this was kitchen. In the refectory, four customers sat on either side of a table. The Success, it was said, was "never empty."[14]

That the Success should have supported two owners implies that the restaurant business in the mining region was a good one to pursue. In fact, like mining itself and the provisions trade, running an eatery was inviting but highly speculative and risky. The fortune of the restaurateur followed the fate of the camp and his or her own skill and luck in a sometimes fierce competition. When the price of silver collapsed in the 1870s, and the Comstock Lode appeared to be exhausted, Virginia City restaurants closed at the rate of one to three a month for over two years. According to Mrs. M. M. Mathews, their owners were saddled with debts because of cutthroat competition. "The expensive tables which they set is the secret of so many restaurants breaking up. . . . They will lose on the same men they have been feeding so high."[15]

Development in Arizona in the 1880s recapitulated the experience in older mining fields. The future of Bisbee, Arizona, was certainly "on paper" when its first restaurant was more or less founded, but the town's present was hardly "under canvas" by then.

On the 15th of June, Manuel Simas, a Portuguese, and his Mexican wife appeared in camp and started the first eat shop. The place for preparing the food (some people would call it a kitchen) was under a large tree. The dining room was large, the ceiling was the sky, and the table was in this big room. During the meals, the participants had the benefit of all sorts of weather conditions. The wind when it blew (which was about fourteen hours out of the twenty-four) carried the dust and dirt into the food, giving it a very disagreeable flavor which was far from palatable. However, after a time this was remedied in a great measure by a house being built. Sour beans continued to be served with commodities of various kinds for seasoning.[16]

At Bisbee's Can-Can (not to be confused, as the proprietor surely intended, with the more famous restaurant by that name in Tombstone), "the table was covered with oil cloth, spotted with droppings from a candle stuck in a beer bottle. The cups and plates were thick and the spoons were of tin. There were no napkins, so here my boy, you had better close your eyes tight or you will see the men wiping their moustaches on the backs of their hands as they push back their chairs."

Like other camps, Bisbee soon boasted far grander houses, including the Copper Queen Mining Company's Copper Queen Hotel—four stories and hardwood panelling "leading the traveller across the frontier Southwest to feel he has stopped into a veritable paradise in a desert oasis." Looking back from 1933 and recalling another Arizona camp's flush times, John C. Hancock felt constrained to clear up some common misapprehensions.

Most writers seem to have the idea that Tombstone was just a cheap rawhide coco town and that long-haired cowboys and rustlers stalked the streets with a six-shooter in each hand shooting at everything that did not suit their fancy. Such was not the case. Tombstone was a big rich mining camp filled with mining men from California, Nevada, Colorado, and other places in the Pacific slope. The service at the Can-Can, Fountain, and other first-class restaurants were as good in those days as the dining service is today on our railroads.[17]

Elsewhere in Arizona, Jerome's Bartlett Hotel fed the copper camp's visitors. The Montana and Jerome Hotels and the Hampton House fed miners, as did the Little Daisy. At Prescott, Ben Butler's Chop House offered "all the delicacies of the home, San Francisco, and Kansas City markets." Dinner there was from four to seven (unusually short hours for a mining town, as we shall see), with "elegant private rooms" available (a rather more common feature of miner restaurants).[18]

The story in Alaska was little different. Even before the news of the Klondike and Yukon strikes had been quite digested in Seattle, Anton Stanish and Louis Ceavich were wrestling several tons of restaurant equipment from shipboard to beach at Skagway. Their Pack Train Inn, in a tent at first, reserved space in Skagway's first commercial building when it was still in blueprint. In September 1897 arrived

The beachhead at Dyea in southeast Alaska became an open-air warehouse and a starting point for the trail over Chilkoot Pass to the Klondike region after the discovery of gold in 1896–97. (Courtesy Hegg Collection, University of Washington, Seattle)

147

The frigid summit of Chilkoot Pass. Prospectors were required by Canadian authorities to have a year's supplies with them when entering the Yukon Territory. (Courtesy Anchorage Historical and Fine Arts Museum)

Harriet Smith Pullen of Mount Hope, Wisconsin, who found a job cooking in another tent for eighteen men constructing Skagway's wharf. As soon as the job was done, she put her skills to work at her own Pullen House, which soon merited reviews of the sort lavished on the Hotel de Paris. At one banquet for the visiting worthies of the Seattle Chamber of Commerce, the Pullen House served caviar, radishes, salted almonds, ripe olives, cream of tomato soup, Alaska halibut with cream sauce, new Bermuda potatos, fried Alaska chicken, spinach and Alaska wild raspberries, shrimp salad, assorted cakes, ice cream, and all the appropriate wines.[19]

More likely to host sourdoughs still seeking their fortune was the White Pass Hotel and Restaurant that offered ninety-eighters (indeed, ninety-seveners) doughnuts, a choice of German pancakes or French pancakes, Boston baked beans and brown bread, corned beef hash, ham and eggs, steak, veal chops, tea, coffee, chocolate, and milk. Another worker's restaurant had a variety of steaks, hamburgers, and "all kinds of fish, game, and poultry in season."[20]

A PLEASANT, NATURAL CO-MINGLING

It is hardly remarkable that booming gold or silver centers should have included among their amenities an elegant restaurant or two. Surely the West's elite, like those elsewhere, were entitled to premises at which to sup pleasantly after a night at the opera. By the late nineteenth century wealthy Americans had decisively adopted the long, leisurely, "gourmet" dinner as one of their favorite recreations. In the mining towns, a fine restaurant was one of the gems by which hosts demonstrated to eastern or European guests (who were never in short supply) that, despite their geographical isolation, they were thoroughly cosmopolitan. The meal the Virginia City banker Blauvelt served a touring English lord at the Washoe Club, dished out on a solid gold service and washed down with, allegedly, six thousand bottles of champagne, was far from unique in the intermountain West.[21]

What is noteworthy in the foodways of the mining camps is that, like the opera houses, premier *public* restaurants such as Georgetown's Hotel de Paris and Tombstone's Can-Can (but not Virginia City's Washoe Club) counted as a major part of their patronage the ordinary miners of the camp and their companions, regular and otherwise. Unlike in our own era, when the social standing and status of an eating establishment's clientele may reliably be guessed after a glance at the interior trappings and the menu, the young mining camp was as democratic at table as it was at the polls and stock exchanges.

"The social life of Silver City," reads a promotional brochure that any of two dozen camps might have published, "is free from the petty jealousies and heart-burnings that are so common in small places, where the 'upper ten' and 'codfish aristocracy' swell over their inferiors. Here there is a pleasant, natural co-mingling between all classes, and a cordial hospitality."

Of course, not all found it so pleasant. Bill Nye wrote of a waiter in Montana who, while he recited the card, leaned "his full weight on my back, while he evaded the revenue laws by retailing his breath to the guests without a license." An English tourist found the easy informality of Montana waitresses "very funny but not very comfortable."[22]

The egalitarian temper of the American mining frontier has, of course, been noticed and analyzed since its earliest days. In his pioneering sociological study of American miners published in 1884, Charles H. Shinn observed that

the mines put all men for once upon a level. Clothes, money, manners, family connections, letters of introduction, never before counted for so little. The whole community was given substantially an even start in the race. Gold was so abundant, and its sources seemed for a time so inexhaustible, that the aggrandizing power of wealth was momentarily annihilated. Social and financial inequalities between man and man were together swept out of sight.[23]

If such a Jacksonian idyll ever really existed in such purity, it did not last very long. The expense of ever more sophisticated and expensive technology to win precious metal from the earth, and the resulting flow of capital into the West, created clear class lines in the mining towns between capitalist and worker, between employer—and his superintendents and professional associates—and employee.

This transformation took place with dizzying speed at the scene of each rich strike. However, the evolution of an egalitarian "prospector society" into a typically American industrial capitalist society occurred at different times in different places. By the time Colorado and the Comstock came in, reviving the vitality of 1849, California's mines were mature, even "old." Goldfield, Nevada, was culturally "younger" in 1904—as wide open socially as Placerville in 1849 or Virginia City in 1859—than Leadville, Cripple Creek, Telluride, Tombstone, or the Coeur D'Alenes. These periodic reinvigorations of the congenial old egalitarian ideals consequently gave them new life again even in the more mature camps where modernization had already had its way. A number of historians have seen this repeated, rapid social transformation as the source of western miner radicalism and the peculiar character of western miner unionism, including the violence common in mining country strikes.[24]

If not precisely an old "ideal," fancy eating was an old practice that, significantly, was one of the prospector ways that persisted into the era of industrial capitalism. It was an obvious aspect of the egalitarian hopefulness of gold miners. Sir Henry Huntley, who liked little of what he saw in California in 1849, was appalled that "every labourer, miner, teamster, or other person who happens to be at the house, sits down together" to dine. In 1849 the waiters in San Francisco insisted on being called *steward* in their belief that *waiter* was a demeaning term. The Clarendon Hotel in Leadville, Colorado, which hired Chef M. LaPierce from Delmonico's in New York, advertised itself as "Headquarters for Miners and Capitalists." In Butte a fracas occurred in a "higher class of cafe" when a miner became indignant that the elaborate menu, which otherwise pleased him, included no stirabout. The Tortoni in Denver, which featured "elegant private dining" and a discreet "second floor entrance from the street," was a trysting place for the well-to-do. But by maintaining a twenty-four-hour schedule to accommodate the shift workers, the Tortoni put out the call to miners as well. Only the fact that they appealed to a broadly based clientele can explain why there were so many pretentious eating houses in the mining camps. Indeed, fine restaurants were among the first businesses to fail in Nevada during the silver depression of the 1870s.[25]

Miners took their sometimes disreputable companions to the fanciest restaurants. Louise Palmer, a proper lady of the middle class, was relieved to report to readers of the *Overland Monthly* in 1869 that the Comstock Lode's "ladies of the *demi-mode* no longer expect to eat the

This clever display in Denver of fruit, plus colored Easter eggs heaped in a plum-pudding box, would have graced any city in the world. (Courtesy Colorado Historical Society, Denver)

dinners and grace the parties of the *haut ton*." Nevertheless, the undesirables continued to frequent the restaurants. It is tempting to speculate that it was, among other things, the sight of prostitutes on the arms of miners in the finest restaurants that impelled the managerial and capitalist classes in the developing towns toward an increasingly private social life, away from the hoi polloi.

Mrs. Palmer and her friends increasingly found their society at invitation-only lunch parties. "All protest against lunch parties," she wrote, yet they continued to give and attend them. "It is stupid to dress in one's newest silk to partake of chickens, creams, ices, and Champagne with a dozen of one's own sex." But, unspoken yet clearly understood, the alternative was to socialize at public restaurants, whatever their quality, where they would have to rub elbows with the lower orders. Mrs. Hugh Brown, wife of a prominent lawyer in Tonopah and Goldfield, the last of the frontier mining camps, told of a similarly private social whirl insulated from the common folk. As a proper lady, she did not even walk past the doors of saloons, which, we shall see, were also eating places and occasionally eating places quite grand.[26]

As for the menfolk of the middle and upper classes, during the 1880s they established membership clubs like Virginia City's Washoe. During the 1890s, these associations of owners, managers, and "citizens" (independent businessmen and professionals) became centers of the anti-union movement, the places where strategies for fighting industrial conflicts were hammered out. By contrast the public restaurant, to which admission depended only upon having a golden eagle or even just a silver dollar in the pocket, remained a workers' preserve.

When the Consolidated Virginia mine collapsed in 1877, followed by a severe depression within a depression on the Comstock, restaurants joined butchers and greengrocers in contributing goods to a soup kitchen set up by a group of Virginia City women. The protests against wage cuts in Virginia City and Gold Hill that led to the formation of the first miners' unions in the West were written after supper in Comstock restaurants. During labor troubles in Butte, Kenoffel's Spokane Cafe and other miner eateries refused to release the bucket lunches they usually prepared, or even the buckets, to workers who were ignoring the call to strike. In Bisbee the Citizens' Protective League offered a subsidy to boarding houses and restaurants that *would* pack lunches for scabs. Apparently few did; at least seven food service owners and employees were among those "deported" from Bisbee in the infamous incident of 1917. Earlier, in 1914, a pro-employer candidate for governor of Arizona, Thomas E. Campbell, had ostentatiously eaten at a restaurant boycotted by members of the local union, Truax's English Kitchen. His opponent, George W. P. Hunt, just as noisily shunned it. Hunt's political enemies took satisfaction (as did, perhaps, his supporters) in the anti-Hunt slur, "he eats with his knife."[27]

A MAN'S WORLD

Neither Kenoffel's Spokane Cafe nor Truax's English Kitchen claimed, as so many miners' restaurants did, to be the "one and only," the old original "Delmonico's of the West," "only better." Like the large majority of mining camp eating houses, they unpretentiously provided ordinary everyday all-American meals of bacon and eggs, soups, stews, steaks, roast beef, chops, potatoes—and almost always oysters, of course—and the like for reasonable prices. There never was a day on which an argonaut could not get a substantial fill in San Francisco for a dollar. A full meal in Virginia City could run as little as fifty cents, one dollar for both breakfast and dinner if paid in advance. In rawer camps like Telluride, one-dollar to two-fifty-a-plate was the list price although Rose's ("the only place in town to get a No. 1 corn fed juicy beefsteak") marked its two-fifty plates down to a dollar seventy-five, and its dollar plates down to seventy-five cents when the competing Saddle Rock Restaurant advertised a dinner for a quarter. The mining towns teemed with cheap eateries.[28]

In fact, San Francisco and the rawest camps of the Sierra slope teemed with homey eating houses (or tents). They were "numerous, plenteous, inviting and even cheap." Restaurants were among the very first businesses at the scene of every strike. Keeping a public table was one of the first nonmining occupations to be found in a hundred "No Name cities." A "restaurant rush" followed closely on—when it did not lead in!—the provisions rush. There are more than a few examples of "starving" forty-niners and Pike's Peakers who allayed their famine not by grubbing on wild plants, snaring beasts, seeking charity, or by fortuitously buying a sack of flour, but by throwing their weary legs under a table at a not-too-distant restaurant.[29]

The reason for this is not obscure. In a society in which domestic cooking remained woman's work, the first flood of population in every mining region was overwhelmingly male. "This circumstance," wrote the chroniclers of gold rush San Francisco, as usual a prototype of miner culture, "naturally tended to give a peculiar character to the aspect of the place and habits of the people."

There was no such thing as a *home* to be found. Scarcely even a proper *house* could be seen. Both dwellings and places of business were either common canvas tents, or small rough board shanties, or frame buildings of one story. Only the great gambling saloons, the hotels, restaurants, and a few public buildings and stores had any pretentions to size, comfort, or elegance. . . . Meals were taken at eating-houses, of which there was an immense number in every portion of the town. These were of every description, good, bad, and indifferent, and kept by every variety of people. . . . Besides the common eating-houses or restaurants there were a number of fashionable saloons, where a delicate meal of small game or oysters could be obtained at exorbitant prices.[30]

A good meal, and certainly a *delicate* one, meant more than a meal that was merely healthful. On the mining frontier, an appropriate meal was often a meal that was "extravagant," as men trafficking in precious gold were inclined to be, and "tasty" in the sense of the spicy foods for which the miners yearned. At the very least, "good" meant food decently prepared. For all their experience on the overland trail, for all the hundreds of thousands of meals they had prepared in "cabins rude" on the western slope of the Sierra, in the canyons of the Rockies, and across the deserts of Nevada and Arizona, the menfolk of the mining frontier seem to have produced few amateur cooks who both enjoyed and were competent in the craft.

"There is little use of my telling the following incident," one forty-niner put it.

None but those who crossed the plains can have the slightest notion of its significance. We were coming down where the road veers off to Hangtown . . . when what do you think burst out through the air? A rooster's crow. O godlings! Chicken! Eggs! The train pulled up as if a warship had thrown a shell across our bows, and you should have heard the yelling from our maudlin mob! They had yet to learn that chickens were sixteen dollars each and eggs fifty cents apiece—but not one to his dying day will forget that welcoming salute of civilization by said chanticleer on the Hangtown Road that morning.[31]

Reminiscent of John Johnson's self discovery in Nebraska was Horace Snow's awakening at Agua Frio Creek:

I am in great trouble! Troubled exceedingly in my domestic affairs. Good bread being an indispensable article in promoting health and happiness, I am sorry to say I have not got it. But the trouble lies with the yeast. Whether by accident or neglect or whether by carelessness or some other misdemeanour, I know not, but we are out of yeast. Twice have we made trial according to directions and twice have we failed. For two long days has our last batch been exposed to the sun and for twice as many long nights has the homogenous mass occupied a space on the warm hearth but, in spite of our ill looks, our indignant rhetoric, and all violation of chemical laws, this aforesaid compound is just as sweet as the moment we had it prepared.[32]

There were exceptions, of course. Looking back from a comfortable middle age on his own gold rush experience, Prentice Mulford

Dinner at Strawberry, known as "the best stopping-place on the route to Washoe" and the last station before crossing the summit of the Sierra Nevada. Dilapidated gentlemen, peddlers, miners, teamsters, *vaqueros*, and traders packed into the barroom to drink and warm themselves by the log fire. The dining room was invaded at intervals by hungry men demanding pork and beans, biscuits, coffee, beefsteak, sausages, potatoes, ham and eggs, and mince pies. The waiters, panting and swearing, then cleared away the carnage, and in half an hour the battlefield was again ready for action. (from J. Ross Browne, "A Peep at Washoe")

remembered mealtimes with fond nostalgia. "Each one has some favorite duty," he wrote of his mess, "Smith's knack is that of slicing tomatoes; Sutton can fry potatoes better than any man in the Southern Mines; Brown prides himself on chile stews, learned in South America, involving a strong application of red peppers; Dan's forte is broiling steak."

But Mulford was describing life in a declining camp, a place where meals were cooked not in cabins but "in tenantless stores and offices" by men who, in the tranquility of dearly bought wisdom, had learned to listen philosophically to proclamations of new eldorados over the far ridge. In their capacity to enjoy "long and social meals" with "no business to hurry off on; nothing to do save wash up the dishes, light the pipes, and then sit on the street in the shade of the locust tree," Mulford's crew was hardly typical of its time and place. The majority of the miners still believed they might yet strike it rich. They continued to find meal preparation an inconvenience at best and, often enough, an onerous burden. In any case, cooking remained a task that they believed should clearly rest in a woman's hands or, lacking hers, those of a professional restaurateur.[33]

If women were rare and exotic in California during the first months of every new excitement, they remained a minority even when a rich camp stabilized. The two males to one female ratio recorded on the Comstock remained typical of the mining frontier, when it did not represent simply wishful thinking on the part of the lonely men.

The masculine character of miner society hardly needs documentation. However, just as vivid and striking as any eyewitness account of the longbeards agog before the first woman in Angel's Camp, or Saturday night in a Leadville brothel, is J. Ross Browne's account of what the absence of women meant at table. He described dinner at the Strawberry House in Placerville, considered the best eating place on the Sacramento–Virginia City Road. "Chiefly remarkable in the crowd," he wrote in April 1859, "was the regiment of light infantry, pressed in double file against the dining room door awaiting the fourth or fifth charge at the table. At the first tinkling of the bell, the door burst open with a tremendous crash, and no Crimean avalanche of troops dealing death and destruction around them could have equaled the terrific onslaught of the gallant troops of the Strawberry."[34]

155

Small wonder that Andrew J. Fisk gushed when he was invited to dine at the Widow Degan's ranch. "She gave me a splendid dinner—oyster soup—Butter—cheese and *such* a piece of *Mince Pie. Lord,* but twas good." Little surprise that the miners of Indian Bar were, lacking company of the fair sex, mesmerized by the strains from the violin of Ned, "the Paganini of the Hotel Humboldt." One guest "found that Ned had not overstated his powers. The dinner, when one considers the materials of which it was composed, was really excellent. The soup was truly a great work of art; the fried oysters dreamily delicious; and as to the coffee, Ned must have got the receipt for making it from the very angel who gave the beverage to Mahomet to restore that individual's decayed motive."[35]

When the restaurateur also happened to be a woman, it often meant the birth of at least local legend. Harriet Pullen's restaurant was the pride of Skagway for two decades. Luzena Wilson was renowned in Grass Valley for having raked ten thousand dollars over a table made of two doors that she set up in the open air. Augusta Tabor, later to be jilted by millionare husband Horace in favor of the beauty fabled in Colorado history as Baby Doe, ran a boarding restaurant when Horace was still struggling to make money.[36]

By far the most legendary mine country hostess was Nellie Cashman of Tombstone and the Klondike. Born about 1850 in Ireland, Nellie joined the stampede to British Columbia's Fraser River in 1877. Although it is not clear that she ran a restaurant there, it would appear likely because, when a long, severe winter resulted in a scurvy epidemic, Nellie rushed in vegetables, especially potatoes. Her reputation for holding distribution superior to acquisition—always a recommendation among the frequently socialist miners—was launched.

Not that Nellie was averse to profit. In 1878 she traveled to Virginia City via California and, the next year, was in Tucson. By 1880 she was the proprietress of Tombstone's Russ House at the corner of Fifth and Tough Nut streets. A modest place serving meals for twenty-five cents and up, it became something of a shrine as Nellie continued her good works. In 1883, it was said, she saved a party of prospectors in the Muleje desert of Mexico by getting water to them. The men reciprocated. According to one tale, when a traveling salesman complained about his dinner at the Russ House, a "tall miner" unlimbered his six-shooter and said, grimly, "Stranger, eat them beans."

According to another memorialist, "her principal business" at the Russ House "was to feed the hungry and shelter the homeless"; her "chief divertissement was to relieve those in distress and to care for the sick and afflicted." Nellie raised five children not her own, sponsored many benefits for injured miners, and broke up sandlot fistfights by leading the gangs of boys "over to her pie bakery where each member was served with a generous cut." (It was said in the town that fights were cordially prearranged "for the sole and lofty purpose of obtaining—MORE PIE.")

In 1897, although getting along in years, Nellie joined one more rush, to the Klondike and Yukon, where at Fairbanks she opened a grocery. Her stature is perhaps best measured by this lovely fragment of western sentimental excess:

She was inclined to associate more generally with men than with members of her own sex, and on several occasions she joined in stampedes with men, tramping with them over rugged lands and sharing the vicissitudes and discomforts of their rude camps. Nevertheless, she maintained an unimpeachable reputation, and her character and conduct commanded the universal respect and admiration of every community in which she lived.[37]

It is unlikely that an Indian woman, "Virgin Mary," who came to Prescott with "Nigger Brown," was lavished with such encomia. Nevertheless, her boarding restaurant in the Goose Flat section of town was favored by local miners over her chief competition, Jackson's Restaurant, "if you liked goat milk in your coffee."[38]

How prominent were women as owners of restaurants? It is difficult to say with any assurance. Beyond those famed few whose names we know, the record is unclear. According to *The Annals of San Francisco,* that city's "fashionable saloons . . . were generally kept by dashing females," but the authors hasten to add,

or such were employed at high wages to decoy and entertain customers. Particular regard was paid to beauty and other attractions in their selection, and those who possessed the rarest charms to please, drew the most patronage and received the heaviest wages. Women were scarce in those days, and men were frequently willing to pay largely for the slight privilege of addressing one even in the way of business.[39]

Widows of miners, particularly "silicosis widows" (women whose husbands died of that dreaded occupational disease), seem frequently to have gone into the boarding restaurant trade. And here and there a statistic appears that implies that a good proportion of mining camp restaurateurs were female. For example, of six miners' restaurants in Silver City, New Mexico, in 1915, three were operated by women, as was one of the two hotels. In a survey of women's occupations in Cripple Creek, historian Elizabeth Jameson found that from 21 to 29 percent of the working women were proprietresses of restaurants, boarding houses, or lodging houses.[40]

However, most women in food service in the mining regions appear to have been employees. In 1880 in Leadville, 26.6 percent of the people waiting table were women or girls, at that time almost precisely the female proportion of the town's population, 27 percent.[41]

As in San Francisco, mining camp restaurants sometimes touted "pretty waiter girls" as one of the house's attractions. Mine host Jackson in Prescott, Arizona, could offer in competition with "Virgin Mary's" goat milk only the promised presence of "his 16 year old stepdaughter and stewed apples occasionally." At Madge's Boarding House in Castle Rock, Colorado, owner P. J. Muzan told Swedish quarrymen that he was "setting up a first class chuck." According to the newspaper, "The boys are well-pleased, especially with the lady who waits in the tables." A Leadville theater was direct in its advertisement for feminine help: "50 *Waiter Girls!* Pay in Gold Promptly every week. Must appear in SHORT CLOTHES or no engagement."[42]

Such spectacles prompted moralists to depict waitressing as a way-station to prostitution. In fact, a survey of 471 California whores in 1888 found that only two had previously waited table in restaurants. Working as a maid (presumably in respectable middle and upper-class homes) was a much more common background. Waitressing in miners' restaurants was more likely seen as an opportunity to find a husband. Of 412 western waiters and waitresses, a study by Mary Lou Spence has shown, 12 percent of the waiters were over forty-five years of age but only 2.7 percent of the waitresses were as old. It is reasonable to guess that most of the young waitresses, from a quarter to a majority in the occupation, were regularly trading the public dining room for the domestic kitchen:

> And Who will know
> > Or who will care,
> If some day I
> > Grab a millionaire.

A waiters' union official in Denver seemed to take this pleasant reverie seriously. He complained that "our girls are getting married so fast to these rich ranchers and mine owners that it is hard for us to keep a line on them."[43]

More likely the husband of a former waitress occupied a more modest station in life. Mary Grace Paquette has discovered that "Keskydees" in the Kern River diggings often chose their wives from among French waitresses and maids at the French hotels of East Bakersfield. No doubt the possibility of a marriage induced many girls from the old country to accept jobs there because employers, also French, had no difficulty securing a constant supply of help from their native towns and villages. Then, however, there was the occasional mining restaurant waitress who joined proprietresses like Augusta Tabor and Nellie Cashman in western legend. Colorado's "Unsinkable Molly Brown" began her career as a waitress.[44]

STRICTLY AN INCIDENTAL

One additional explanation of, to borrow Professor Spence's phrase, the miners' "eating out mentality," remains to be explored. As Dan DeQuille wrote of Virginia City, "the people of the town eat at restaurants and have their rooms at lodging houses, . . . except that a restaurant is seldom found in the same building as a lodging house. Those who live in lodging houses patronize the restaurant which best suits them. Restaurants and lodging houses are therefore even more numerous in the town than saloons." An editor from nearby Gold Hill added a moralistic fillip: "men live in restaurants and sleep in bunks. They feed on whiskey and that diet causes to rowdyism as naturally as turtle soup lays fat on an alderman's ribs."[45]

However that may have been—Comstock miners spent up to an hour and a half at dinner—it is clearly true that miners and other denizens of the camps chose to eat and room in different places, so

Boarding in Shasta

"I pay fourteen dollars a week for my board without lodging and sleep in a barn. I have slept in a barn or on a haymow for the last four or five months. I have not slept in a house more than three or four nights in a year. . . . I have never been able to sleep in the public houses without being infested with vermin."

H. W. Garfield, Letter from Shasta City, April 7, 1854

much so that evidence of room *and* boarding houses in the mining camps, where bed and meals were sold for a single fee, is difficult to find. An analysis of the residences of a hundred Comstock miners of 1878, selected at random from the city directory, revealed twenty-one living at houses providing both room and board (but not necessarily in a package), seventy-six with addresses in lodging houses that served no meals, and three at European plan "hotels" where they may or may not have eaten. On the Comstock that year there were sixty-four boarding-only houses, eighty-five establishments offering rooms without meals, and twelve "hotels" providing room and board on separate tickets.

The majority of miners preferred, apparently even insisted on, exercising the prerogative of choosing where they would eat by the day or, at most, by the week. This represented a departure from conventional American boarding practice. The term *boarding house* meant to most Americans a place where one both ate and slept for a weekly sum. On the mining frontier, however, it would more accurately have been called a *boarding restaurant*. This curious institution will be examined more closely in the next chapter. Here it is enough to emphasize that the miner's boarding house provided no beds and served meals singly as well as on short-term contract (usually a week).[46]

This seems to have been an arrangement particularly associated with gold and silver miners; in Tombstone, Arizona, teamsters and clerks typically worked for wages *plus* board while miners received straight wages and provided their own meals. Moreover, while employer-operated cookhouses were common in copper camps, they were virtually unknown where gold and silver were the metals men dug.[47]

The peculiarity of this arrangement derives in part from the fact that boarding restaurants in mining camps kept long hours, often remaining open twenty-four hours a day. Meeting such a schedule was too much for the operator of a lodging house, the maintenance of which was itself a fulltime job. Although there were exceptions, particularly in Butte, Montana, the vast majority of lodging houses were small businesses, run by owner-operators in their homes with few employees.

A TABLE FOR THE CAMP

INTERIOR OF COOK HOUSE HENDRICKSON & JOHNSON 10 BELOW CLEARY CREEK. WOLF & PHOTO 75

Was it Christmas? Possibly, although the photographer found it pertinent to note only that it was ten below outside this comfortable eatery near Cleary Creek in the Yukon Territory. (Courtesy Idaho State Historical Society, Boise)

The miners' strong sense of personal independence—the same ornery individualism that gave miners' unions their strident, even aggressive and violent character—also helps account for their insistence on choosing the time and place they took their meals weekly, daily, or even on the spur of the moment. They were a mobile people, of course; 80 percent of the miners of Virginia City in 1875 had left by 1880. But beyond that, the miners were irregular in their habits and impulsive in camp. The standard American room *and* boarding house arrangement would have limited the miner's choice of viands to the choice of his landlady, and compelled him to breakfast, dine, and sup at the landlady's appointed hour. People who found it difficult to accept an absentee mineowner's right to his property were unlikely to accept petticoat tyranny. Just as they liked their saloons and casinos open around the clock, gold and silver miners insisted on the freedom to pop into a boarding restaurant at their pleasure, at any hour of the day or night, present a dollar or a ticket, and chow down.[48]

Like so much in the mentality of the mining West, the custom of eating out when and where a freeborn American chooses has its roots in gold rush days. The earliest California restaurants, like the "boarding shanties" on Mormon Island and Ned's Humboldt House and Alexander Gault's Antelope Restaurant in Nevada City, provided "meals at all hours." The City Bakery in Auraria and other restaurants in Denver in 1859 never closed. In Juneau as early as 1888, the Enterprise Restaurant kept its doors open twenty-four hours a day. So did Albuquerque's Exchange Hotel, from where "a coach leaves . . . every Tuesday morning for the New Placers."[49]

Restaurants also were ubiquitous in California in 1849 because, with gold fever burning at its hottest, the men wanted to think of nothing but gold, to be at nothing during their waking hours except digging gold. With good reason Edward Austin thought he could make a fortune as a truck farmer in Sacramento because, while "garden tools are very cheap" in the mines, and seeds available, "no one will take the trouble to plant them." Nascent restaurateurs were presented with a similar opportunity. To the men cooking was, as John W. Caughey nicely puts it, "to be dispatched as quickly as possible and strictly as an incidental."[50]

162

C. H. Randall wrote his parents from Sacramento that "the reasons for so much sickness and death in this country is that every one is so much engaged in getting money that their health becomes a secondary object to them." William Elder moved a little closer to the cookfire. "I do not say that much attention is paid to washing dishes," he wrote from the diggings to his wife, "but I might make the remark that the woman did about her boy's face, that it could not be dirty as she washed it every week herself."[51]

But it would be unseemly for a sedentary writer or reader from the age of convenience foods to patronize the miners of the nineteenth century for preferring that others prepare their meals for them at their convenience. Mining was, pure and simply, "intense and unremitting" toil. Keeping house in addition was simply too much for most men. "Only think of working all day," Horace Snow wrote to a boyhood friend, and then "going home at night, rolling up your sleeves, making biscuits, doughnuts, flapjacks, frying pork or ham, washing dishes and all such things as pertain to domestic duties?"[52]

Although Snow took pride in that the demands of his life were making him "an accomplished young man," versatile in both man's and woman's work, he had no apologies when on occasion he shirked his duties. "The evening that I received your letter," he wrote to a friend, "it happened to be my turn to prepare the supper, but I just seated myself in the most comfortable part of the cabin and told the boys that I should visit America for a short time and they must supply their insufficiency as best suited them."[53]

Others in the ravines had long since thrown it all over and looked for someone who would feed them for a fee. If they did not laze over the heat of every western summer day at "commercial establishments," decidedly including restaurants as well as the better-known types of dispensaries, it was the widespread, nigh universal, custom to eat out on Sunday. One group did this in order to have "something extra." Another, "older hands" at Sutter's Mill, "every Sunday had made a custom of visiting [Little's Hotel in] Coloma for the express purpose of having one good dinner in the week."[54]

To some extent the social stability that hard-rock mining and marriage brought to the mining West kept the husbands at home.

TREADWELL MINE.
ECONOMICAL VEGETABLE PEELING MACHINE,
TREADWELL BOARDING HOUSE.

CASEYDRAPER   93

Chinese kitchen workers watch as a
potato-peeling machine is timed at the
massive Treadwell mine boardinghouse.
(Courtesy Alaska Historical Library,
Juneau)

A TABLE FOR THE CAMP

Nevertheless, a substantial proportion of the underground workforce in most mining camps, from Virginia City to Goldfield, was made up of young, unmarried males for whom restaurant meals remained the rule. More striking is that many married couples continued to eat out often. "Two thirds of the inhabitants" of Virginia City "board at restaurants," a disapproving Mrs. M. M. Mathews wrote, "many of them with whole families of children. . . . Even those families that do board themselves, when they want a square meal, as they call it, go out and get it; and nearly everybody goes out on Sunday and the holidays to one meal." To make matters worse, she felt, husband and wife did not even dine together on weekdays.

The male portion of a family generally get up and go to the restaurant, eat their breakfast, and go to work at six and seven o'clock; and the miners especially. At ten and eleven o'clock you will see the ladies go stringing into the restaurants with their children. . . . A lady who eats her breakfast at ten and eleven o'clock, as many of them do, can scarcely start in on a Virginia City dinner before one or two o'clock.

So, while "miners and businessmen want to eat their meals when they come home from work," Madame was not hungry again until seven or eight. Husband and wife have their supper separately too.[55]

Now and then, no doubt, the married miners enjoyed their evenings out with a splurge at one of the camp's finer French eating houses. But, for all the importance of *haute cuisine* in miner culture, they more often went to the cheaper boarding restaurants where the miners supped. The institutions of everyday eating—the boarding houses, saloons, and Chinese restaurants—are the subject of the final chapter.

AND WON TON SOUP

Negroes from the Southern States swaggering in the expansive feeling of runaway freedom; mulattoes from Jamaica trudging arm-in-arm with Kanakas from Hawaii; Peruvians and Chileans claiming affinity with the swarthier Mexicans; Frenchmen, Germans, and Italians fraternizing with one another and with the cockney fresh from the purlieus of St. Giles; an Irishman, with the dewdrop still in his eye, tracing relationship with the ragged Australian; Yankees from the Penobscot chatting and bargaining with the genial Oregonians; a few Celestials scattered here and there, their pigtails and conical hats recalling the strange pictures that took my boyish fancy while studying the geography of the East; last of all, a few Indians, the only indigenous creatures among all these exotics, lost, swallowed-up, out of place. . . .
At home one would associate such a crowd with the deck of a Mississippi

For half a century after 1849, fresh strikes of precious metal in the intermountain West, British Columbia, the Klondike, and the Yukon resulted in repeated rushes and those brief heady epochs when a camp was "wide open." Then the dream of sudden riches kindled anew in the breasts of the miners and those who accompanied them in their zig-zagging, criss-crossing odyssey from California to Colorado, from Alaska to southern Arizona. The repeated reinvigoration of notions and practices born in California led to the creation of a culture, or at least a mentality, that included within it a number of foodways that, had they thought about them much, Americans "back East" would have found peculiar. "Eating out" at restaurants, which comparatively few Americans did in the nineteenth century, was common practice among gold and silver miners until the high-grade veins of ore beneath Goldfield, Nevada, pinched out during the 1910s.

The frontier miners' taste for spicy, saucy, fancy, "Frenchy" food, at least on special occasions, was a foodway most Americans would have found pretentious, if not subversive and risky to the digestion. To most Americans during the late nineteenth and early twentieth centuries, quantity, and not particularly the quality of the feed, was the index of a special meal.

Ironically, it is unnecessary to look any further for a prototype of the food-loving American in those times than to that political hero of the western silver miners, William Jennings Bryan. The Great Commoner was the most appreciative guest the hostesses at a thousand church picnics and county fairs ever entertained. His eyes rolled, his

168

nostrils flared, and his hands rubbed warmly together at the vision of a
board groaning under mountains of roast and boiled and scarcely
seasoned meats, piles of home-baked bread and biscuits, and mounds
of starchy salads. The gluttony that left him in the kind of stupor
usually associated with multiple nights in a barroom was an object of
mockery for his many political enemies. But none of them ever accused
Bryan of hankering for galantine truffles or anything garlicked, let
alone a well-selected wine for each of seven or eight courses at a
restaurant operated by someone named Jean-Claude. The miners who
voted for him, on the contrary, often enjoyed with distinct relish
precisely such dainties, *carte,* and host.

Another curiosity among the miners' foodways is that while the
customs forged in California in the 1850s were passed along from new
camp to new camp, there was comparatively little "development" in
the food culture. When Jim Butler, as crusty a sourdough as ever
Hollywood could create, hammered his pick into a mountain in southern Nevada in 1900 and discovered it was "solid silver," his burro was
carrying the same utilitarian grub—beans, bacon, flour, and saleratus—with which, five decades earlier, the forty-niners trudged from
Sacramento or Stockton into the Sierra. The only advantage over his
predecessors Butler might have enjoyed was in canned goods. But even
that cannot be said for certain. Despite the high prices of tinned meat,
fish, and fruits at the middle of the nineteenth century, before cans
were mass-produced, the rusted artifacts were conspicuous at every
camp's dump.

The most elegant meal offered at Tonopah's or Goldfield's finest
hotel in the sunset of the mining frontier was much the same as the
"good champaign dinner" wagered by the passengers of two ships of
1849 over which would first enter the Golden Gate. Both began with
oysters, the *sine qua non* of miner dining. Both were organized into
seven or eight courses with French names, served *à la russe,* and both
were composed of dishes described in that same language. Quantity
was *trés formidable,* quality of ingredient and preparation *la même
chose.* Both meals were heavy on the rich buttery and creamy sauces of
haute cuisine and the wine lists were long.

The miners' boarding restaurant was not unique to the West, but in
its centrality in the meal-taking customs of the mining frontier, the

eating house at which one could board by the week or buy a meal as a "walk-in" was peculiar. Virtually unique to the mining country was that such eateries often—usually—remained open twenty-four hours a day. We owe our own all-night businesses to the age of cheap electrical power, of course. But the western miners developed them first, for better or for worse, even before the gaslit age.

Another foodway that the folks back East may have adopted from the mining frontier was the saloon's free lunch. We cannot be certain about this. Details surrounding the origin of that institution are feverishly debated to this day. Unlike the case of most bastard children—and anything associated with the saloon at the turn of the century was illegitimate—numerous towns, cities, and even specific bibbing houses have claimed to be father to the free lunch. Chronologically, however, the claims of the too-many and therefore highly competitive saloons of the mining West are most persuasive.

Finally, the mining West introduced the United States to a cuisine that has been almost universally adopted, albeit in frequently modified form, as a cheap "eat out" or "take home" meal, the cooking of the Cantonese Chinese who swarmed to "the Golden Mountain," as they called California. The Caucasian miners feared, hated, or ridiculed John Chinaman. But they liked what he ate.

BOARDING HOUSES

It is not always possible to determine whether the eating places the miners called "boarding houses" looked more or less like what we would call hotels, with sleeping chambers upstairs and a lobby and dining restaurant on the ground floor. Perhaps some were more like ordinary counter-and-tables restaurants where one could walk in and buy a meal from the menu. Sometimes they meant places where one could contract for a week of breakfasts and dinners, with box lunches to carry on the job. Or it might mean simply a room in a home—usually a woman's—where meals were served and lunches packed on weekly contract.

The miners used the term loosely to apply to all sorts of eateries. San Francisco's What Cheer and Butte's "Big Ship," which served thousands of meals daily, were sometimes called boarding houses, as was the table set for two or three boarders in the silicosis widow's small house, and the "boarding tent" kept for ten men at Fairview,

The What Cheer Restaurant was one of San Francisco's most famous eating establishments. (Courtesy Huntington Library, San Marino, Calif.)

WHAT CHEER RESTAURANT

NEAT, GOOD AND CHEAP!

NEAT, GOOD AND CHEAP!

WHAT CHEER HOUSE.

527 and 529 Sacramento Street, corner of Leidesdorff,
SAN FRANCISCO.

E. P. BUCKLIN, - - Proprietor.
Orders Cooked from 5 A. M. to 10 P. M.

Nevada, "by a big raw-boned farm woman from Kansas . . . who smoked a corncob pipe filled with Bull Durham tobacco."[2]

Whatever the miners meant, their "boarding house" was not the "room *and* boarding house" that most Americans visualized when they used the term. With the occasional exception of an isolated mine such as Colorado's Tomboy, which because of its high elevation was cut off from the outside world much of the winter, gold and silver miners shunned the practice of eating and sleeping at the same address, and particularly at company-operated cookhouses. Even at very small mines, employees expected to find their own dining accommodations.[3]

Like the miners' yen for highly spiced foods, this preference contrasted sharply with the habits of western loggers, who virtually insisted on company-provided meals as part of their pay. But while logging company cookhouses were almost always described as serving good food, "as good as at a first-class hotel," the odd mining company cookhouse is typically execrated. For example, it was said about "Baxter's awful grub" at Utah's Apex Mine:

The coffee has the dropsy; the tea it has the grippe.
The butter was consumptive, and the slapjacks they had fits;
The beef was strong as jubilant; it walked upon the floor.
The spuds got on their dignity and rolled right out the door.
The pudding had the jimjams; the pies was in disguise.
The beans came to the table with five hundred thousand flies.
The hash was simply murdered, just as hard as 'dobe mud.
We howl, we wail, our muscles fail on Baxter's awful grub.[4]

In addition, while mining towns were, like logging camps, usually far from major urban centers, they were fixed sites and often cities, with a remarkably full range of urban services and amenities. The logging camp really was a camp, highly portable because after a season or two the nearby timber was harvested. With the workplace moving frequently, loggers expected their employers to provide meals because there was no one else nearby to offer an alternative. The miners, on the other hand, lived in cities, however small, where private entrepreneurs offered competitive prices, variety, and, in the case of

BOARDING HOUSES AND WON TON SOUP

the finer houses, some extraordinary meals. A company cookhouse, particularly if eating there was compulsory, would have been an unacceptable imposition.

Finally, because capital preceded labor in the forests—there had to be an employer before there was large-scale logging—the loggers were inclined to "think proletarian." Being employees was fundamental to their self-perception. Their camaraderie on the job carried over to collective ways after hours, including while at table. Eating together at the expense of their employers was a logical extension of their work experience and the origins of the industry.[5]

The world of the miners, however, was shaped by strong individualism and entrepreneurship. Neither the wild-eyed forty-niner nor the tens of thousands of men who rushed to the site of new strikes throughout the second half of the nineteenth century thought in terms merely of "a good job," with or without good meals. The gnawing hope that, just maybe, they would strike it rich and retire to the good life on Nob Hill, or to nothing more than a spree at some high desert hog ranch, continued to inform miner mentality to the very last days of the mining frontier.

The last bonanza mining camp in the United States was Goldfield, Nevada. Within two years of its excited beginnings at the turn of the century, when fifteen thousand people rushed there from as nearby as Tonopah and as far away as Dawson, Yukon Territory, the town was locked in an all-too-modern strike and lockout. The leader of the most radical faction among Goldfield's workers was Vincent St. John. Later St. John became the head of the Industrial Workers of the World, the "Wobblies," who regarded themselves as the vanguard of the labor movement, people who understood what industrialization had done to traditional concepts of work and worker organization. Even later, however, St. John returned to prospecting, working on a claim that he hoped would prove as rich as the mines in which he had labored in Goldfield and Telluride. He had no such luck. But it is not safe to assume that if Vincent St. John had struck pay-dirt, he would have used his riches to finance an experiment in post-capitalist social structure. Whatever their politics, however cold the reality that they punched a clock just as did the factory hands of the East, the miners of

1849–1914 could never quite shake their gold fever. In their world, labor—themselves—had preceded capital. The miners were not inclined to brook regulation of their lives by latecomers from outside the workplace.[6]

The cost of boarding varied from a low of seven dollars a week paid by Emmett Arnold, who lived in a shack in Goldfield, and eight dollars a week by J. Ross Browne on the Comstock during the 1860s, to fourteen dollars a week ("invariably in advance") in the earliest days of Silver City, Idaho. Most boarding houses charged ten to twelve dollars, almost always a third less than customers paid for the same meals bought one at a time. This fee paid for breakfast, a box lunch for work, and an evening meal. Some used meal tickets, like the War Eagle Restaurant in Silver City, Idaho, which sold a twenty-one-meal strip for sixteen dollars. Other smaller boarding houses simply recognized the eligible diners by sight. The principle of payment in advance was necessary, according to the operator of a Virginia City lodging house, because the miners did not regard the cost of board as a "debt of honor." That category seems reserved for subscriptions to aid a stricken fellow worker or support some civic or union project, and drinking, gambling, and whoring debts.[7]

Boarding house meals were picked from the regular menu if the place was also a per-meal restaurant. They usually charged for "all you can eat" although "restaurants commonly charged extra for delicacies such as seafoods." Some menus were clearly marked with restrictions along the lines of: "Guests requested not to carry fruit from the table." Mrs. Mathews of Virginia City turned up her nose at the intelligence that one boarding restaurant skimmed four gallons of grease from its soup pot each day but she also conceded that most houses provided excellent meals at reasonable prices. Her assessment was echoed by both Charles Shinn ("the well-fed . . . miners of the Comstock") and Eliot Lord ("men . . . fed on the choicest foods the Pacific Coast affords"). Indeed, it is difficult to imagine an inferior boarding house remaining open long in a mining town. The trade was as crowded as the saloon business. Competition was fierce and customers were inclined to go elsewhere on a whim.[8]

Perhaps because the finest of *haute cuisine* was also available in mining towns, the documents yield few ecstatic comments about boarding house food. (Loggers, by way of contrast, have left behind volumes of praise for cookhouse gastronomy.) Of Ma Reilly's of Brewery Gulch, Arizona, however, Joe Chisholm's review is worth quoting at length.

> Ma's board was like calling the turn with your last stack of chips. Never had such scrumptious grub been absorbed in a mining camp. Not even in mighty Butte, where miners dwelt in regular brick hotels with steam heat and fat Swede chambermaids and all other modern improvements. The miners, naturally, were distrustful of Ma. Such good grub for nothing extra could mean only one thing—that the old squaw was trying to get them foundered or salivated or something so they'd spend all their *dinero* over Pa's bar getting themselves cured.
>
> But Ma Reilly continued to have grapes and other unreasonable delicacies shipped in on the freight wagons from Tombstone and Bisbee for the boys. She had Molly the cook to break graham bread and such unusually good stuff to take the curse off powder smoke. And after awhile the boys began to realize that Ma Reilly was doing it just because she liked the darned roughnecks and wanted to mother them.[9]

Was running a boarding restaurant profitable? The Pearce family of Tombstone sold silver claims to a mining company but explicitly insisted that they retain the right to continue operating their boarding restaurant on the property. The Pearces obviously believed that shoveling food out held more promise than shoveling silver ore. Ma and Pa Reilly, on the other hand, seem to have taken a loss on their eating house, making it up on their saloon and brothel. "We have no foolish notions, Pa and I," Ma told Joe Chisholm. "Sometimes I wish we had children to educate and care for. But perhaps it's just as well. We're not respectable."

"No," agreed Pa, "but we pay our bills."[10]

Financial borrasca, which periodically plagued silver mining during the late nineteenth century, pulled boarding houses down with it. The men "went to cabining" first, abandoning the lodging houses for a shack on the outskirts of town. Only later did they drop out of boarding arrangements. In the case of extended slumps, however, as during the late 1870s, restaurants closed their doors along with the mining companies.[11]

During bonanza, according to the folklore, the worst the "all you can eat" restaurant operator had to beware was the big eater. In Butte, it was said, Fat Jack Jones lost his false teeth in a game of faro. For a week he could eat nothing but mush. When he redeemed his teeth for coin, he ate three T-bone steaks. Dan DeQuille tells of a regular scourge of the restaurateur. Instead of boarding, the "check guerilla" starved himself for several days at a time. Semiweekly, he paid for an "all you can eat" meal.

The landlord paces the room wringing his hands, eyes red, face flushed, brows corrugated, general aspect venomous. In his walk, as steak after steak disappears, he eyes his customer in a malignant, yet helpless manner. In case of fifteen or twenty such customers arriving in one day, the restaurant-keeper generally goes out into his back yard and cuts his throat.[12]

LUNCHES FREE AND
OTHERWISE

Check guerrillas must all have been steak-eaters for there was another extremely cheap alternative for the mining camp diner, the saloon. It may even be that, in the West at least, saloons have been somewhat misdefined as merely "public houses, barrooms, drinking places." Historian Elliot West's more careful formulation is closer to the mark: saloons were "places that seem to have relied on the sale of liquor by the drink for most of their income."[13]

Our image of swinging doors, whiskey neat, poker in the corner, spittoons in the sawdust, fists flying, and soiled doves akimbo on the mezzanine is by no means a delusion. Plenty of places were like that and, in booming mining towns, saloon-keepers did indeed compete with one another by importing opulent velvet drapes, carved rosewood bars, huge mirrors, and paintings of naked women that now seem the epitome of proper good taste in the genre. However, the implication that all saloons were exclusively or even primarily drinking, gambling, and whoring places is not borne out by the evidence. On the contrary, it would appear that the provision of food for customers was at least a sideline of most saloons, an essential loss-leader in others, and in yet others a major source of income, even a *raison d'etre*. If lodging and boarding were rarely combined in mining camps, drinking and eating almost always were.

Elliott West found saloons places that kept separate rooms "where gentlemen can call and be made comfortable." That is an ambiguous

This Wallace, Idaho, brewery wagon
delivered Pabst from Milwaukee as well
as its own beer. Was there status in
ordering a bottle of "imported"?
(Courtesy Barnard-Stockbridge
Collection, University of Idaho
Library, Moscow, Idaho)

description, but the image is not of a place whose primary purpose was to book a speedy passage to oblivion. Other saloons were clearly eating places, some quite posh, definite bidders for the discriminating diner's dollar. The Occidental Saloon in Tombstone offered for Sunday dinner a chicken giblet consomme with egg, Columbia River salmon "au Buerre Noir," and no mere beefsteak but "Filet a la Financier." In addition, the Occidental listed a choice of six entrees including "Pinions a Poulett, aux Champignons" and "Casserole d'Ritz au Oufs, a la Chinoise," not to mention cold boiled meats, roasts, and five different kinds of pastry. "And we will have it all or perish," the Occidental boasted, leaving no question as to the income level of the clientele desired, all "for 50 cents." While not neglecting the other activities of Tombstone's Bird Cage, Can-Can, and Fountain saloons, an old desert rat remembered that they were also "first-class restaurants."[14]

Only a few saloons seem to have been as ambitious as the Occidental in the table they set. But it is clear that food service was an important part of the business at many. Nearly half the saloon-keepers of whom Elliott West was able to construct an occupational biography had previously operated hotels or restaurants (or livery stables) before they became publicans. Butte's saloons were famous for their "Merchants' Lunches," fair-sized meals of stew, baked beans, roast beef, and mashed potatoes with gravy for ten cents, including beer. The saloon-restaurant combination, like Ma and Pa Reilly's complex in Brewery Gulch, and the adjoining Pack Train Inn and Pack Train Saloon in Skagway, was a fixture in the mining camps.[15]

So was, apparently, the "Miners Saloon and Bakery." At least Denver, Central City, Colorado, and Thunder Mountain, Idaho, had an establishment bearing that name. A saloon in Kendall, Montana, was called the Wedge Buffet. Grass Valley had its Occidental Saloon and Chop House that advertised not shipments of Scotch but "Fresh Oysters in Every Style." Sacramento's Metropolitan Saloon crowed, "A Tip-Top Lunch Always Available." And in the River City's earliest days, a large tent saloon known as the Polka was graced by all the predictable accoutrements including twenty games of monte, two faro tables, and two roulette wheels, but it also sported "a forty-foot bar and lunch counter jammed three deep with thirsty and hungry custom-

Exterior of the tent restaurant in Thunder Mountain. (Courtesy Idaho State Historical Society, Boise)

ers." A Walker, Arizona, social center was J. W. Johnson's Saloon and Restaurant. Perhaps most convincing that when a miner read *saloon,* he thought food as well as drink, was the fact that several diarists remarked on the large number of "restaurants" in Nevada City while the city directory listed only three under that rubric. There were, however, thirty-one "saloons" in town.[16]

Most mining camp saloons that served no sit-down meals offered a free lunch. (William S. Greever has concluded that they all did, including the "bit houses" where drinks sold for a "short bit," a dime.) The most extraordinary spreads of which we have records were laid out in Butte, one of the cities with a claim to having invented the custom. "Unusual is an inadequate word as used in describing the free lunch as served by the town's thousand or so saloons in the pre-Prohibition days. For quantity and variety, it is doubtful if these gratuitous repasts could be equalled in any city of the country with the possible exception of New York's Bowery." Twenty feet of Butte's Council Bar—which was half a block long—was periodically cleared of bibbers and heaped with bologna, liverwurst, anchovies, summer sausage, pickled tripe, pig's snout, kippered fish, various sorts of cheeses, rye and white and whole wheat and pumpernickel bread, crackers, pickles, whole and sliced beets, radishes, green onions, sliced bermudas. Few could compete with such munificence but, instead, offered a more substantial free "special" on different days: barbecued meat on Saturdays, buffalo or bear meat (advertised by hanging the hide of the appropriate beast out front), chili or franks, turkey on Thanksgiving.[17]

Because no money was made on the free lunch, we are inclined to define the institution from the publican's point of view: as a competitive gambit designed to lure in drinking customers whose highly profitable thirsts were fiercely aroused by the salt, vinegar, and spice that characterized the spread. From the customer's vantage, however, the free lunch was as often a satisfying meal as a stimulant to drink. Since the free lunch never really returned after the repeal of Prohibition in 1933, it might be concluded that it was not "cost-effective" as a promotion and, therefore, historically more important as a meal.

In Butte, at least, "there was little occasion for a miner to go hungry if he could provide the five cents necessary for the accompanying glass of beer." William S. Greever adds that "the proper etiquette for a patron was never to appear hungry or hurried." Writing in the third

The saloon in remote Gold Reef, Nevada, was also a restaurant. (Courtesy Nevada Historical Society, Reno)

person, Horace Snow explains how he cultivated his free meal routine, down to the subtlest gesture.

> Divers ways did he manage in Sacramento to save dimes. One meal a day was all he could afford and sometimes none, but he was a very zealous advocate and patronizer of free lunches. At ten in the forenoon and nine in the evening the most fashionable dandy saloons furnished roast beef, pickled cabbage, crackers and cheese, etc., for their patrons, with the expectation that all will step up and take a drink before taking a bite, thus giving permanency to the custom, but Snow, with more *sense* than *cents* at the time, would walk in and carelessly peruse a newspaper or two till a right opportunity afforded and then he would pitch in with a good relish and in the same quiet manner take his exit! thus saving his money and not troubling the proprietor. Two such friendly visits in the forenoon would be sufficient till nine in the evening, for you are aware that gentility and quantity at such places is as much a virtue as moderation while masticating. Therefore, it was necessary to be ettiquettic-al and not partake more than a sufficiency. In the evening Snow usually fared better, as the elements combined in his favor and gave him more confidence.[18]

Nor was Sacramento the only city where the free lunch was more than a midday affair. In Las Vegas, New Mexico, Billy's Saloon and Billiard Parlor, at the "sign of the red and blue lamp, south side of the plaza," advertised "Open Day and Night: Lunch at All Hours." With the men working shifts around the clock, free mealtime was as irregu-lar—and as universal—as the hours when a patron with gold jingling in his pockets might purchase a dinner in other kinds of eateries.[19]

OF THE CONSERVATISM
OF FOODWAYS

Given the miners' adventurousness in adopting *la cuisine française*, and the innovation of the free lunch, it is curious that they did not take a keen interest in most of the other "ethnic" foods and modes of preparation to which they were exposed. The argonauts who traveled by sea to California sometimes commented, even favorably now and then, on the way people ate in the Caribbean and in the Latin Amer-ican ports at which they called. But the typical notice of edibles in their diaries dwells on the abundance, lushness, and cheapness of fruits in Sao Paolo, Valparaiso, Acapulco, or wherever. With the occasional exception of the man who prepared "chili" for his mates, and the appearance of the odd enchilada on the free lunch bar at Skagway's Mascot Saloon—despite the fact that Chileans and Mexicans were numerous in California—South American and Mexican foods and styles of preparation had little impact on the Californians and, over several generations, their cultural heirs.

To be sure, groups of non-Americans that were large enough on the mining frontier to create and sustain an ethnic community clung to familiar foods and forms of cookery. Archaeologist Julia G. Costello discovered that Italian gold miners on Angel's Creek in Calaveras County, California, shunned the regulation biscuits, cornbread, and sourdough in favor of the classic loaves of their homeland, even though this meant taking considerable pains to construct the beehive oven required to bake them properly. (Most miners took fewer pains with their cabins than the Italians did with their bread ovens.) Forty-niners from South Wales had their "dampers"—flour, water, and salt dough covered with hardwood coals—which were said to have been durable for a week. A grocer in Terlingua, Texas, learned quickly enough "just about what the Mexicans [working in the quicksilver mines there] were going to buy so we were ready with them with their daily staples wrapped in small packages: rice, 10¢; beans, 15¢ or 25¢; dried whole corn for tortillas, 25¢; dried chili for seasoning, 5¢; . . . and always last on the list was *dulces*. This was a daily must." Mexicans manning a pack train, described by German-Californian Carl Meyer, cooked tortillas on a sheet of iron, frijoles (described as such), and "charqui fried in hot mantequilla."[20]

Grass Valley had its German Boarding House, "H. Otte, Prop." If Professor Greever is correct that the eating places considered best in the mining country were run by Germans, French, or Italians, it may be that their menus reflected the national cuisines of their proprietors. Mary Grace Paquette, an expert on the French in California, is convinced that was true of that group. A chastened Chilean gold-seeker ran a hotel for his countrymen in Stockton and, presumably, served victuals familiar to them. In the Midvale-Murray District of Utah, South Slav smelter workers found countrywomen running boarding houses that approximated in their ambience the *biltiya* of old Croatia. Sometimes taking payment in foodstuffs, the hostesses prepared "a potluck cuisine," including box lunches, with a pronounced Yugoslavian flavor. Christmas in Bingham Canyon, Utah, saw Swedes, Danes, and Serbians preparing their distinctive feasts. Otis E. Young has found additional evidence that immigrant miners frequently sought out boarding houses run by a countryman or countrywoman.[21]

Any number of boarding restaurants that give no hint in their names of an ethnic orientation were well known at the time to cater to specific groups. As they were on opposite sides in so many matters, the Irish and Cornish miners inclined to patronize different eateries. One tale of a rare fraternal moment tells of a Cornish "Cousin Jack" nicknamed "Hard Rock" accompanying an Irish friend to his favorite haunt.

> It happened to be a Good Friday. When the waitress asked Hard Rock for his order he decided on a "ribber." The girl looked frustrated. Con came to her rescue.
>
> "Hell, man, ye can't eat meat in an Irish boarding house av a Good Friday. I thought even Cousin Jacks wasn't so dumb as that."
>
> "Oh, that belong being all right," said the agreeable Hard Rock, "Just as soon 'ave a bit of 'am."[22]

"Hard Rock" had nothing to apologise for. With the exception of the French (whose contribution was to very special meals) and the Chinese, the Cornish almost alone among mining country ethnic groups had a significant impact on the general eating habits of the region. Cornish women were reputed to be excellent cooks, peerless in the use of citron, jellies, raisins, currants, and saffron. (Saffron cake was a bright yellow dainty in which saffron took the place of eggs.) A Cornish miner's box lunch might also include "kiddley broth," marinated pilchards, saffron "boons" (buns), "figgy hobbin," and "junket and cream." Most distinctive and most durable, however, was the pasty. "Fortunate indeed, is the miner so steeped in connubial bliss as to possess a better half who in her loving care, as a token of her affection, places a pasty or two in the lunch box of her miner spouse. 'A letter from home,' is what the miners term such a setup."[23]

But the enduring popularity of the pasty in Montana, in the foothills communities of California, and in other mining districts is exceptional. The followings that other ethnic cuisines now enjoy in the West stem not from the days when gold and silver were the basis of the western economy, but from developments in our own times. Nor, when cuisine is considered as part of the larger social history of the mining West, should this be surprising.

The Gracey family pose at home in front of their kitchen table in Atlanta, Idaho. (Courtesy Idaho State Historical Society, Boise)

THE CALIFORNIOS   On the face of it, the *cocina* of the *californios,* the Hispanics who had California almost to themselves in 1848, should have had a great deal of influence on the arrivals of forty-nine. Much as Lansford Hastings, one of the most thoroughgoing of the pre-gold rush guidebook writers, attempted to disdain it, the meal he describes in his *Emigrant Guide* of 1845 sounds ready-made for camping out on the slopes of the Sierra.

Should you call at the residence of one of these Mexicans, even of the highest class residing in the interior, you would not only be received very kindly, but you would also be annoyed with continued proffers, of all the luxuries which they possess. And should you remain until noon, a large quantity of beef will be roasted before the fire, which, when done, will be attached to a few sticks, which are driven into the ground for that purpose, in the middle of the room, when you are invited to sit down with them, and partake of the rich repast; at the same time you are offered a stool of beef's head as a substitute for a chair, if there happens to be one convenient, if not, you are expected to sit upon the ground. Being thus located, you now commence the dissection and mastication of the half, or quarter of a beef, as the case may be, with which you are now confronted, but in this operation you labor under the disadvantage of having none of the ordinary instruments used upon such occasions; hence you are under the necessity of using your pocket knife, or such other knife as you may chance to have in your possession.[24]

Despite his broad generalization, Hastings must have dined with few if any *californios* of real means. There is plenty of evidence of a grander cookery among them that was as much Spanish as it was what we call Mexican. One feast-day menu that survives would excite any gastronome:

Chicken Meat Ball Soup
Tongue Salad and Toasted Red Chile Sauce
Roast Fowl Drenched with Red Chile Sauce
Young Chicken Stewed with Rice and
Served with Tomatoes and Green Chile Relish
Leafy Green Salad
Tamales and Enchiladas
Beans
Tortillas
Red Wine and White Wine
Turnovers, Buns, Shortbreads, Fruit Dainties
Candied Pumpkin Boiled Custard
Angelica Wine[25]

Instead of such a menu, however, the forty-niners chose French dishes for their feasts. And there is virtually no mention of other distinctively *californio* dishes in the everyday cooking of the Mother Lode: no *tortillas de maíz, pozole, frijoles refritos, chile colorado, masa,* or even *nixtamal,* a hominy prepared much like the famous dish of the southern states. Nor were the favorite *californio* seasonings— anise, *chia* (the seed of the purple sage), cilantro, *hinojo* (fennel)—to be much found on miner tables.[26]

Californio cookery failed to influence the new Californians because few of the latter visited in the homes of the former and fewer yet were invited, particularly by the *caballero* class that could afford to eat so well. The inundation of their sleepy, oft-romanticized land by tens of thousands of foreigners and the annihilation of their hide and tallow economy by gold instantly transformed the *californios* into a resentful minority that was ignored when not despised.

184

Californio Hospitality
"California, inhabited as it was by the generous Ranch owners and their help, was a land of ideal hospitality, and one could travel for a year throughout its length and breadth without the opportunity of expending anything for entertainment."

William Lemuel Beebe, Reminiscence, Society of California Pioneers

Nor did the somewhat different foodways of the Mexicans who swarmed to California have much effect on the habits of other forty-niners. Even those American gold-seekers who crossed Mexico on their way to California—even miners who worked in the Hispanic borderlands of Arizona and New Mexico—tended to cling to their own diet and modes of preparation and shun that of the Sonorans.

This is worth remark because, on the face of it, some Mexican foods were better adapted to life in the mines than were their American equivalents. Whereas baking saleratus biscuit or sourdough bread required considerable time and a makeshift oven, tortillas could be cooked in a minute on a sheet of iron or flat rock. Refried beans were more easily whipped up than a crock of baked beans, a dish requiring no small culinary skill.

However, tortillas called for a much more finely ground meal than the Americans or Europeans were accustomed to using in California. And while cooking time was brief, preparing the tortilla for cooking was time-consuming. The process involved mixing, kneading, rolling, and shaping whereas biscuit dough could be mixed, even carelessly, and then baked untended. It may also be wondered how many of the Sonorans in California were themselves masters of the craft. Making tortillas in Mexico was considered women's work. While *masa* and *harina* are conspicuous orders at groceries in camps of the Southwest where Mexican families lived, they are not found in grocers' ledgers or daybooks farther north even when other sources reveal that Mexican men were present.[27]

There are exceptions to the rule. John W. Caughey found forty-niners bringing *pinole* (one form of powdered corn) and *hijote* (a kind of jerky mixed with onions and pepper) from Chihuahua. The enchiladas at Skagway's Mascot Inn have been mentioned. The first hotel in Prescott, Arizona, the Juniper House, opened its doors on July 4, 1865, offering fried venison and chile for breakfast, and the same plus "Chili Baked Beans" and "Chili and Tortillas" for dinner. H. C. Bailey recalled eating tortillas with an *Italian* merchant in Puntas Arenas in 1853.[28]

But Bailey also provides us with an insight to why he and his generation shunned *cocina mexicana*. "Any of us could have eaten three or four times our allowance," he remembered, while the Mexicans "lived chiefly on the native fruits, which cost very little, using

185

Mexican Coffee and Chocolate
H. C. Bailey did not like much about Mexican food. But there was an exception in his judgement. "Their coffee and chocolate surpassed anything I ever tasted. One cup of the coffee would in strength make at least six American. Such chocolate I never tasted, almost like soup, and such flavor."

H. C. Bailey,
"California in '53,"
Bancroft Library

little meat or grease of any kind and little bread. One Englishman or American could eat as much bread as a dozen of them."[29]

Too little: it was the key to much of the American image of the Mexicans. The Americans and at least the English-speaking forty-niners from abroad despised the Mexicans for, among other things, their poverty. They "ate French" because *cuisine française* represented to them what the rich ate back East. By the same principle, they were unlikely to adopt the foodways of a people whom they had just defeated in war, whom they were driving from the mines with force and the Foreign Miner Tax of 1850, and whom they associated with Indians and therefore with an inferior race. Perhaps the most curious of the anti-Mexican canards was the remark that coyotes would not eat the flesh of dead Mexicans because it was so infused with chile peppers that it burned their innards. This from a people whose passion for spicy foods appalled visitors from back East.[30]

And yet the principle does not necessarily hold true in the case of the most exotic and, along with *cuisine française,* the most important cuisine in the mining West, the cookery of the Cantonese Chinese immigrants.

INSCRUTABLE CUISINE

When James Marshall discovered gold there could not have been more than a handful of Chinese in California, probably seamen either shipwrecked or deserted. In February 1849 there were only 54 on the rolls and a year later but 791. Only in 1852 began the deluge that was to lead to a cycle of racial hostility more violent than any in the United States since the reprisals visited on the blacks of southern Virginia in the wake of Nat Turner's rebellion. In 1852 about twenty thousand "Celestials" sailed through the Golden Gate, almost all of them under contract to what became the famous "Six Companies" of San Francisco. They fanned out over abandoned placer mines, making do with diggings the whites found unattractive when news came of a new El Dorado in another part of the mountains.

This was to prove the pattern. Never in the vanguard, rarely competing for rich gravels, Chinese miners followed the rushes in a self-contained, self-sufficient phalanx little interested in anybody else's culture. This clannishness, centered around old country ways, was a minor cause of their persecution, "convenient grist for anti-Chinese propaganda," as a Christian assimilationist Chinese immigrant put it. But the major source of the pogroms in places otherwise as diverse as Oroville and San Francisco was economic competition complicated by racism. As long as there were placer deposits and they were permitted to moil in them, most of the Chinese were miners. Only after the poor man's poorest diggings played out did the Chinese begin to drift into jobs white men wanted, as in construction. Then came sinophobic movements such as the Workingmen's Party of Denis Kearney and the chronic, often violent, persecution, legal exclusion, and de facto restriction of the Chinese to ghettos and low paying and menial service occupations, such as launderer, cook, waiter, and gardener.[31]

The place of the Chinese in the food history of the mining West is as enigmatic as was, to Caucasian eyes, the impassive Chinese face. It is not hard to agree with a writer of 1927 that food service was "natural" to the Chinese because they were "a people . . . traditionally brought up to appreciate fine cuisine and its preparation." Food plays a central part in Chinese popular culture, unlike in America or Europe, except in France and Italy. Even Huie Kin, who wanted his countrymen to adopt American ways and Christian religion, wrote of an early job in an American household that "there lingers still in my mind the vision of the ubiquitous apple sauce on the table, which I soon got so sick and tired of that I would have given anything for a Chinese meal."

Our culinary tastes play an important part in the psychology of homesickness. We were told on Scriptural authority that the one thing that marred the otherwise joyous exit of the Israelites from the land of their serfdom and their triumphal journey to their new home in Canaan was the longing for the meats and drinks they were accustomed to in Egypt, and when the good Lord heard their pleading and sent them a flock of wild geese, or something of that sort, the people ate so heartily that many died of acute indigestion.[32]

To many Caucasians of the mining frontier, however, Chinese in the kitchen were reviled as "filthy Chinese cooks." Common and monotonously similar were solemn tales such as John Clampitt's of a Chinese cook making biscuits who squirted water into the dough from his mouth, "his own Asiatic saliva sweetened by the mouldering gums

A yellow pennant signaled the presence
of a Chinese restaurant. (Courtesy
Society of California Pioneers,
San Francisco)

and decayed teeth born of opium joints." Bernice Johnson of Lynx Creek was shocked "to see cats sleeping in the open boxes of dried fruit" at a Chinese-run boarding restaurant. A Virginia City woman gave thanks that "many of the best restaurants" had fired their Chinese chefs and now employed only "good respectable white people." In Bisbee, Arizona, and many other mining camps, "no member of the celestial kingdom" was permitted to "remain in town overnight," which, given the odd hours of miner mealtimes, may have excluded Chinese from food service.[33]

On the other hand, it is clear that Chinese were often actively sought as cooks in private homes and in restaurants serving sturdy, conventional American fare. Chinese restaurants, too, were popular from San Francisco to the remotest mining camp. The extent of "Charlie's" presence in the kitchen is not immediately apparent in the sources, in part because any mention of food is rare and in part because many employers were ambivalent toward the race of their workers. Russell Wahmann, historian of Jerome, Arizona, believes that mining camp restaurants called "English Kitchen"—it was a common name—were places attempting to conceal their Chinese cooks, even Chinese owners. In the diaries, letters, and other writings of middle-class people of the mining towns who employed Chinese cooks, the color of their servants emerges only accidentally, in the odd, unguarded reference or the humorous tale. For instance, a Mrs. Hillyer of Virginia City realized one day that her cook looked different. "Why, you're not Charlie," she said. The new cook answered, "Charlie he go two weeks. Charlie go China."[34]

In San Francisco, a forty-niner "put up a 12 by 15 shack on the spot afterwards occupied by the stage of the Metropolitan Theater, hired a Chinese cook, opened a restaurant and acted as waiter himself, on the two tables covered with black oil-cloth." Mark Twain's *Territorial Enterprise* retained a Chinese cook. According to one source, "all" the miners' boarding houses in Silver City, Idaho, had Chinese cooks, as did the pack trains hauling provisions into the high camp. Silver City's teenaged boys favored a restaurant that sold a bowl of noodles for ten cents. Lewiston's Raymond House, reputed for its steaks, chops, and cutlets, was run by Chinese. Quong Kee headed the kitchen of Tombstone's famous Can-Can. In tiny Richmond Basin, Arizona, twenty miles outside of Globe, a Chinese cook prepared meals that were decidedly not celestial. "The menu never varied. . . . It consisted of a platter of thin, evil tasting stake [*sic*], cooked until it was like leather, this was passed around the table; bread, coffee, condensed milk and nearly always sugar, sometimes this was missing. Occasionally boiled rice or stewed, dried fruit. For this we paid nine dollars each, a week."[35]

Economics explain the ubiquity of the Chinese in home kitchens, conventional hash houses, and boarding restaurants. Except for head chefs in the elegant French restaurants, kitchen workers were paid wages that were low by mining camp standards, and domestic servants earned even less. Andrew Smith Church noted that when he looked for a cheap restaurant serving "American food," he usually found a Chinese man waiting tables or toiling in the kitchen.[36]

Despite the sinophobia of the mining West, restaurants run by Chinese and serving Cantonese fare, both "chop suey joints" and fine restaurants, were also quite popular. Within a few years of his arrival with the first wave of gold-seekers, San Francisco's Tsing Tsing Lee built the Balcony of Golden Joy and Delight into a restaurant seating four hundred customers at a time. As was done at the What Cheer, he sold meal tickets, twenty-one for twenty dollars. Other early "dollar houses" in the city were Kong Sung's on the waterfront, Whang Tong's on Sacramento Street, and Tong Ling's on Jackson.[37]

While originally intended for Chinese patrons, these restaurants soon attracted Occidental customers. Like boarding restaurants in the mining towns, most Chinese restaurants appear to have charged a flat price for "all you can eat." Parsimonious argonauts in San Francisco or Sacramento looked for the triangular yellow silk flags that designated Chinese food and, when in the camps, simply asked around for "John Chinaman." Virginia City's "Restaurant Row" was on South C Street, the town's Chinatown. According to Mrs. Mathews, "all the popular restaurants" were there. In Silver City, Idaho, H Street was the address for Hinky Jack's, Av Dick's Star, and at least two or three others. In Silver City, New Mexico, O. D. Wing and Wah Hop catered to miner tastes. Butte, where Chinese were banned from the mines, nevertheless supported a large if shifting number of Chinese eateries.[38]

In part, Chinese restaurants were popular because they were cheap. John McMillen of Jerome, later resident manager for the Phelps-

Chinese grocers, like Lee Tan of Tucson, were not so numerous as Chinese restaurateurs, but Orientals were identified with food from the beginning of the mining frontier. (Courtesy Arizona Historical Society, Tucson)

Dodge Corporation, remembered as a young miner preferring beef-steak after payday but eating Chinese when money was low. Unlike American cooks, Chinese restaurateurs could take a pound of meat, chop it up, cook it quickly with bamboo shoots, mushrooms, and perhaps an imported bottled sauce, and serve a delicious "light, hot and tasty" meal.[39]

Imported ingredients such as sauces, dried oysters and abalone, bamboo shoots, bean sprouts, and noodles were expensive. Nevertheless, by the 1860s, Chinese importers were paying half a million dollars a year in comparatively low duties on such goods. Moreover, Cantonese cooks showed incredible ingenuity (for those who noticed) in adapting to local ingredients. James Beard tells of the mother of a distinguished Chinese restaurateur who followed her husband, a Christian preacher, in his far-ranging search for heathen souls. "For years they trekked to small towns and villages—wherever there might be a colony of Chinese workmen. She cooked Chinese food with almost none of the necessary ingredients, substituting what she found at hand, creating new dishes with a traditional style of cooking."[40]

According to popular legend, two "Chinese" dishes now known universally in the United States were invented on the mining frontier. Hangtown fry, tradition has it, was invented in the Cary House of Placerville, California, then called Hangtown, when a lucky forty-niner blew in with a pouch spilling over with gold. Give me the most expensive dish in the house, he probably roared. The most expensive *ingredients,* he was told, were oysters and eggs. (These were the dollar apiece days.) The cook promptly scrambled the eggs with some onions and folded in the oysters. Although no version of the tale identifies the cook as Chinese, surely he was: hangtown fry is an egg foo yung, a fundamental of Cantonese cookery.

The second famous "Chinese-American" dish to come out of the mining frontier is chop suey, the subject of some historical controversy. It has been common wisdom to say that chop suey (*tsap sui,* Cantonese for "miscellaneous stuff" or even "slops") did not exist in old China. The stir-fried hash was invented, according to tradition, in a San Francisco restaurant during the wee hours one morning when a rowdy group of holidaying miners would not hear of the Chinese cook's plea that he had no food. Rather than risk a drubbing, the cook concocted chop suey of the day's scraps.

Perhaps. At least one Chinese authority, however, insists that chop suey was intimately familiar to emigrants from Toisan, the region south of Canton that is the ancestral home of more than half the American Chinese. It does seem hard to believe that a people wracked by poverty had not thought to put together "miscellaneous stuff" before they arrived at the "Golden Mountain."[41]

Whatever the origin of chop suey, and however deep the sinophobic bitterness of the Caucasian miners, some of them were willing to go on record with their enthusiasm for Cantonese food. "There are houses of refreshment at every turn," wrote William Kelly of California.

Amidst the host of competitors the Celestials carry off the palm for superior excellence in every particular. They serve everything promptly, cleanly, hot and well-cooked; they give dishes peculiar to every nation over and above all their own peculiar soups, curries, and ragouts, which cannot be even imitated elsewhere; and such are their quickness and civil attention, that they anticipate your wants and of course secure your patronage.[42]

William Shaw was another afficionado. "The best eating houses in San Francisco are those kept by the Celestials and conducted Chinese fashion. The dishes are mostly curries, hashes, and fricassees served up in small dishes and as they are extremely palatable, I was not curious enough to enquire as to the ingredients."[43]

Shaw's reminiscence of California was called *Golden Dreams and Waking Realities*. If the Chinese contribution to American diet is the only reality left from the mining frontier, then it was a golden dream indeed. At one feast for themselves, to which a few white friends were invited, three hundred-and-twenty-five dishes were served. Among them were "bamboo soup, bird's nest soup, stewed seaweed, stewed mushrooms, fried fungus, banana fritters, shark fins, shark sinews, reindeer sinews, dried Chinese oysters, pigeons, ducks, chickens, scorpions' eggs, watermelon seeds, fish in scores of varieties, many kinds of cake, and fruits ad infinitum." A dazed Caucasian commented that "the Celestials drank champagne and claret as if to the manner born."[44]

This was, of course, a feast of American Mandarins, of merchant princes with some interest in and perhaps some illusions about friendly relations with California's white elite. The vast majority of Chinese westerners remained subsistence laborers, servants, or frugal operators of small businesses able to survive with notoriously low expenditures in part because, coming from a food-scarce and even famine-stricken land, their ancestors had created a cookery that chopped expensive meat finely and distributed it thinly among the grain and vegetables.

This genius won a place in every western town for a chop suey house and a more or less secure niche for at least one Chinese family. But the Chinese frugality at table was also deplored by the sinophobic demagogues of the late nineteenth century, and given as a reason for driving the Chinese away. It is interesting to note just how prominent were references to food—"They eat dogs and rats!"—in those broadbased social movements that, by the end of the century, forced the retreat of the Chinese—save for that restaurant family or two—to the big city Chinatowns. One is reminded of the ambivalent relationship between better-established Americans and Italian immigrants in the next generation. Americans took zestfully and quickly to "Italian food." They also scorned and ridiculed the "spaghetti-benders."[45]

The peculiar foodways of the mining frontier were reinvigorated in every new boomtown. The miner arriving in Goldfield, Nevada, in 1905 would have found much the same restaurant scene his father (or he) had known in Virginia City in 1865. Every new strike was, briefly, 1849 all over again. That meant, along with the dreams and the all-night tumult of the saloons, casinos, and bordellos, the gastronomy of 1849. But when the high-grade ore played out, when the veins pinched into worthless quartz, mining towns became more and more like other relatively isolated American towns, including their eating habits. The moving on and settling down of the young, footloose, single male population wrote an end to their ubiquitous peculiar institution, the boarding restaurant. After World War I, the mining town was no more likely to boast an elegant French eatery than was any farmtown, cowtown, or even small manufacturing city. In our own era—with its gourmet mania, interest in various ethnic foods, and an "eating out mentality" of rather different origins than that of the mining frontier—western towns have, if anything, lagged far behind the country's trend-sensitive metropolises. George DuPuy's Hotel de Paris is now a museum. There is a microwave oven in "the Delmonico's of the West." The best meal in Tombstone is a steak. In Virginia City the tourists order hamburgers and frozen yogurt. Back on the Mother Lode the restaurateurs are ex-urbanites whose customers are hungry from mining the antique shops. Gastronomically, at least, San Francisco is no longer "next to GRASS VALLEY, the pride of the Pacific Coast."

Historians warn, and rightly, against falling prey to the "Golden Age Syndrome," the misguided nostalgia that finds an idyll in the past we know only from selected and fragmentary sources. For the West that was built on gold and silver, however, in the matter of comestibles a dispensation has been granted.

ASSIGNING NUTRITIONAL VALUES

As explained in the text, the nutritional values assigned to the diets of the overlanders should not be regarded as "scientific fact." As with the already-scant records of almost all historical diets, one must work with records of what food was available rather than with actual consumption. The "weight watchers" of our own time seem to be unique in charting meticulously the quantities they actually consume.

Moreover, it would be foolish to assume that the nutritional components of, say, nineteenth-century "side bacon," are the same as those listed by Bernice K. Watt and Annabel Merrill in their *Composition of Foods* for "Bacon, cured: raw, slab." The nutritional composition of apparently identical foods can vary widely. For example, the niacin content of various contemporary wheat flours listed by Watt and Merrill range from 19.7 mg per pound to 3.0. We have no idea of the variety of wheat from which the forty-niners milled their wheat nor how thoroughly it was refined. There is probably no commodity on the market today much like the "biscuit" and "pilot bread" found so commonly in the diets of the transcontinental crossing or the sea passage.

In all cases of measurement, therefore, I have played my calculator conservatively, estimating food values at what seemed reasonable minimums, and constantly reminding myself of how cavalierly I was guessing. The tables that follow indicate how I arrived at the totals cited in Chapter 3.

	Quantity per person per day (lb)	Calories	Protein (g)	Thiamine (mg)	Riboflavin (mg)	Niacin (mg)	Vitamin C (mg)
Flour	.85	1284	51.3	2.1	.45	16.6	-
Bacon	1.5	4254	53.7	2.31	.735	10.2	-
Sugar	.32	541	-	.016	.05	.25	-
Beans	.4	633	5.18	.76	.19	2.02	-
Lard	.4	1636	-	-	-	-	-
Saleratus	trace	-	-	-	-	-	-
Coffee	.15	154	8.56	.48	.35	11.5	-
Dried Fruit	.3	480	1.92	trace	trace	.87	14.1

	Quantity per person per day (lb)	Calories	Protein (g)	Thiamine (mg)	Riboflavin (mg)	Niacin (mg)	Vitamin C (mg)
Flour	1.2	1812	72.36	2.98	.65	23.6	-
Biscuit	.5	995	20.9	.03	.10	2.4	-
Bacon	.8	2269	28.64	1.23	.39	6.2	-
Sugar	.2	338	-	.01	.03	.16	-
Beans	.4	633	5.18	.76	.19	2.02	-
Lard	1.6	6546	-	-	-	-	-
Saleratus	trace	-	-	-	-	-	-
Coffee	.12	123	6.85	.38	.27	9.2	-
Tea	trace	trace	trace	trace	trace	trace	-
Dried Fruit	.5	801	3.2	trace	trace	trace	23.5

[Professor Faragher's keg of whiskey has not been subjected to analysis. Spirits are high in calories but have no nutrients.]

APPENDIX

NOTES

In the following notes several libraries and historical societies are referred to by their initials: AHS, Arizona Historical Society, Tucson; CHS, California Historical Society, San Francisco; HEH, Henry E. Huntington Library, San Marino, Calif.; HHB, Hubert Howe Bancroft Library, Berkeley, Calif.; ISHS, Idaho State Historical Society, Boise; NHS, Nevada Historical Society, Reno; NYHS, New York Historical Society, New York; SCP, Society of California Pioneers, San Francisco; SSHP, Shasta State Historic Park, Calif.; UNM, University of New Mexico Library, Albuquerque.

INTRODUCTION

1. Silver City, Nevada, *Lyon County Times*, April 10, 1876; Eliot Lord, *Comstock Mining and Miners* (Washington: Government Printing Office, 1883).

2. Louise Amelia Knappe Smith Clappe, *California in 1851: The Letters of Dame Shirley* (San Francisco: Thomas C. Russell, 1922); Mrs. Hugh Brown, *Lady in Boomtown: Miners and Manners on the Nevada Frontier* (Palo Alto, Calif.: American West Press, 1968).

   In 1952, ninety-eight-year-old Ellen Lucy Clapp was asked by an oral historian to explain what Lake Valley, New Mexico, a silver camp of some 350 miners, was like during her girlhood: "Why, there were just these sporting houses there and . . . ah . . . saloons and so forth and that's about all . . . [except for] eating houses." Transcript, Pioneers' Foundation, Oral History Project, University of New Mexico.

3. The best recent social histories of the western miners, which I borrow from much more often than I cite, are: Richard E. Lingenfelter, *The Hard Rock Miners: A History of the Mining Labor Movement in the American West, 1863–1893* (Berkeley: University of California Press, 1974); Mark Wyman, *Hard Rock Epic: Western Miners and the Industrial Revolution* (Berkeley:

University of California Press, 1979); Ronald C. Brown, *Hard-Rock Miners: The Intermountain West, 1860–1920* (College Station, Tex.: Texas A. & M. University Press, 1979); T. H. Watkins, *Gold and Silver in the West* (New York: Bonanza Books, 1971).

4. Peter Farb and George Armelagos, *Consuming Passions: The Anthropology of Eating* (Boston: Hougton Mifflin, 1980), p. 4.

5. Ibid., pp. 4–6.

CHAPTER *1*
HOME COOKING

1. John W. Caughey, *Gold is the Cornerstone* (Berkeley: University of California Press, 1948), p. 40; J. S. Holliday, *The World Rushed In: The California Gold Rush Experience* (New York: Simon and Schuster, 1981), p. 36.

2. Caughey, *Gold,* p. 40.

3. Ibid., p. 42.

4. Holliday, *World,* p. 297.

5. William Swain, diary, April 15, 1949, in Holliday, *World,* p. 73. In his essay "The Outfitting Posts," Walker D. Wyman notes that St. Joseph was so overstocked in provisions in 1849 that much had to be shipped back to St. Louis. Wyman also quotes a Missourian who may have the key to the contradictory reports about prices in the trailhead towns: "Eastern men particularly are sadly out of fix here, and we have almost incalculable advantage over them in fixing up for the trip. . . . The Missourians are skinning them most horribly." (In John W. Caughey, ed., *Rushing for Gold* [Berkeley: University of California Press, 1949], pp. 18, 19.)

6. Holliday, *World,* p. 95.

7. Unidentified Sacramento newspaper, October 13, 1849, in William Ralston Balch, comp., *The Mines, Miners, and Mining Interests of the United States in 1882* (Philadelphia: Mining Industrial Publishing House, 1882), pp. 790–92.

8. Somewhat less conjectural than this estimate are the calculations for 1879 made by Merrill K. Bennett and Rosamund H. Peirce in "Change in the American National Diet, 1879–1959," *Stanford University Food Research Institute Studies* I (1961), pp. 95–119. They posit a 3,750 per capita per diem calorie intake in 1879. As that total declines steadily by 550 calories, 15 percent, over the eighty years to 1959, 4,000 sounds about right for 1849.

9. My own statements and speculations dealing with the diet of American slaves have been published only in part, in "What the Slaves Ate," (California State University at Chico) *University Journal* (Spring 1983). I hope to publish a book-length study of the subject in the near future. Although my conclusions there are somewhat different from those found here, see R. W. Fogel and Stanley Engerman, *Time on the Cross: The Economics of American Negro Slavery* (Boston: Little Brown, 1974), and the critique by Richard Sutch in F. A. David et al., *Reckoning with Slavery: A Critical Study in the Quantitative History of American Negro Slavery* (New York: Oxford University Press, 1976).

10.	Department of Commerce, Bureau of the Census, *Statistical Abstract of the United States, 1982–1983*, p. 128; J. V. G. A. Durnin and R. Passmore, *Energy, Work and Leisure* (London: Heinemann, 1967), pp. 42, 61, 66, 91–92.

11.	S. G. Goodrich, *A System of Universal Geography, Popular and Scientific, Embracing Numerous Sketches from Recent Travels* (New York: Collins and Hanney, 1832), p. 100; John Mack Faragher, *Women and Men on the Overland Trail* (New Haven, Conn.: Yale University Press, 1979), pp. 44, 52; Poe to Mrs. Clemm, April 1844, in William Bittner, *Poe: A Biography* (Boston: Little Brown, 1962), p. 196.

12.	Eugen Weber, *Peasants into Frenchmen: The Modernization of Rural France, 1870–1914* (Palo Alto, Calif.: Stanford University Press, 1976), pp. 132, 139–40.

13.	Frances Trollope, *Domestic Manners of the Americans,* ed. Donald Smalley (New York: Alfred A. Knopf, 1949); Elborg and Robert Forster, eds., *European Diet from Pre-Industrial to Modern Times* (New York: Harper and Row, 1975); Robert Forster and Orest Ranum, *Food and Drink in History* (Baltimore: Johns Hopkins University Press, 1979); Waverley Root and Richard de Rochemont, *Eating in America: A History* (New York: William Morrow, 1976), pp. 143–44.

14.	Werner Sombart, *Why Is There No Socialism in the United States?* (1906, reprint White Plains, N.Y.: International Arts and Sciences Press, 1976); Peter H. Shergold, " 'Reefs of Roast Beef': The American Worker's Standard of Living in Comparative Perspective," monograph, 1976, pp. 5, 17, tables 2, 7; Root and de Rochemont, *Eating*, p. 139; Weber, *Peasants*, p. 300.

15.	The standard works on pellagra as a social phenomenon are Elizabeth W. Etheridge, *The Butterfly Caste: A Social History of Pellagra in the South* (Westport, Conn.: Greenwood Press, 1972) and Daphne A. Roe, *A Plague of Corn: The Social History of the Pellagra* (Ithaca, N.Y.: Cornell University Press, 1973). The argument that slaves did suffer from pellagra but it was not diagnosed is found in Kenneth F. and Virginia H. Hiple, "Black Tongue and Black Men," *Journal of Southern History* 43 (1977), pp. 411–28.

16.	Peter Farb and George Armelagos, *Consuming Passions: The Anthropology of Eating* (Boston: Houghton Mifflin, 1980), pp. 74–75; John M. Hunter, "Geophagy in Africa and in the United States: A Cultural-Nutritional Hypothesis," *Geographical Review* 63 (1973), pp. 170–95.

17.	Frederick Law Olmsted, *A Journey in the Seaboard States* (1856, reprint, New York: Negro Universities Press, 1968), p. 65; Robert Beverley, *The History and Present State of Virginia*, ed. Louis B. Wright (London: R. Parker, 1705; reprint, Chapel Hill, N.C.: University of North Carolina Press, 1960), p. 318; Gerald Carson, *Cornflake Crusade* (1957, reprint, Salem, N.Y.: Ayer Co., 1976), pp. 28–29.

18.	Bureau of the Census, *Eighth Census* (Washington: Government Printing Office, 1860).

19. Dr. John S. Wilson, "Health Department," *Godey's Lady's Book* 60 (February 1860), p. 178.

20. John H. Moore, *Agriculture in Ante-Bellum Mississippi* (New York: Octagon, 1971), p. 111.

21. Root and de Rochemont, *Eating*, pp. 137–38; *American Heritage Cookbook* (New York: American Heritage Press, 1964), p. 24.

22. Eliza Leslie, *Directions for Cookery* (Philadelphia: E. L. Carey, 1837); Root and de Rochemont, *Eating*, p. 139; Georgia Willis Read, "Diseases, Drugs, and Doctors on the Oregon-California Trail in the Gold-Rush Years," *Missouri Historical Review* (April 1944), p. 264.

23. *See,* for example, W. J. Rorabaugh, *The Alcoholic Republic: An American Tradition* (New York: Oxford University Press, 1979).

24. Root and de Rochemont, *Eating*, p. 139; St. Paul *Minnesota Pioneer,* March 20, 1850. *See also* Joseph R. Conlin, "Consider the Oyster," *American Heritage* (February–March, 1980), p. 65ff.

25. *See* Root and de Rochemont, *Eating*, p. 139, and Richard J. Hooker, *A History of Food and Drink in America* (Indianapolis: Bobbs-Merrill, 1981), pp. 110–11.

26. Harvey Levenstein, "The New England Kitchen and the Origins of American Eating Habits," *American Quarterly* (Fall 1980), pp. 20–6.

27. Root and de Rochemont, *Eating,* pp. 136, 141; on American salads at mid-century *see* Heather Maisner, ed., *Bon Appetit Country Cooking* (New York: Knapp, 1978), p. 254; Carl Meyer, *Prospectus to Form a Society for Emigration to California,* trans. Ruth Frey Axe (1852, reprint, Claremont, Calif.: Saunders Studio Press, 1938), p. 11; Lansford W. Hastings, *The Emigrant's Guide to Oregon and California* (1845, reprint, Princeton, N.J.: Princeton University Press, 1932), p. 143.

28. Harriet Beecher Stowe, *House and Home Papers* (Boston: Little Brown, 1865), p. 263; Susan Strasser, *Never Done: A History of American Housework* (New York: Pantheon, 1982).

29. In Bill Gilbert, "The Cry Was: Go West, Young Man, and Stay Healthy," *The Smithsonian* (March 1983), p. 442.

30. Helen Carpenter, diary, June 19, 1857, in Sandra L. Myres, ed., *Ho for California!: Women's Overland Diaries from the Huntington Library* (San Marino, Calif.: Huntington Library, 1980), p. 115; *Country Cooking,* p. 254.

31. James Beard, *American Cookery* (Boston: Little Brown, 1972), p. 4.

32. In Gilbert, "The Cry Was," p. 142. References to the American talent for rushing meals are as numerous as the travel books about the United States in the nineteenth century. *See,* for example, Phil Robinson, *Sinners and Saints* (Boston: Roberts Brothers, 1883), p. 267; Maria Theresa Longworth [Thérèse Yelverton], *Teresina in America* I (London: R. Bentley, 1875), p. 284; Emily Faithfull, *Three Visits to America* (Edinburgh: D. Douglas, 1884), p. 49; Robert

Tomes, "Before, At, and After Meals," *Harpers* (April 1856), p. 729; J. J. Aubertin, *A Fight with Distances* (London: K. Paul, Trench and Co., 1888), pp. 66–67.

CHAPTER 2
ADVICE TO EMIGRANTS

1. Joseph E. Ware, *The Emigrants' Guide to California*, ed. John Caughey (1849, reprint, Princeton, N.J.: Princeton University Press, 1932); Lansford W. Hastings, *The Emigrant's Guide to California and Oregon* (1845, reprint, Princeton, N.J.: Princeton University Press, 1932); John C. Frémont, *Report on the Exploring Expedition to the Rocky Mountains in the Year 1842 and to Oregon and North California in the Years 1843–1844* (Washington: Gates and Seaton, 1845); Seymour E. Sanford, *Emigrant's Guide to the Gold Mines of Upper California* (Chicago: 1849); John Bidwell, *A Journey to California in 1841* (Liberty, Mo.: 1842); Edwin Bryant, *What I Saw in California . . . in the Years 1846–1847* (New York: D. Appleton, 1849). For the most complete listing of the guides (and diaries of travelers), *see* Merrill Mattes, *The Great Platte River Road* (Lincoln, Nebr.: Nebraska State Historical Society, 1969), pp. 523–71.

2. *Ohio Statesman*, April 26, 1843, and *Iowa Capital Register*, March 25, 1843, in *Oregon Historical Quarterly* (December 1902), pp. 390–92; ibid. (December, 1914), p. 296; Alonzo Delano, *Across the Plains and among the Diggings* (1854, reprint, New York: Wilson-Erickson, 1936).

3. Iowa City *Iowa Capital Reporter*, March 25, 1843; circular letter from Independence, Missouri, to various midwestern newspapers, February 15, 1847, in *Oregon Historical Quarterly* (September 1910), p. 360.

4. See John W. Caughey, *Gold is the Cornerstone* (Berkeley: University of California Press, 1948), p. 113.

5. William Johnstone, diary, June 14, 1866, in Helen McCann White, ed., *Ho! For the Goldfields: Northern Overland Wagon Trains of the 1860s* (St. Paul: Minnesota Historical Society, 1966), p. 10; Richard F. Burton, *The City of the Saints, and Across Rocky Mountains to California* (New York: Harper and Brothers, 1862), p. 53; John Ritchie Schultz, "Features of Colorado Life as Seen by Bayard Taylor in 1866," *Colorado Magazine* (September 1939), p. 164; Richard A. Van Orman, *A Room for the Night: Hotels of the Old West* (Bloomington: Indiana University Press, 1966), pp. 7–8, 10; J. S. Holliday, *The World Rushed In: The California Gold Rush Experience* (New York: Simon and Schuster, 1981), p. 82.

6. Le Roy R. Hafen and Francis Marion Young, *Fort Laramie and the Pageant of the West* (Glendale, Calif.: Arthur H. Clark, 1938), pp. 157–58.

7. J. W. Cooper, oral recollection, December 3, 1889, HHB Library; Caughey, *Gold Rush*, pp. 118–19; L. Dow Stephens, *Life Sketches of a Jayhawker of '49* (San Jose, Calif.: Nolta Brothers, 1916), p. 20; Brigham D. Madsen, *Gold Rush Sojourners in Great Salt Lake City, 1849 and 1850* (Salt Lake City: University of Utah Press, 1983), pp. 19–20.

8. The Bloomington Company planned inadequately across the board, listing in addition to the skimpy pork ration only one hundred pounds of flour and "1 pack" of salt per person. They were inexperienced, as the first to do a thing are apt to be, and probably overly sanguine about the prospects of living off the land. Other groups from the same period insisted on the hundredweight of bacon. *Oregon Historical Quarterly* 3 (1902), pp. 390–92; White, *Ho!,* p. 12. For comparable material on later rushes in Colorado, *see* Amanda M. Ellis, *Bonanza Towns: Leadville and Cripple Creek* (Colorado Springs, Colo.[?]: 1954), pp. 2–3; Edward N. Wentworth, "Meat in the Diet of Westward Explorers and Emigrants," *Mid-America* 29 (April 1947), pp. 75–91.

9. Hastings, *Emigrant's Guide,* p. 143.

10. Circular letter from Independence, Missouri, p. 360; Holliday, *World,* p. 82; White, *Ho!,* p. 12.

11. On the importance of all that bacon in the overland larders, *see* Wentworth, "Meat in the Diet."

12. Frémont, *Report,* pp. 100, 191.

13. Holliday, *World,* p. 111; Margaret Frink, journal, in Sandra L. Myres, ed., *Ho for California!: Women's Overland Diaries from the Huntington Library* (San Marino, Calif.: Huntington Library, 1980), p. 35; Holliday, *World,* p. 143.

14. Frémont, *Report,* pp. 175, 223.

15. Ware, *Emigrants' Guide;* Andrew Child, *Overland Route to California: Description of the Route, . . .* (1852, reprint, Los Angeles: N. A. Kovach, 1946), pp. vi–vii; John Mack Faragher, *Women and Men on the Overland Trail* (New Haven, Conn.: Yale University Press, 1979), p. 192.

   For recommendations from the later Pike's Peak and Comstock Lode period, *see* John Mullan, *Miners and Travellers' Guide to Oregon, Washington, Idaho, Montana, Wyoming, and Colorado* (New York: William M. Franklin, 1865) and *The Rocky Mountain Gold Regions* (Denver: Rocky Mountain News Printing Co., 1861), p. 98. Like these, the account of Helen Carpenter is also of interest. She crossed the plains in 1857 and inasmuch as her larder was substantially the same as that of the forty-niners, she tells us that their estimates were pretty nearly correct: "A Trip Across the Plains in an Ox Wagon," May 26, 1857, in Myres, *Ho for California!,* p. 93.

16. For all calculations of nutritional values of food, I have relied on Charles Frederick Church and Helen Nichols Church, *Food Values of Portions Commonly Used,* 12th ed. (Philadelphia: Lippincott, 1975); and Bernice K. Watt and Annabel L. Merrill, *Composition of Foods* (Washington: U.S. Department of Agriculture, Handbook No. 8, 1975).

17. Swain to George Swain, May 6, 1849, in Holliday, *World. See also* William Ogilvie, *The Klondike Official Guide* (Buffalo, N.Y.: Matthews-Northrup, 1898), p. 126.

18. John C. Frémont, *Report,* p. 174; Virginia Wilcox Ivins, *Pen Pictures of Early Western Days* (Keokuk, Ia.[?]: 1905); E. Allene Dunham, *Across the Plains in a*

204

Covered Wagon, in Faragher, *Men and Women,* pp. 70, 78; Camper, "Why I Crossed the Plains," p. 57.

19.   John H. Bean, diary, MS. 28, University of Utah; Bennett C. Clark, diary, July 15, 1849, and "The Overland Diaries of J. P. Hamelin Jr.," both in Madsen, *Gold Rush Sojourners,* pp. 12–13, 16–18; Howard Stansbury, *Exploration and Survey of the Great Salt Lake of Utah* (Washington: U.S. Army, Corps of Topographical Engineers, 1853), p. 52; Carpenter, "A Trip," June 13, 1857, in Myres, *Ho for California!,* p. 105; James D. Lyon, letter in the *Detroit Advertiser,* September 10, 1849.

20.   Holliday, *World,* pp. 189, 202; Johnstone, diary, in White, *Ho!,* p. 10; James Barnett, *Overland Journey to California* (New Harmony, Indiana: 1906), p. 20.

21.   Charles Dexter Cleveland, "Reminiscence," typescript, SCP Library; Juanita Brooks, ed., *A Mormon Chronicle: The Diary of John D. Lee, 1848–1876,* vol. 1 (San Marino, Calif.: Huntington Library, 1955) p. 109; Madsen, *Gold Rush Sojourners,* p. 23.

22.   Brooks, *Mormon Chronicle,* vol. 1, p. 109; Madsen, *Gold Rush Sojourners,* p. 25.

23.   Mary Stuart Bailey, journal, July 30 and September 19, 1852, in Myres, *Ho for California!,* pp. 75–76, 85; Charles C. Ferguson, *California Gold Fields* (Oakland: Biobooks, 1946), p. 45; Madsen, *Gold Rush Sojourners,* pp. 35, 40, 42, 57, 61; Dale S. Morgan, "Letters by Forty-Niners," *Western Humanities Review* (April 1949), p. 99.

       Visiting Salt Lake City in 1861, Mark Twain found an identically comforting reception: "We had a fine supper, of the freshest meats and vegetables—a great variety, and as great abundance. . . . At the end of our two days sojourn, we left Great Salt Lake City hearty and well-fed and happy." *Roughing It,* pp. 93, 120.

24.   J. S. Shepherd, *Journal of Travel across the Plains to California and Guide to the Future Emigrant* (Racine, Wisconsin: privately published, 1851), p. 44.

25.   Bailey, journal, May 3, 1852, in Myres, *Ho for California!,* pp. 56–57; Holliday, *World,* p. 124.

26.   Carpenter, "A Trip," June 13, 1857, in Myres, *Ho for California!,* pp. 105–06.

27.   John F. Hoyt, letter in *St. Paul Press,* June 10, 1862; Holliday, *World,* p. 194; Camper, "Why I Crossed," p. 59; Caughey, *Gold Rush,* p. 108; Carpenter, journal, July 24, 1857, in Myres, *Ho for California!,* pp. 108, 139. *See also* Richard J. Hooker, *A History of Food and Drink in America* (Indianapolis: Bobbs-Merrill, 1981), p. 185.

28.   Faragher, *Women and Men,* p. 78; Carpenter, "A Trip," August 6, 1857, in Myres, *Ho for California!,* p. 147. See Joseph R. Conlin, "Old Boy Did You Get Enough of Pie?: The Social History of Food in the Logging Camps," *Journal of Forest and Conservation History* (October 1979), and Joseph R. Conlin, "What the Slaves Ate" (California State University at Chico) *University Journal* (Spring 1983), pp. 6–10.

In *A Room for the Night,* p. 109, Richard A. Van Orman suggests that "early days Western food" was "highly seasoned." While I have found this piquantly true of the food to which the western miners took in the diggings, it surely does not apply to the comestibles served on the overland crossing. The staples were so bland that to some extent the later desire, nay *lust,* for spicy food was in part inspired by their insipidity.

29.   Frémont, *Report,* p. 154. Tobacco root is mentioned in few forty-niner diaries.

30.   Note, however, that some midcentury Americans considered cholera a diet-related disease. *See,* for example, Georgia Willis Read, "Diseases, Drugs, and Doctors on the Oregon-California Trail in the Gold-Rush Years," *Missouri Historical Review* (April 1944), p. 264, and Stephen Nissenbaum, *Sex, Diet, and Debility in Jacksonian America* (Westport, Conn.: Greenwood Press, 1980).

31.   Octavius Thorndike Howe, *Argonauts of '49: History and Adventures of the Emigrant Companies from Massachusetts, 1849–1850* (Cambridge: Harvard University Press, 1923).

206

CHAPTER 3
EATING ON THE RUSH

1.   Richard A. Dwyer and Richard E. Lingenfelter, *The Songs of the Gold Rush* (Berkeley: University of California Press, 1964), p. 41.

2.   See the Articles of Association in J. S. Holliday, *The World Rushed In: The California Gold Rush Experience* (New York: Simon and Schuster, 1981), pp. 461–63; Octavius Thorndike Howe, *Argonauts of '49: History and Adventures of the Emigrant Companies from Massachusetts, 1849–1850* (Cambridge: Harvard University Press, 1923), pp. 4–5.

3.   Very occasionally a professional cook hired expressly for his trade appears; for example, see Sandra L. Myres, ed., *Ho for California!: Women's Overland Diaries from the Huntington Library* (San Marino, Calif.: Huntington Library, 1981), pp. 43–44; and Lucy Rutledge Cooke, *Crossing the Plains in 1852: Narrative of a Trip from Iowa to "The Land of Gold"* . . . (Modesto, Calif.: privately published, 1923), p. 61.

4.   William Swain to George Swain, May 6, 1849, in Holliday, *World,* p. 102.

5.   John Mack Faragher, *Women and Men on the Overland Trail* (New Haven, Conn.: Yale University Press, 1979), table AI-10, pp. 19, 34, 39.

6.   Faragher, *Men and Women,* table AI-11, p. 195. However, the *family-size* mess had proved its utility in other ways and, on the trail of 1849, remained the norm.

7.   The diet and food customs of the cowboys invites a systematic study, of which there is none. There are, however, several excellent sources of information, among them: Wesley L. Fankhouser, "Son-of-a-Gun to Pate de Foie Gras: Chow on Early Great Plains Ranches," *Journal of the West* (January 1977), pp. 29–36; Ruth Tressman, "Home on the Range," *New Mexico Historical Review* (January 1951), pp. 11–12; John L. Sinclair, "Chuck-Wagon Chow," *New*

Mexico Magazine (March 1938); and the illuminating notes in Verne Carlson, *The Cowboy Cookbook* (Los Angeles: Sonica Press, 1981).

8. Helen Carpenter, "A Trip Across the Plains in an Ox Wagon," June 22, 1857, in Myres, *Ho for California!*, pp. 114ff.

9. Oliver Goldsmith, *Overland in Forty-Nine: The Recollections of a Wolverine Ranger . . .* (Detroit: privately published, 1896), p. 23.

10. Carpenter, "A Trip," June 12, 1857, in Myres, *Ho for California!*, p. 104.

11. Wellman Packard and Greenberry Larison, *Early Emigrants to California* (Bloomington: University of Indiana Press, 1928), pp. 6–7.

12. John King, letter, June 16, 1850, in his diary, Yale University Library; Isaac Jones Wistar, *Autobiography of Isaac Jones Wistar, 1827–1905* (Philadelphia: Wistar Institute of Anatomy and Biology, 1914); Franklin Langworthy, June 27, 1850, *Scenery of the Plains, Mountains and Mines: Or a Diary Kept Upon the Overland Route to California* (Ogsdenburg, New York: privately published, 1955).

13. Samuel Langhorne Clemens [Mark Twain], *Roughing It* (New York: Harper and Brothers, 1913), p. 16.

14. Noah Brooks, "The Plains Across," *Century Magazine* 63 (1902), p. 805; Carpenter, "A Trip," June 22, 1857, in Myres, *Ho for California!*, pp. 114–15.

15. Mary Stuart Bailey, journal, June 1, June 24, 1852, in Myres, *Ho for California!*, pp. 57, 66; Andrew S. McClure, *The Diary of Andrew S. McClure* (Eugene, Ore.: Lane County Pioneer Historical-Society, 1959), pp. 9, 53; Cecilia Emily McMillin Adams, "Crossing the Plains in 1852," *Transactions of the Oregon Pioneer Association* (1904), pp. 292–321; James Clyman, *James Clyman, Frontiersman: The Adventures of a Trapper and Covered-Wagon Emigrant as Told in His Own Reminiscences and Diaries,* ed. Charles L. Camp (Portland, Ore.: Champoeg Press, 1960), p. 71.

16. Cooke, *Crossing the Plains,* p. 61; Catherine Haun, "A Woman's Trip Across the Plains in 1849," manuscript, HEH Library, p. 18; Rebecca Ketcham, "From Ithaca to Clatsop Plains," *Oregon Historical Quarterly* 62 (1961), p. 275; William S. Greever, *The Bonanza West: The Story of the Western Mining Rushes, 1848–1900* (Norman: University of Oklahoma Press, 1963), p. 14.

17. Brooks, "The Plains Across," p. 805.

18. John A. Johnson to his wife, April 1, April 22, 1849, in Faragher, *Women and Men,* pp. 81–82.

19. Ibid., April 29, May 3, 1849, p. 101.

20. Ibid., May 10, 1849, p. 108.

21. James Lyne to his wife, May 4, 1849, in Holliday, *World,* pp. 97–98.

22. Carpenter, "A Trip," July 4, 1857, in Myres, *Ho for California!*, pp. 127–28.

23. Ibid., June 22, September 5, 1857, pp. 114–15, 171.

24. *See,* for example, Haun, "A Woman's Trip," p. 18; Sabrina Swain to William Swain, May 27, July 26, 1849, in Holliday, *World,* pp. 138, 195.

25. Swain to his mother, May 29, 1849, in Holliday, *World,* p. 129.

26. Swain, diary, April 25, May 12, June 10, June 13, July 4, August 6, August 24, and September 4, 1849; Swain to Sabrina Swain, May 10, 1849, in Holliday, *World,* pp. 73, 104, 105, 132, 167, 169, 186, 219, 235.

27. Ibid., May 12, May 22, June 20, August 16, August 24, 1849; pp. 105, 123, 129, 155, 215, 219. *See also* Vincent Geiger and Wakeman Bryarly, *Trail to California: The Overland Journey of Vincent Geiger and Wakeman Bryarly,* ed. David M. Potter (New Haven, Conn.: Yale University Press, 1945), July 25, 1849. p. 107.

28. Thomas O. Clark, ed., *Gold Rush Diary: Being the Journal of Elisha Douglas Perkins on the Overland Trail* (Lexington: University of Kentucky Press, 1967), June 16, 1849, p. 67.

29. Swain, journal, July 26, 1849, in Holliday, *World,* pp. 102, 196.

30. Hezekiah John Crumpton, "Reminiscence," typescript, vol. 1, p. 59, SCP Library; Cave J. Couts, *From San Diego to the Colorado in 1849,* ed. William McPherson (Los Angeles: Arthur M. Ellis, 1932), p. 21.

31. Charles Dexter Cleveland, "Reminiscence," typescript, vol. 5, p. 61, SCP Library.

32. Carpenter, "A Trip," September 7, 1857, and Bailey, journal, September 3, September 19, 1852, in Myres, *Ho for California,* pp. 82, 85, 172; Niles Searls, *The Diary of a Pioneer . . . ,* comp. Robert Searls (San Francisco: Pernau-Walsh, 1940), p. 31; Swain, diary, October 10, 1849, in Holliday, *World,* pp. 229, 274.

33. Joseph Middleton, diary, October 4, 1849, YU Library; Greever, *Bonanza West,* p. 14; J. Goldsborough Bruff, *Gold Rush: The Journals and Other Papers,* ed. Georgia W. Read and Ruth Gaines (New York: Columbia University Press, 1949), vol. 1, p. 218.

34. Alonzo Delano, *Across the Plains and Among the Diggings* (1853, reprint, New York: Wilson-Erickson, 1936); George W. Evans, *Mexican Gold Trail: Journal of a forty niner,* ed. Glenn S. Dumke (San Marino, Calif.: Huntington Library, 1945.

35. Middleton, diary, August 26, 1849.

36. Unidentified Sacramento newspaper, October 13, 1849, in William Ralston Balch, comp., *The Mines, Miners and Mining Interests of the United States in 1882* (Philadelphia: Mining Industrial Publishing House, 1882), p. 790; Holliday, *World,* pp. 269–71.

37. Daniel H. Rucker and John H. Peoples, correspondence, Senate Executive Documents, 31st Cong., 1st sess., 1852, no. 52.

CHAPTER 4
THE ARGONAUTS

1. Octavius Thorndike Howe, *Argonauts of '49: History and Adventures of the Emigrant Companies from Massachusetts, 1849–1850* (Cambridge: Harvard University Press, 1923), p. 90.

NOTES

2. See John W. Caughey, *The California Gold Rush* (Berkeley: University of California Press, 1975), p. 96.

3. J. S. Holliday, *The World Rushed In: The California Gold Rush Experience* (New York: Simon and Schuster, 1981), p. 50.

4. Howe, *Argonauts,* p. 19; Caughey, *Gold Rush,* pp. 58, 62.

5. H. C. Bailey, "Reminiscences," typescript, p. 18, HHB Library; Howe, *Argonauts,* p. 26; Photograph Collection, SCP; "Bill of Fare," *Crescent City,* November 14, 1849, HEH Library.

6. Howe, *Argonauts,* pp. 22, 25, 27; Julian Dana, *The Sacramento; River of Gold* (New York: Farrar and Rinehart, 1939), p. 119; Taylor quoted in Caughey, *Gold Rush,* p. 62.

7. Caughey, *Gold Rush,* p. 64; Albert C. Wells, letter, June 4, 1850, NYHS.

8. Bailey, "Reminiscences," p. 22.

9. Wells to Bailey, June 4, 1850; Bailey, "Reminiscences," p. 22.

10. Bailey, "Reminiscences," p. 34. Menu in Photograph Collection, SCP; Howe, *Argonauts,* pp. 21, 22.

11. Jane McDougal, diary, May 1, 1849, in Sandra L. Myres, ed., *Ho For California!: Women's Overland Diaries From the Huntington Library* (San Marino, Calif.: Huntington Library, 1980), p. 9; Holliday, *World,* p. 415.

12. Isaac Lord, diary, February 15, February 16, March 4, 1851, HEH Library.

13. Benjamin Baxter, diary, August 17, 1850, HEH Library.

14. McDougal, diary, May 14, 1849, in Myres, *Ho For California!,* p. 19.

15. Howe, *Argonauts,* pp. 220–21; Oscar Lewis, *Sea Routes to the Gold Fields: The Migration by Water to California in 1849–1852* (New York: Alfred A. Knopf, 1949), p. 107.

16. Howe, *Argonauts,* pp. 13, 48; Lewis, *Sea Routes,* p. 20.

17. Lewis, *Sea Routes,* pp. 21, 24; Howe, *Argonauts,* p. 90.

18. Carolyn Hale Russ, *The Log of a Forty-Niner* (Boston: B. J. Brennan, 1923), p. 22.

19. Edward E. Chever, "Reminiscence," typescript, SCP Library, vol. 5, pp. 22–23.

20. John Runyon Fouratt, "Reminiscence," typescript, SCP Library, vol. 1, p. 85; Howe, *Argonauts,* p. 48; Lewis, *Sea Routes,* p. 106.

21. Howe, *Argonauts,* pp. 49–50; Lewis, *Sea Routes,* p. 107.

22. George G. Webster and Linville Hall, *The Journal of a Trip Around the Horn* (1849, reprint, Ashland, Ore.: Lewis Osborne, 1970), p. 15.

23. Howe, *Argonauts,* pp. 48, 82, 96.

24. Ibid., pp. 82, 93, 94.

25. Charles H. Randall to his parents, May 10, 1849, HHB Library; Lewis, *Sea Routes,* p. vii; Caughey, *Gold Rush,* p. 86; Howe, *Argonauts,* p. 64.

26. Howe, *Argonauts,* p. 70; Lewis, *Sea Routes,* pp. 59–60, 112.

27. Randall to parents, March 20, 1849, HHB Library.

28. Ibid.

29. Webster and Hall, *Journal of a Trip,* p. 15.

30. Lewis, *Sea Routes*, pp. 98–99; Howe, *Argonauts*, p. 66.

31. *Journals of the California Legislature*, 2d sess., 1851, pp. 921–23; Henry Harris, *California's Medical Story* (San Francisco: J. W. Stacey, 1932), p. 78.

<table>
<tr><td>CHAPTER 5
THE BLACK CANKER
OF THE PLAINS</td><td>1.</td><td>J. Goldsborough Bruff, *Gold Rush: The Journals and Other Papers*, ed. Georgia Willis Read and Ruth Gaines (New York: Columbia University Press, 1949). In my discussion of scurvy in the gold rush and on the mining frontier, I was unable to benefit from Kenneth J. Carpenter, *The History of Scurvy and Vitamin C* (New York: Cambridge University Press, 1986), which appeared after my own book was in print.</td></tr>
</table>

1. J. Goldsborough Bruff, *Gold Rush: The Journals and Other Papers*, ed. Georgia Willis Read and Ruth Gaines (New York: Columbia University Press, 1949). In my discussion of scurvy in the gold rush and on the mining frontier, I was unable to benefit from Kenneth J. Carpenter, *The History of Scurvy and Vitamin C* (New York: Cambridge University Press, 1986), which appeared after my own book was in print.

2. Paul B. Beeson, ed., *Cecil Textbook of Medicine* (Philadelphia: W. B. Saunders Co., 1979), p. 1,691.

3. Charles D. Ferguson, *California Gold Fields* (Cleveland: Williams Publishing Company, 1948).

4. Edward Gould Buffum, *The Gold Rush: An Account of Six Months in California* (London: The Folio Society, 1959); George W. Groh, *Gold Fever* (New York: William Morrow, 1963), pp. 236–37.

5. Oliver Goldsmith, *Overland in Forty-nine: The Recollections of a Wolverine Ranger* (Detroit, privately published, 1896); Groh, *Gold Fever*, p. 236.

6. See, for example, the discussion in Thomas M. Logan, "Reports from California: Land Scurvy—Its Pathology, Symptoms, Causes and Treatment; Poisonous Properties of Food and Water in a State of Fermentation or Putrefection," *Southern Medical Reports* (New Orleans: 1850), pp. 468–80. Another excellent discussion of alternative medical theories of scurvy may be found in Alfred F. Hess, *Scurvy Past and Present* (Philadelphia: Lippincott, 1920). A theory winning some adherents in 1849 had it that scurvy was a postassium-deficiency disease: see A. B. Garrod, "On the Nature, Cause, and Prevention of Scurvy," *Journal of Medical Sciences* (1848), p. 457.

7. Logan, "Reports from California," pp. 471, 476; H. S. B. Schell, "Medical History of Fort Laramie," 1868, Records of the Office of the Adjutant General, National Archives, Washington, D.C.; H. H. Bancroft, *History of California* (San Francisco: Bancroft, 1886–1888), vol. 6, p. 231; J. D. B. Stillman, *Seeking the Golden Fleece* (San Francisco: 1877), p. 121; George W. Evans, *Mexican Gold Trail: Journal of a forty niner,* ed. Glenn S. Dumke (San Marino, Calif.: Huntington Library, 1945); Groh, *Gold Fever*, p. 115.

8. John H. Crandon, "Ascorbic-acid Deficiency in Experimental and Surgical Subjects," *Proceedings of the Nutrition Society of London* (1953), pp. 273–79; Richard W. Vitter, "Effects of Ascorbic Acid Deficiency in Man" in W. H. Sebrell and Robert S. Harris, eds., *The Vitamins: Chemistry, Physiology, Pathology, Methods* (New York: Academic Press, 1967), vol. 1, pp. 457–85, 462–67; Beeson, *Cecil Textbook* p. 1,690.

9. Richard W. Vitter, a "conservative" in the vitamin C debate, recommends 75–100 mg per diem: see his "Ascorbic Acid Requirements in Man," in Sebrell

and Harris, *The Vitamins*, vol. 1, p. 50. Nobel Laureate Linus Pauling is the best known of the scientists who hold that megadoses of vitamin C are a prophylactic against the common cold and other diseases, possibly even some forms of cancer.

10. Charles F. Church and Helen Nichols Church, *Food Values of Portions Commonly Used* (Philadelphia: Lippincott, 1975); Bernice K. Watt and Annabel L. Merrill, *Handbook of the Nutritional Contents of Foods* (Washington: U.S. Department of Agriculture, 1975).

11. Church and Church, *Food Values*, p. 44.

12. Georgia Willis Read, "Diseases, Drugs, and Doctors on the Oregon-California Trail in the Gold-Rush Years," *Missouri Historical Review* (October 1943), pp. 260–77; Anthony J. Lorenz, "Scurvy in the Gold Rush," *Journal of the History of Medicine* (October 1957), pp. 473–510. That sentence is a little misleading. Without saying just so, the implication is that scurvy was responsible for the fact that most overland parties suffered fatalities en route. In fact, "most historians" of the gold rush do not even mention scurvy and there are any number of documented examples of overland companies that arrived in California quite "intact." Two historians of food and nutritional disease in the United States who apparently found it unnecessary to notice scurvy in the gold rush are: Howard N. Simpson, *Invisible Armies: The Impact of Disease on American History* (Indianapolis: Bobbs-Merrill, 1980) and Richard J. Hooker, *Food and Drink in America* (Indianapolis: Bobbs-Merrill, 1981).

13. Bruff, *Gold Rush;* J. T. Kerns, "Journal of the Crossing of the Plains in 1852," *Oregon Pioneer Association*, 42, pp. 148–93; Reuben Cole Shaw, *Across the Plains in '49* (Chicago: Lakeside Press, 1948); Daniel H. Rucker and John H. Peoples, correspondence, Senate Executive Documents, 31st Cong., 1st sess., 1850; Lorenz, "Scurvy," pp. 479–80; Charles Dexter Cleveland, "Reminiscence," SCP Library, vol. 5, p. 61; Groh, *Gold Fever*, p. 116.

14. Another example of "negative evidence" is folklorist C. Grant Loomis' failure to find a mention of scurvy in his survey of "Indications of Miners' Medicine," *Western Folklore*, 8 (April 1949), pp. 117–22.

15. Beeson, *Cecil Textbook*, p. 1690; Crandon, "Ascorbic-acid Deficiency," p. 277; Lorenz, "Scurvy," p. 474.

16. Edwin Bryant, *What I Saw in California . . . in the Years 1846–47* (New York: D. Appleton, 1849); Schell, "Fort Laramie," 1868; Joseph Cain and A. C. Brown, *The Mormon Waybill, Advice to Emigrants* (Salt Lake City: 1851), cited in L. R. Hafen and A. W. Hafen, *Journals of forty niners* (Glendale, Calif.: Arthur H. Clark, 1954); Captain Howland, *Reminiscences* (San Francisco: The Pioneer Society Book Club of California), p. 473; Lorenz, "Scurvy," p. 475; Francis Galton, *The Art of Travel, or Shifts and Contrivances Available in Wild Country* (London: John Murray, 1867); Vincent Geiger and Wakeman Bryarly, *Trail to California: The Overland Journal of Vincent Geiger and Wakeman Bryarly*, ed. David M. Potter (New Haven: Yale University Press, 1945); Groh, *Gold Fever*, pp. 236, 116.

17. Catherine M. Haun, "A Woman's Trip Across the Plains," manuscript, HEH Library; Mary Stuart Bailey, journal, July 30, 1852, in Sandra L. Myres, *Ho for California!* (San Marino, Calif.: Huntington Library, 1980), pp. 75–76; Holliday, *World,* p. 202; Cain and Brown, *Mormon Waybill;* Lorenz, "Scurvy," p. 479; Richard F. Burton, *The City of the Saints* (New York: Harper and Brothers, 1862), pp. 308–9.

18. Roger S. Baldwin, Jr., "Tarrying in Nicaragua: Pleasures and Perils of the California Trip in 1849," *Century,* (October 1891), p. 911; John W. Caughey, *The California Gold Rush* (Berkeley: University of California Press, 1975), p. 64; Photograph Collection, SCP Library; Octavius Thorndike Howe, *Argonauts of 1849* (Cambridge: Harvard University Press, 1923), p. 26.

19. Julius H. Pratt, "To California by Panama in '49," *Century Magazine* (April 1891), p. 905; Baldwin, March 20, May 24, and October 4, 1849, in "Tarrying," pp. 914, 918, 931.

20. J. Praslow, *Der Staat Californien, in Medizinischer, Geographischer Hinsicht,* trans. F. C. Cordes (Gottingen: Vandenhoek, 1852; reprint, San Francisco: Newbegin, 1939); Groh, *Gold Fever,* p. 68.

21. Charles H. Williams, "Journal of a Voyage to San Francisco in the Good Ship 'Pacific'," August 22, 1849, manuscript, HEH Library; Shaw, *Across the Plains,* p. 107; Lorenz, "Scurvy," pp. 482, 500.

22. Charles H. Randall to his parents, May 10, 1849, HHB Library; William H. DeCosta, "Voyage of the Charlestown Company," April 19, 1848, manuscript, HEH Library; Williams, "Journal of a Voyage," February 22, 1849, typescript, HEH Library; James Wood, journal, in Lorenz, "Scurvy," pp. 483–84.

23. Robert Hutchinson, "Journal of a Voyage from Cherryfield, Maine, on the Bark 'Belgrade'," manuscript, HEH Library; Lewis Sanger, "Round the Horn," manuscript, HEH Library; Williams, "Journal of a Voyage," June 1, 1849, HEH Library; unnamed forty-niner cited in Howe, *Argonauts,* p. 97.

24. W. H. Herbert, "Round the Horn on the Bark 'Elvira'," in Lorenz, "Scurvy," p. 485.

25. Henry Harris, *California's Medical Story* (San Francisco: J. W. Stacey, 1932), p. 77.

CHAPTER 6
THE FOOD RUSH

1. J. T. Kincade, in Anthony J. Lorenz, "Scurvy in the Gold Rush," *Journal of the History of Medicine,* October 1957, p. 490.

2. Lorenz, "Scurvy," p. 506.

3. *Memoirs of the Crusades by Villehardouin and de Joinville,* trans. F. T. Marzails (New York: Dutton, 1958), 210–11. The Census of 1850 listed a population of 93,000 in California, a number which, given the size of the immigration and the thousands of men whom we know were holed up in wooded canyons beyond the reach of the most industrious counters, is surely low. Nevertheless, 93,000 is significantly more than the total that some historians have estimated, and to say that one Californian in 10 or 12 or 14 died of scurvy between 1848

and 1850 is simply not borne out in the tenor of the sources. For an example of a Mariposa County miner, *see* Horace Snow, *Dear Charlie Letters: Recording the Everyday Life of a Young 1854 Gold Miner as Set Forth by Your Friend, Horace Snow* (Fresno: Mariposa County Historical Society, 1979). *See also* John W. Caughey, ed., *Rushing for Gold* (Berkeley: University of California Press, 1949), p. 179.

4. John Hovey, "Journal of a Voyage from Newburyport, Mass., to San Francisco in the Brig *Charlotte,*" manuscript, HEH Library; George F. Kent, diary, HEH Library; Lorenz, "Scurvy," pp. 494–95; Edward Gould Buffum, *Six Months in the Gold Mines* (Philadelphia: Lea and Blanchard, 1850), pp. 98–99.

5. Charles H. Shinn, *Mining Camps: A Study in American Frontier Government* (New York: Alfred A. Knopf, 1948).

6. William Taylor, *California Life Illustrated* (New York: Carlton and Porter, 1858), p. 11.

7. William R. Grimshaw, "His Narrative of Life and Events in California," manuscript, HHB Library, pp. 29–30; Columbia *Tuolumne Courier,* April 6, 1861; William Downie, *Hunting for Gold: Reminiscences of Personal Experiences and Research in the Early Days of the Pacific Coast* (San Francisco: California Publishing Company, 1893), p. 26; Edna Bryan Buckbee, *The Saga of Old Tuolumne* (New York: Press of the Pioneers, 1935), pp. 91–92; Joan Margo, "The Food Supply Problem of the California Gold Miners, 1848–1855," Master's thesis, University of California, n.d., pp. 15–16; John Todd, *The Sunset Land* (New York: Lee, 1871); unidentified contemporary account in William Ralston Balch, comp., *The Mines, Miners, and Mining Interests of the United States in 1882* (Philadelphia: The Mining Industrial Publishing House, 1882), p. 792; Joseph H. Jackson, *Anybody's Gold: The Story of California's Mining Towns* (New York: Appleton, 1941), p. 385; Edward Austin to George Austin, August 19, 1849, Honeyman Collection, HHB Library. *See also* Frank Soule, John H. Gihon, and James Nisbet, *The Annals of San Francisco and History of California* (New York: D. Appleton, 1855), pp. 243–63.

8. Charles D. Ferguson, *California Gold Fields* (Cleveland: Williams Publishing Co., 1948); *See also* Taylor, *California Life,* p. 30; Caughey, *Rushing for Gold,* p. 35; Daniel B. Woods, *Sixteen Months at the Gold Diggings* (New York: Harper and Brothers, 1851), pp. 18, 19, 91.

9. Elizabeth L. Gunn, *Records of a California Family* (San Diego: privately published, n.d.); Holliday, *World,* p. 303.

10. Taylor, *California Life,* pp. 48–49.

11. William Dinkel, "A Pioneer of the Roaring Fork," *Colorado Magazine* 21 (September 1944), p. 189.

12. William D. Howard to Benjamin T. Reed, June 11, 1848, Howard Papers, CHS Library; C. F. Winslow, "Nantucket to the Golden Gate," *Proceedings of the California Historical Society,* 1950, p. 29; Margo, "Food Supply," pp. 88–97; Walter Colton, *Three Years in California* (New York: A. S. Barnes & Co., 1850), p. 279.

13. Edward Austin, letter to George Austin, September 21, 1849, Honeyman Collection, HHB Library.

14. Franklin A. Buck, letter, March 11, 1851, private collection, Bath, Maine, in Lorenz, "Scurvy," p. 505.

15. Edward Austin, letters to George Austin, September 21, October 14, and November 8, 1849, Honeyman Collection, HHB Library; Jacques Moerenhout (French consul in Monterey), quoted in Margo, "Food Supply Problem," p. 9; Colonel R. B. Mason, *Report* to Brigadier General R. Jones, August 17, 1848, House Executive Documents, 31st Congress, 1st Session, No. 17, p. 533. See also William S. Greever, *The Bonanza West: The Story of the Western Mining Rushes 1848–1900* (Norman: University of Oklahoma Press, 1963), p. 369; Julian Dana, *The Sacramento: River of Gold* (New York: Farrar and Rinehart, 1939), pp. 155, 158–159, 161, 162.

16. Balch, *Mines, Miners, and Mining Districts*, p. 790.

17. Ralph Mann, *After the Gold Rush: Society in Grass Valley and Nevada City, California 1849–1870* (Palo Alto: Stanford University Press, 1982), pp. 20, 23. *See also* Dana, *Sacramento*, p. 139.

18. Francis George Bornemann, v. 4, p. 21; John Henry Liening, v. 2, p. 39; Edward Percy Reed, v. 2, p. 106, all in "Reminiscences," typescript, SCP Library; Margo, "Food Supply," p. 34.

19. "The California Recollections of Caspar T. Hopkins," *California Historical Society Quarterly*, 25 (June 1946), p. 106.

20. Margo, "Food Supply," pp. 23, 90; Isaac Lord, diary, December 22, 1849, HEH Library.

21. Alonzo Green, "Reminiscences," vol. 3, p. 34, SCP Library.

22. G. Walter Reed, *History of Sacramento County, California* (Los Angeles: Historic Record Company, 1923), p. 67; C. H. Randall, letter, March 12, 1850, SCP Library; Alonzo Delano, letter, April 4, 1850, in Irving McKee, ed., *Correspondence* (Sacramento: 1952), p. 61.

23. Octavius Thorndike Howe, *Argonauts of '49: History and Adventures of the Emigrant Companies from Massachusetts, 1849–1850* (Cambridge: Harvard University Press, 1923), pp. 103–5.

24. Greever, *Bonanza West*, p. 57; unidentified Sacramento newspaper, October 13, 1849, in Balch, *Mines, Miners*, p. 790; Charles H. Randall to his parents, September 24, 1850, HHB Library; Elisha Oscar Crosby, "Reminiscence," typescript, vol. 4, p. 39, SCP Library; Woods, *Sixteen Months*, p. 7.

25. *Rocky Mountain News*, May 7, 1859; Agnes Wright Spring, "Food Facts of 1859," *Colorado Magazine* 22 (May 1945), p. 115; Amanda M. Ellis, "Leadville and Cripple Creek," *Colorado Magazine* (1954), p. 4.

26. In Merle W. Wells, "Rush to Idaho," *Idaho Historical Bulletin* 19 (1963), p. 27.

27. Balch, *Mines, Miners*, p. 790; Louise Amelia Knapp Smith Clappe, *The Shirley Letters from California Mines in 1851–1852* (San Francisco: Thomas C. Russell, 1922), September 13, 1851, p. 10; Downie, *Hunting for Gold*, p. 59.

28. Elisha Oscar Crosby, "Reminiscence," typescript, vol. 4, p. 39, SCP Library; Edward Austin to George Austin, January 12, 1850, Honeyman Coll., HHB Library; *see also* Downie, *Hunting for Gold,* p. 58; Margo, "Food Supply," p. 19.

29. Wells, "Rush to Idaho," p. 27.

30. "California Rainfall Survey: Monthly Total Precipitation, 1849–1980" (Sacramento: State of California Department of Water Resources, July 1981), microfiche supplement.

31. Charles Nelson Teeter, "Four Years of My Life on Adventures in the Far West," typescript, n.d., pp. 225–27, ISHS Library; "Praying Abe Slocum," *San Francisco Argonaut,* November 17, 1877; Daniel A. Cornford, "Lumber, Labor, and Community in Humboldt County, California, 1850–1920" (Ph.D. diss., University of California, Santa Barbara, 1983), p. 63.

32. Edwin F. Bean, comp., *Bean's History and Directory of Nevada County, California* (Nevada City: Daily Gazette Book and Job Office, 1867), pp. 190–91. According to Ralph Mann, 70 percent of Grass Valley's citizens at this time were miners (*After the Gold Rush,* p. 19).

33. Bean, *Bean's History,* pp. 191–92; *see also* Mann, *After the Gold Rush,* p. 13.

34. Clappe, *Shirley Letters,* p. 54.

35. J. S. Holliday, *The World Rushed In: The California Gold Rush Experience* (New York: Simon and Schuster, 1981), p. 303; Caughey, *Rushing for Gold,* pp. 34–35; Margo, "Food Supply," pp. 51–52. An excellent article on the subject of mining camp supply was published after this book was in press: Randall E. Rohe, "Feeding the Mines: The Development of Supply Centers for the Goldfields," *Annals of Wyoming* 57 (Spring 1985).

36. Margo, "Food Supply," pp. 21, 47–48, 52–53; *Sacramento Daily Union,* June 16, 1858; Oscar O. Winther, *Express and Stagecoach Days in California* (Palo Alto: Stanford University Press, 1936), p. 42.

37. Eliot Lord, *Comstock Mining and Miners* (Washington: Government Printing Office, 1883), p. 200; William H. Brewer, *Up and Down California in 1860–1864* (Reprint. Berkeley: University of California Press, 1966), August 23, 1863.

38. William Turrentine Jackson, *Treasure Hill: Portrait of a Silver Mining Camp* (Tucson: University of Arizona Press, 1963), p. 47. For similar data in regard to Idaho's Salmon River rush of the early 1860s and the Thunder Mountain district several decades later, see Wells, "Rush to Idaho"; Teeter, "Four Years," p. 158; *Idaho Daily Statesman,* February 2, 1902; and *Idaho World,* April 28, 1902, and August 29, 1904. For the same story on the road to Globe, Arizona, see Alice Curnow, "The Journey with Tom," typescript, Small Collections, AHS Library, p. 25; Lord, *Comstock Mining,* p. 200; *Gold Hill Daily News,* August 1, 1864, p. 2.

39. Mark Twain, *Roughing It,* I, p. 182.

40. *Grangeville Standard,* January 23, 1902 and April 13, 1902.

215

41. *Elmore County News,* April 18, 1902; *Lewiston Times,* November 7, November 11, and December 3, 1902.

42. *Lewiston Times,* December 25, 1902.

43. Mann, *After the Gold Rush,* pp. 10, 20; *San Francisco Evening Bulletin,* October 17, 1860; Wells, "Rush to Idaho," p. 24; Mrs. M. M. Mathews, *Ten Years in Nevada* (Buffalo, N.Y.: Baker, Jones & Company, 1880), p. 165; Caughey, *Rushing for Gold,* p. 34.

    The fact that provisioners were buffeted by the same forces that formed their lives—the fact that provisioners often were miners—led to the curious phenomenon that retailers were rarely if ever blamed for sudden jumps in prices. The delegates to the Hungry Convention blamed "soul-less speculators" of San Francisco. When beef prices soared in Silver City, Idaho, in 1875, the culprits were not Silver City's butchers but their suppliers. "An honest ranchman is one of the noblest works of the Creator," the *Owyhee Avalanche* sarcastically remarked. Two months later a rise in the price of butter and cheese led to a vilification of dairymen (*Owyhee Daily Avalanche,* June 5 and August 14, 1875). But a thorough scouring of sources turns up no evidence of significant hostility between miner and provisioner.

44. When Florence was opened in November 1861, food costs comprised 22 percent of wages. After declining to 18 percent in the winter of 1861–62, the price of a miner's sustenance rose to 26 percent in late March and to a high of 27 percent in late April, before dropping precipitously to a low of 2.5 percent of the prevailing wage in the fall of 1862. During 1864 and 1865 basic food costs ranged between 3.2 percent and 4.2 percent. (Bartton, Stoddard, & Mulhollin, Consulting Engineers, comps., *Royalties and Gold Production Costs on the Nez Perce Indian Reservation 1860–1867* (Boise, Idaho: U.S. Department of Justice, Indian Claims Section, 1958).

45. The price of the customary daily ration in Virginia City in March of 1860 was $1.02, or between 20 and 29 percent of the prevailing daily wage of mine workers. In January 1864 the cost was 83¢ or 21 percent of wages; through 1867 about 76¢ (22 percent); in January of 1871, 62¢ (16 percent); and in January of 1881, 58¢ (17 percent). These calculations are based on data in Lord, *Comstock Mining,* pp. 95, 200, 371; J. Ross Browne, *Report of J. Ross Browne on the Mineral Resources of the State and Territories West of the Rocky Mountains* (San Francisco: H. H. Bancroft, 1868); and the Virginia City *Territorial Enterprise,* July 20, 1861. See also Duane A. Smith, *Rocky Mountain Mining Camps: The Urban Frontier* (Bloomington: Indiana University Press, 1967), p. 198.

    Prices in Helena and Butte, Montana, Deadwood, South Dakota, Pinal, Arizona, and Silver Reef, Utah, were—once the initial excitement was over—similar in pattern to those in Virginia City. In Leadville, Colorado, and Tombstone, Arizona, food costs were not high even during the flush early years. It is reasonable to extend to the entire region Charles H. Shinn's characterization of

216

Comstock miners as "well fed." Shinn, *The Story of the Mine: As Illustrated by the Great Comstock Lode of Nevada* (New York: Appleton, 1896); reprint, Reno: University of Nevada Press, 1979), p. 239. S. C. Hotchkiss, in his thorough study of "Occupational Diseases in the Mining Industry," *American Labor Legislation Review* 2 (February 1912), pp. 131–39, found no nutritional problems worth noting.

46. Mathews, *Ten Years,* p. 139.

CHAPTER 7
HOW AN ELEPHANT
IS EATEN

1. In Gretchen Adel Schneider, "Pigeon Wings and Polkas: The Dance of the California Miners," *Dance Perspectives* 39 (Winter 1969), p. 6.
2. Louise Cook Walters to Emma Cook [?], n.d., ISHS Library.
3. Francis Marryatt, *Mountains and Molehills* (London: 1855), in Vardis Fisher and Opal Laurel Holmes, *Gold Rushes and Mining Camps of the Early American West* (Caldwell, Idaho: Caxton Printers, 1968), p. 137; the verse is found in several variations in any number of sources, including Fisher and Holmes, *Gold Rushes,* p. 142, and Glenn Quiett, *Paydirt,* p. 153.
4. Daniel B. Woods, *Sixteen Months at the Gold Diggings* (New York: Harper and Brothers, 1851), 57. The mention of poor water is one of the very few I have come across, a fact that discouraged me from pursuing the excellent suggestion of Professor Judith Walzer Leavitt's critique of an early draft of this study that the consequences for mining camp health of polluted water be included as part of the final work. *Hutching's California Magazine* (September 1859), in Marvin Lewis, ed., *The Mining Frontier: Contemporary Accounts from the Mining West in the Nineteenth Century* (Norman: University of Oklahoma Press, 1967), p. 37; German couplet from Erwin G. Gudde, "The Miner's ABC," *Western Folklore* 6 (April 2, 1947), p. 113.
5. E. S. Holden, "Condemned Bar in 1849: An Excerpt from the Journal of Erastus S. Holden," *California Historical Society Quarterly* 12 (December 1933), 316. James L. Cogswell, "Reminiscence," vol. 1, p. 44, SCP Library.
6. Andrew Smith Church, "Reminiscence," vol. 4, pp. 46–47. *See also* the sources quoted in Fisher and Holmes, *Gold Rushes,* p. 137; Hinton R. Helper, *The Land of Gold* (Baltimore: 1855), p. 156.
7. Alice Curnow, "The Journey with Tom," typescript, Small Collections, AHS Library, p. 80.
8. Horace Snow, *Dear Charlie Letters: Recording the Everyday Life of a Young 1854 Gold Miner As Set Forth by Your Friend, Horace Snow* (Fresno: Mariposa County Historical Society, 1979), April 20, 1854, p. 20; William Swain to George Swain, January 6, 1850, in J. S. Holliday, *The World Rushed In* (New York: Simon and Schuster, 1981), p. 319; Elmon Camp, February 17, 1850, in Holliday, *World,* p. 309.
9. H. C. Bailey, "California in '53," memoirs, HHB Library.
10. Snow, *Dear Charlie Letters,* December 4, 1854, p. 78.
11. Lewis, *Mining Frontier,* pp. 96–97.

12. Frank Soule, John H. Gihon, and James Nisbet, *The Annals of San Francisco and History of California* (New York: Appleton, 1855; reprint, Palo Alto: Lewis Osborne, 1966); Octavius Thorndike Howe, *Argonauts of '49: History and Adventures of the Emigrant Companies from Massachusetts, 1849–1850* (Cambridge: Harvard University Press, 1923), p. 101; Daniel Boorstin, *The Americans: The Democratic Experience* (New York: Random House, 1973), 307ff.

13. In Joan Margo, "The Food Supply Problem of the California Gold Rush," (Master's thesis, University of California, n.d.), p. 17; Francis George Borneman, "Reminiscence," vol. 4, p. 20, SCP Library; Edward Austin to Frank Austin, September 26, 1849, Honeyman Collection, HHB Library; William Downie, *Hunting for Gold: Reminscences of Personal Experiences and Research in the Early Days of the Pacific Coast* (San Francisco: California Publishing Co., 1893), p. 62.

14. *See* Joseph R. Conlin, "Consider the Oyster," *American Heritage* (February–March 1980), pp. 65–73; *American Heritage Cookbook* (New York: American Heritage Press, 1969), p. 53; Waverley Root and Richard De Rochemont, *Eating in America: A History* (New York: William Morrow, 1976), p. 135.

15. Willard R. Espy, "Grandpa's Village," *American Heritage* (February 1975), p. 61.

16. Reno *Daily Nevada State Journal,* August 5, 1874; Amelia Clappe, *The Shirley Letters from California Mines in 1851–1852* (San Francisco: Thomas C. Russell, 1922), p. 107; Margo, "Food Supply," p. 17; On the matter of oysters, see almost any menu of a mining region restaurant or banquet between 1849 and 1914.

17. Soule, Gihon, and Nisbet, *Annals,* pp. 639, 641; William Taylor, *California Life Illustrated* (New York: Carlton and Porter, 1861), p. 178; quotation from Remi Nadeau, *Ghost Towns and Mining Camps of California* (Los Angeles: Ward Ritchie Press, 1965), p. 81.

18. The records of the California Trademark Office are in the California State Archives, Sacramento: *see* vol. 1, p. 350; Edwin F. Bean, *Bean's History and Director of Nevada County, California* (Nevada City: Daily Gazette Book and Job Office, 1867), pp. ii, 157, 160, 285.

19. Lucius Beebe, in Helen Evans Brown et al., *The Virginia City Cook Book* (Los Angeles: Ward Ritchie Press, 1953), p. 6; Kruse & Euler Co., San Francisco, to Frank Litsch, January 22, 1874, Litsch Papers, SSHP; Curnow, "Journey," 101–2.

20. Tombstone *Epitaph,* September 9, 1880. *See also* Denver *Rocky Mountain News,* August 28, 1862; John W. Reps, *Cities of the American West: A History of Frontier Urban Planning* (Princeton, N.J.: Princeton University Press, 1979), p. 475.

21. Daphne Overstreet, *Arizona Territory Cookbook 1864–1912* (Globe: Pimeria Press, 1975), p. 26; *Prescott Journal Miner,* 1886, in Overstreet, *Arizona Territory Cookbook,* p. 31; Barton Wood Currie, "Housekeeping in Alkali

Land," *Good Housekeeping* 49 (August 1909), p. 119; Soule, Gihon, and Nisbet, *Annals,* pp. 644–45.

22.   Menus from banquets commemorating special occasions and from restaurants are to be found in most historical society libraries in the mining states. Those cited are from the SCP Library.

23.   Menu in SCP Archives.

24.   Menu, HEH Library.

25.   Louise Palmer, "How We Live in Nevada," *Overland Monthly* (May 1869), p. 457; Virginia City Collection, NHS; Richard A. Van Orman, *A Room for the Night: Hotels of the Old West* (Bloomington: Indiana University Press, 1966), pp. 43–44; *Reno Evening Gazette,* July 8, 1896.

26.   Sandra Dallas, *Yesterday's Denver* (Miami: E. A. Seemann Publishing, 1974), p. 41; William S. Greever, *The Bonanza West: The Story of the Western Mining Rushes, 1848–1900* (Norman: University of Oklahoma Press, 1963), p. 177; Amanda M. Ellis, *Bonanza Towns: Leadville and Cripple Creek* (Colorado Springs, Colo. [?]: 1954), p. 4.

27.   Greever, *Bonanza West,* p. 37; *Daily Arizona Citizen,* July 29, 1879; Menu of unidentified restaurant, June 27, 1901, in Herbert L. Heller, ed., *Sourdough Sagas* (Cleveland: World Publishing Company, 1967), p. 149. *See also* collections of menus in the HHB and HEH Libraries; Heller, *Sourdough Sagas,* p. 72. For another miner satire of their own gastronomic pretensions, albeit with Hockheimer wine, see *Omaha Times,* February 17, 1889; A. D. Grew, "Denver's First Christmas," *Colorado Magazine* 14 (January 1937), p. 19; Fisher and Holmes, *Gold Rushes,* p. 43.

28.   *Gold Hill Daily News,* August 1, 1864.

29.   Richard A. Lingenfelter, *The Hard Rock Miners* (Berkeley: University of California Press, 1974). For a curious comparison with miners who were by no means extravagantly paid, *see* D. A. Brading, *Miners and Merchants in Bourbon Mexico 1763–1810* (Cambridge: University Press, 1971), passim; *Telluride Daily Journal,* December 28, 1900.

30.   Lord, *Comstock Mining and Miners* (Washington: Government Printing Office, 1883), p. 372.

31.   Sam Churchill, *Big Sam* (New York: Doubleday, 1965), p. 129; Bert Webber, *Swivel-Chair Logger: The Life and Work of Anton A. "Tony" Lausmann* (Fairfield, Wash.: Ye Galleon Press, 1976), p. 140.

32.   Irma Lee Emmerson with Jean Muir, *The Woods Were Full of Men* (New York: David McKay Company, 1963), pp. 140–44; "Why I Am a Member of the I.W.W.," *4 L Bulletin* (October 1922), p. 9. For a detailed study of logger diet, *see* Joseph R. Conlin, "Old Boy, Did You Get Enough of Pie? A Social History of Food in Logging Camps," *Journal of Forest History* (October 1979), 164–85.

33.   I have developed—some would say beaten to death—the idea of the tenacity of "prospector culture" among the hard-rock miners in other matters. *See Big Bill Haywood and the Radical Union Movement* (Syracuse, N.Y.: Syracuse Univer-

sity Press, 1969); "Goldfield High-Grade," *American West* (May–June 1983), pp. 31–37; "William D. Haywood," in *American Labor Leaders*, ed. Melvyn Dubofsky and Warren Van Tine (Urbana: University of Illinois Press, 1986.)

34. *Idaho Daily Statesman*, April 13, 1902; Overstreet, *Arizona Territory Cookbook*, p. 29.

35. Curnow, "Journey," p. 57; Mathews, *Ten Years*, p. 171.

36. Edward Vollmer and Company Letterbook, pp. 447–48, Vollmer and Company Collection; John McGrath Stock Account, January 16, 1897, NHS Library; Litsch Papers, SSHP Archives. In fact, virtually any of the numerous surviving grocers' daybooks and ledgers will tell the same story.

37. Ellen Rockwell, interview with the author, Paradise, California, March 7, 1979.

38. Joe Chisholm, *Brewery Gulch: Frontier Days of Old Arizona* (San Antonio: Naylor, 1949), p. 131. Chisholm says that these circumstances made miners "indifferent to food" and "cynical of all edibles as such," leaving nothing "in the world worthwhile except red licker with beer chasers." I have made somewhat different deductions.

39. Lord, *Comstock Mining,* p. 436. The starvation death occurred in February 1880, obviously not a result of the shortages sometimes attendant on development. Lord also reported one case of marasmus, a deficiency of protein relative to calorie consumption and usually associated with children in undeveloped nations. The age of the sufferer on the Comstock is not known and the newspapers reveal nothing. One suspects that both cases involved prospectors from the back country.

40. Alexander Delmar, "The History of Precious Metals," in William Ralston Balch, *The Mines, Miners, and Mining Interests of the United States in 1882* (Philadelphia: The Mining Industrial Publishing House, 1882), p. 791.

CHAPTER *8*
A TABLE FOR
THE CAMP

1. J. Ross Browne, *Report of J. Ross Browne on the Mineral Resources of the States and Territories West of the Rocky Mountains* (San Francisco: H. H. Bancroft, 1868), April 1859.

2. "Restaurants and Food Services," Bank of America *Small Business Reporter* (1977) p. 1; 1983, p. 22; *Historical Statistics of the United States* (Washington: Department of Commerce, Bureau of the Census, 1975), Section T 79-115, p. 843; "Food Service Business Rang Up $133 Billion in Sales," *Variety* (February 9, 1983).

3. Louise Amelia Knapp Smith Clappe, *California in 1851: The Letters of Dame Shirley* (Thomas C. Russell, 1922) vol. 1, p. 27; Frank Marryatt, *Mountains ad Molehills* (London: 1855), p. 223; Charles B. Gillespie, "A Miner's Sunday in Coloma," *Century* (June 1891) p. 263; Gretchen Adel Schneider, "Pigeon Wings and Polkas: The Dance of the California Miners," *Dance Perspectives* 39 (Winter 1969), p. 8; Edwin F. Bean, comp., *Bean's History and Directory of Nevada County, California* (Nevada City: Daily Gazette Book and Job Office, 1867), p. 392.; William Swain to George Swain, January 6, 1850, in J. S.

Holliday, *The World Rushed In: The California Gold Rush Experience* (New York: Simon and Schuster, 1981), p. 315.

4. Menu of El Dorado Hotel, SCP Library; S. W. Holladay, "Reminiscence," vol. 5, p. 156, SCP Library.

5. Bean, *Bean's History*, p. 160.

6. Edward Percey Reed, "Reminiscences," SCP Library, vol. 2, p. 109; N. B. Malville had the same experience in Placerville, ("Reminiscences," vol. 2, p. 55, SCP Library.)

7. Frances Moffat, *Dancing on the Brink of the World* (New York: Putnam's, 1977), p. 17; Ward House Menu, December 27, 1849, SCP Library.

8. Johann Knocke, "Reminiscence," vol. 3, p. 81, SCP Library; III, Richard A. Van Orman, *A Room for the Night: Hotels of the Old West* (Bloomington: Indiana University Press, 1966), p. 33; C. N. Teeter, "Four Years of My Life, or, Adventures in the Far West," typescript, n.d., ISHS, p. 181.

9. San Francisco *Commercial Advertiser*, April 6, 1854; George Soule, John H. Gihon, and James Nisbet, *The Annals of San Francisco and History of California* (New York: Appleton, 1855), pp. 643–44; Mary Lou Spence, "They Also Serve Who Wait," *Western Historical Quarterly* 14 (January 1983), p. 12. This essay was first delivered as Professor Spence's presidential address before the Western History Association in October 1982.

10. *Territorial Enterprise*, July 20, July 21, 1861; Emmett L. Arnold, *Gold Camp Drifter, 1906–1910* (Reno: University of Nevada Press, 1973), pp. 62–63; Henry C. Morris, *Desert Gold and Total Prospecting* (Washington, D.C.: privately published, 1955), pp. 18–19; Van Orman, *Room for the Night*, p. 103.

11. "Diary of Mrs. A. C. Hunt, 1859," *Colorado Magazine* 21 (September 1944), p. 169; Lawrence W. Marshall, "Early Denver History as told by Contemporary Newspaper Advertisements," *Colorado Magazine* 8 (September 1931), p. 162; Sandra Dallas, *Yesterday's Denver* (Miami: E. A. Seamann Publishing, 1974), p. 40; John W. Reps, *Cities of the American West* (Princeton, N.J.: Princeton University Press, 1979), p. 475; Van Orman, *Room for the Night*, pp. 43–44; Duane A. Smith, *Rocky Mountain Mining Camps: The Urban Frontier* (Bloomington: Indiana University Press, 1967), p. 223; *Corbett, Hoye and Co.'s Eighth Annual City Directory of the Inhabitants, Institutions, Incorporated Companies, Manufacturing Establishments, Business, Business Firms, Etc., in the City of Denver for 1880* (Denver: 1880), p. 35; Spence, "They Also Serve," p. 11.

12. *Telluride Daily Journal*, December 17, 1900; "Ashes Senior," letter in the *Rocky Mountain News*, April 17, 1861; "Colorado in 1867 as Seen by a Frenchman," *Colorado Magazine* 14 (March 1937), p. 61; Vardis Fisher and Opal Laurel Holmes, *Gold Rushes and Mining Camps of the Early American West* (Caldwell, Idaho: Caxton Printers, 1968), p. 143; *Corbett, Hoye and Co.'s First Annual City Directory . . . Leadville,* (Leadville, Colo.: 1880); Spence, "They Also Serve," p. 11.

13. *Owyhee Avalanche,* June 22, 1867.

14. Federal Writers' Program, Works Progress Administration, *Copper Camp: Stories of the World's Greatest Mining Town, Butte, Montana* (Helena: Montana State Department of Agriculture and Industry, 1943), pp. 245, 251.

15. M. M. Mathews, *Ten Years in Nevada, or, Life on the Pacific Coast* (Buffalo, N.Y.: Baker, Jones & Co., 1880), p. 171.

16. Mrs. Opie Rundle Burgess, in Frank L. Wentworth, *Bisbee with the Big B* (Iowa City, Ia.: Mercer, 1938), pp. 257–58.

17. Wentworth, *Bisbee,* pp. 130–31; Epler, *Bisbee Vignettes,* n.p.; John C. Hancock, "Reminiscences," typescript, 1933, p. 24, Hancock Collection, AHS.

18. Russell Wahman, interview with author, May 16, 1982; *Prescott Journal Miner,* 1886, in Daphne Overstreet, *The Arizona Territory Cook Book, 1864–1912* (Globe: Pineria Press, 1975), p. 27.

19. Howard Clifford, *The Skagway Story* (Anchorage: Alaska Northwest Publishing Company, 1975), p. 75; Menu, in Klondike National Historical Park Archives, Skagway, Alaska.

20. *Skagway News,* December 31, 1897; documents on exhibit, 1982, Trail of '98 Museum, Skagway.

21. Lucius Beebe, in Helen Evans Brown et al., *Virginia City Cook Book* (Los Angeles: Ward Ritchie Press, 1953), p. 6. Also see any number of banquet menus in manuscript collections in major mining states, such as those in the Society of California Pioneers, Nevada Historical Society, Colorado Historical Society, and Arizona Historical Society.

22. *A Historical Descriptive and Commercial Directory of Owyhee County, Idaho* (Silver City: Press of the Owyhee Avalanche, 1898), p. 28; Edgar Wilson Nye, *Bill Nye's Remarks* (Chicago: 1891), pp. 341–42; Rose Pender, *A Lady's Experience in the Wild West in 1883* (London: 1888), p. 77; Spence, "They Also Serve," p. 19.

23. Charles H. Shinn, *Mining Camps: A Study in American Frontier Government* (New York: Alfred A. Knopf, 1948), p. 2.

24. In an influential essay, "Origins of Western Working Class Radicalism," *Labor History* (Spring 1966), pp. 131–54, Melvyn Dubofsky traces the origins of miner union radicalism in the West to the suddenness with which the old egalitarianism was inundated by capital. I have also played with this theme in *Big Bill Haywood and the Radical Union Movement* (Syracuse: Syracuse University Press, 1969), pp 9–19. Another presentation of the idea is in Joseph R. Conlin, "Goldfield High-Grade," *American West* (May–June 1983), pp. 38–45.

25. Fisher and Holmes, *Gold Rushes,* p. 137; Bayard Taylor, *Eldorado; or Adventures in the Path of Empire* (New York: Alfred A. Knopf, 1949), p. 116; M. M. Mathews, *Ten Years in Nevada: Or, Life on the Pacific Coast* (Buffalo, N.Y.: Baker, Jones, & Co., 1880), p. 170; Van Orman, *Room for the Night,* p. 42; Federal Writers' Program (WPA), *Copper Camp: Stories of the World's*

Greatest Mining Town, Butte, Montana (Helena: Montana State Department of Agriculture, Labor, and Industry, 1943), p. 246; Dallas, *Yesterday's Denver,* p. 49.

26. Louise Palmer, "How We Live in Nevada," *Overland Monthly* 22 (May 1869), p. 461; Mrs. Hugh Brown, *Lady in Boomtown: Mining and Manners on the Nevada Frontier* (Palo Alto, Calif.: American West, 1968).

27. Brown, *Virginia City Cook Book,* p. 28; Gold Hill *Daily News,* August 1, 1864; Virginia City *Daily Union,* August 2, 1864; *Copper Camp,* p. 252; James W. Byrkit, *Forging the Copper Collar,* (Tucson: University of Arizona Press, 1982), pp. 38, 53, 89–91, 198–99, 237, 243.

28. Mathews, *Ten Years,* p. 170; Alonzo Green, "Reminiscence," vol. 3, p. 32, SCP Library; *Telluride Daily Journal,* December 17, 1900; Virginia City *Territorial Enterprise,* July 20, 1861.

29. Charles Erastus Lester, *Atlantic to the Pacific* (Boston: 1873), p. 106.

30. Soule, Gihon, and Nisbet, *Annals,* pp. 244–45, 640, 641.

31. Hulbert, "Reminiscence," vol. 4, p. 294, SCP Library.

32. Snow to Charles E. Fitz, October 9, 1954, in Horace Snow, *Dear Charlie Letters . . .* (Fresno: Mariposa County Historical Society, 1979), p. 65.

33. Prentice Mulford, "Camp," May 1870, in Lewis, *Mining Frontier,* p. 107.

34. Browne, *Report of J. Ross Browne.*

35. Andrew J. Fisk, diary, September 1860, in Sandra L. Myres, ed., *Ho for California! . . .* (San Marino, Calif.: Huntington Library, 1980), p. 221; *The Pioneer,* September 1854, p. 107.

36. Archives and Exhibits, Trail of '98 National Historic Park, Skagway, Alaska; Mann, *After the Gold Rush,* p. 44; Margaret S. Woyski, "Women and Mining in the Old West," *Journal of the West* (April 1981), p. 45.

37. Noble Burns Waller, *Tombstone: An Iliad of the Southwest* (New York: Grosset and Dunlap, 1929), p. 37; John P. Clum, "Nellie Cashman," *Arizona Historical Review* (January 1931); Daphne Overstreet, *Arizona Territory Cookbook* (Globe: Pineria Press, 1975), p. 28.

38. Alvina N. Potter, *The Many Lives of the Lynx: A Century of Mining on Lynx Creek between 1863 and 1963* (Prescott, Ariz.: privately published, 1964), p. 60.

39. *New Mexico State and El Paso, Texas, Business Directory* (Albuquerque: Gazeteer Publishing Company, n.d.), pp. 640–53; Elizabeth Jameson, "Imperfect Unions," *Frontiers* 1 (1976), p. 61; Soule, Gihon, and Nisbet, *Annals,* pp. 4–41.

40. Mary Grace Paquette, *Lest We Forget: The History of the French in Kern County* (Bakersfield, Calif.: Kern County Historical Society, 1978), p. 18; Woyski, "Women and Mining," p. 45

41. Spence, "They Also Serve," p. 13.

42. Castle Rock *Record Journal,* December 28, 1888; Don L. and Jean Griswold, *The Carbonate Camp Called Leadville* (Denver: 1951), p. 207; Spence, "They Also Serve," p. 13.

43. Spence, "They Also Serve," pp. 16, 17, 23–24.

44. Woyski, "Women and Mining," p. 45.

45. Spence, "They Also Serve," p. 11; Dan De Quille [William Wright], *The Big Bonanza* (New York: Alfred A. Knopf, 1947), p. 268; Gold Hill *Daily News*, p. 268.

46. D. M. Bishop, *Bishop's Directory of Virginia City, Gold Hill, Silver City, Carson City, and Reno* (San Francisco: B. C. Vandall, 1879); Mathews, *Ten Years*, p. 172.

47. Odie B. Faulk, *Tombstone: Myth and Reality* (New York: Oxford University Press, 1972), pp. 127–28. There were exceptions to the rule that company cookhouses were absent from the mining frontier. James B. Allen, *The Company Town in the American West* (Norman: University of Oklahoma Press, 1966), listed only one company town involved in gold or silver mining, but he found the company cookhouse used widely in coal, copper, and quarrying. Russell R. Elliott, the distinguished historian of labor relations in Nevada, grew up in Ely, a copper camp where, he remembered, most miners ate at the company boardinghouse by choice because the meals there were cheaper and better than at private restaurants. (Elliott to the author, January 9, 1980).

48. Thomas H. Kinnersley, "Virginia, Nevada, 1859–1890: A Study of Police, Water and Fire Problems" (Ph.D. diss., University of California, Los Angeles, 1974), p. 70. *See also* Conlin, *Big Bill Haywood,* and Conlin, "Goldfield High-Grade."

49. Mathews, *Ten Years*, p. 140; Lawrence W. Marshall, "Early Denver History as Told By Contemporary Newspaper Advertisements," *Colorado Magazine* 8 (September 1931), p. 162; Juneau *City Mining Record*, April 19, 1888; Bean, *Bean's History*, p. 157; *Complete Business Directory*, p. 18; Holliday, *World*, p. 39.

50. John W. Caughey, ed., *Rushing For Gold* (Berkeley: University of California Press, 1949), p. 16.

51. C. H. Randall to his parents, November 29, 1849; William Elder to Sara, April 6, 1851, Bancroft Library.

52. Snow, *Dear Charlie Letters,* July 24, 1854, p. 28.

53. Ibid., April 1, 1854, p. 1.

54. Gillespie, "Sunday in Coloma," p. 263.

55. Mathews, *Ten Years*, p. 170; Eureka *Daily Sentinel,* July 9, 1878; Robert E. Ericson, "Touring Entertainment in Nevada during the Peak Years of the Mining Boom, 1876–1878" (Ph.D. diss., University of Nevada, 1970), p. 34.

CHAPTER 9
BOARDING HOUSES,
SWINGING DOORS

1. Charles B. Gillespie, "A Miner's Sunday in Coloma," *Century* (June 1891), pp. 259, 268.

2. Otis E. Young, Jr., *Black Powder and Hard Steel: Miners and Machines on the Old Western Frontier* (Norman: University of Oklahoma Press, 1976), p. 61;

Henry C. Morris, *Desert Gold and Total Prospecting* (Washington: privately published, 1955), pp. 26–27.

3. "North Idaho Miners," letter to Walla Walla *Washington Statesman*, February 10, 1863; "Mining at High Elevations," pp. 177, 179, 182, 184. Separation of domestic functions in mining camp business would seem to have reached new refinement in Grass Valley, California, where an "Occidental Shaving Saloon" was advertised. See Edwin F. Bean, comp., *Bean's History and Directory of Nevada County, California* (Nevada City: Daily Gazette Book and Job Office, 1867), p. 303.

4. Lester A. Hubbard, *Ballads and Songs from Utah* (Salt Lake City: University of Utah Press, 1961), p. 435. By contrast, the food at the Tomboy mine was lauded—"very well furnished table and plenty of good food"—albeit by a company man. (Hubbard, *Ballads and Songs*, p. 177.)

5. *See* Joseph R. Conlin, "Old Boy Did You Get Enough Pie?: A Social History of Food in the Logging Camps," *Forest History* (October 1979).

6. See Sally Springmeyer Zanjani and Guy Louis Rocha, "A Heart for Any Fate: Vincent St. John in Goldfield," *Nevada Historical Society Quarterly* (Summer 1984); Earl Bruce White, "Might is Right: Unionism and Goldfield, Nevada, 1904–1908," *Journal of the West* (July 1977); Guy Louis Rocha, "Radical Labor Struggles in the Tonopah-Goldfield Mining District, 1901–1922," *Nevada Historical Society Quarterly* (Spring 1977); Joseph R. Conlin, "Goldfield High-Grade," *American West* (May–June 1983).

For examples of precious metal mines keeping company cookhouses, *see* Ralph Mann, *After the Gold Rush: Society in Grass Valley and Nevada City, California, 1849–1870* (Palo Alto: Stanford University Press, 1982), p. 30; and J. Ross Browne, *Report of J. Ross Browne on the Mineral Resources of the States and Territories West of the Rocky Mountains* (San Francisco: H. H. Bancroft and Company, 1868). In Clarksdale, Arizona, where Jerome's copper ores were smelted, the mining companies operated cookhouses. In Jerome, miners working for the same employers provided their own meals. (Interview with Russell Wahmann, May 16, 1982.)

7. *Report of J. Ross Browne*; Emmett Arnold, *Gold Camp Drifter, 1906–1910* (Reno: University of Nevada Press, 1973), p. 47; M. M. Mathews, *Ten Years in Nevada: or, Life on the Pacific Coast* (Buffalo, N.Y.: Baker, Jones, and Co., 1880), p. 173; *Owyhee Avalanche*, August 25, 1865, September 29, 1866; Young, *Black Powder*, p. 58; Eliot Lord, *Comstock Mining and Miners* (Washington: Government Printing Office, 1883), pp. 200–1; Violet Boyce, *Upstairs to a Mine* (Logan: Utah State University Press, 1976), p. 54.

8. Robert E. Ericson, "Touring Entertainment in Nevada during the Peak Years of the Mining Boom, 1876–1878" (Ph.D. diss., University of Nevada, 1970), p. 34; Menus, HEH Library; Mathews, *Ten Years*, p. 276; Lord, *Comstock Mining*, p. 312; Charles H. Shinn, *The Story of the Mine, As Illustrated by the Great Comstock Lode of Nevada* (New York: Appleton, 1896; reprint, Reno: University of Nevada Press), p. 239.

9. Joe Chisholm, *Brewery Gulch: Frontier Days of Old Arizona* (San Antonio: Naylor, 1949), p. 131.

10. A. L. Rowse, *The Cornish in America* (New York: Macmillan, 1969), p. 393; Chisholm, *Brewery Gulch*, p. 131.

11. Mathews, *Ten Years*, p. 144.

12. Dan De Quille [William Wright], *The Big Bonanza* (New York: Alfred A. Knopf, 1947), pp. 269–70; William S. Greever, *The Bonanza West: The Story of the Western Mining Rushes, 1848–1900* (Norman: University of Oklahoma Press, 1963), p. 254.

13. Elliott West, *The Saloon on the Rocky Mountain Mining Frontier* (Lincoln: University of Nebraska Press, 1979), p. xv.

14. West, *Saloon*, pp. 40–41; Frank Waters, *The Earp Brothers of Tombstone* (New York: 1960), pp. 94–95; John C. Hancock, "Reminiscences," typescript, 1933, p. 24, Hancock Collection, AHS.

15. West, *Saloon*, pp. 30, 55; Howard Clifford, *The Skagway Story* (Anchorage: Alaska Northwest Publishing Company, 1975), p. 67; Works Progress Administration Writer's Project, *Copper Camp: Stories of the World's Greatest Mining Town, Butte, Montana* (Montana State Department of Agriculture, Labor, and Industry, 1943), p. 250.

16. West, *Saloon*, 55; Photograph file, Montana Historical Society; Bean, *Bean's History*, pp. ii, 285, passim; Andrew Smith Church, "Reminiscence," vol. 4, p. 67, SCP Library; Alvina N. Potter, *The Many Lives of the Lynx: A Century of Mining on Lynx Creek between 1863 and 1963* (Prescott: privately published, 1964), pp. 138–39.

17. Greever, *Bonanza*, p. 138; *Copper Camp*, pp. 249–50.

18. Greever, *Bonanza*, p. 138; Snow to Charles E. Fitz, August 30, 1854, in Horace Snow, *Dear Charlie Letters: Recording the Everyday Life of a Young 1854 Gold Miner* (Fresno: Mariposa County Historical Society, 1979), p. 49.

19. *Complete Business Directory*, Las Vegas, New Mexico, UNM Library.

20. Julia G. Costello, "Gold Rush Archaeology: Excavating the Mother Lode," *Archaeology* 34 (March/April 1981), p. 18ff. I am also grateful to Julia G. Costello for allowing me to see her unpublished paper, "Material Culture of the Mother Lode"; J. D. Borthwick, *Three Years in California* (Oakland: Biobooks, 1948), p. 103; Ragsdale, *Terlingua*, p. 161; Carl Meyer, *Nach dem Sacramento*, in John W. Caughey, *The California Gold Rush* (Berkeley: University of California Press, 1975), pp. 207–8.

21. Bean, *Bean's History*, p. 285; Greever, *Bonanza*, p. 59; Mary G. Paquette, "Charles Meyssan—A Founder of French Camp," *CHISPA* (Quarterly of the Tuolumne County, California, Historical Society); Mary G. Paquette, *Lest We Forget: A History of the French in Kern County* (Bakersfield, Calif.: Kern County Historical Society, 1978) p. 101; Joseph Stipanovich, "South Slav Settlements in Utah, 1890–1935," *Utah Historical Quarterly* 43 (Spring 1975), pp. 157–58; Boyce, *Upstairs to a Mine*, pp. 102–4, 113; Young, *Black Powder*, p. 60.

22. Chisholm, *Brewery Gulch,* p. 119.

23. Lynn I. Perrigo, "The Cornish Miners of Early Gilpin County," *Colorado Magazine* 14 (May 1937), p. 95; Young, *Black Powder,* p. 7; *Copper Camp,* pp. 244–45.

24. Lansford W. Hastings, *The Emigrant Guide to California and Oregon* (1845, reprint, Princeton, N.J.: Princeton University Press, 1932), p. 125.

25. Lee Shippey, *It's an Old California Custom* (New York: Vanguard, 1948), p. 104.

26. Ana Bégué de Packman, *Early California Hospitality: The Cookery and Customs of Spanish California, with Authentic Recipes and Menus of the Period* (Glendale, Calif.: Arthur H. Clark Co., 1938), p. 25, passim; Amelia Clappe, *The Shirley Letters from California Mines in 1851–1852* (San Francisco: Thomas C. Russell, 1922), September 4, 1852, p. 291; Grace S. Dawson, "Dining with the Dons," *California History Nugget* 6 (March 1939), p. 187.

27. I have found numerous examples of customers with Hispanic names ordering "Mexican" foodstuffs in the records of grocers like Andrew Brown, whose store was in Kern County, but none in perhaps a dozen grocers' ledgers from stores in central and northern California, Virginia City, and Colorado. There, the orders of men with Hispanic names were virtually identical to those of the Caucasians (records in HEH Library).

28. Caughey, *Gold Rush,* p. 130; Daphne Overstreet, *Arizona Territory Cookbook 1864–1912* (Globe: Pineria Press, 1975), p. 29; Albert Lyman, diary, October 30, 1850, HEH Library; H. C. Bailey, "Reminiscence," typescript, p. 42, HHB Library.

29. Bailey, "Reminiscences," p. 42.

30. J. D. Borthwick, *Three Years in California* (London: 1857), pp. 64–65; Vardis Fisher and Opal Laurel Holmes, *Gold Rushes and Mining Camps of the Early American West* (Caldwell, Idaho: Caxton Printers, 1968), p. 138.

31. An excellent recent overview of the Chinese role in western mining is Randall E. Rohe, "After the Gold Rush: Chinese Mining in the Far West, 1850–1890," *Montana: The Magazine of Western History* (Autumn 1982), pp. 2–19; Potter, *Many Lives,* p. 137; Huie Kin, *Reminiscences* (Peiping: San Yu Press, 1932), p. 28; *Wood River News Miner,* March 24, 1883; Fern Cable Trull, "The History of the Chinese in Idaho from 1864 to 1910" (Master's thesis, University of Oregon, 1946), pp. 29, 51, 53.

32. I. Jones, "Cathay of the Coast," *American Mercury* (1927), p. 46; Kin, *Reminiscences,* pp. 28–29.

33. Mathews, *Ten Years,* p. 171; J. W. Clampitt, *Echoes from the Rocky Mountains* (Chicago: 1890), p. 146; Will H. Robertson, *The Story of Arizona* (Phoenix: Berryhill, 1919), p. 397; James W. Byrkit, *Forging the Copper Collar,* p. 21.

34. Russell Wahmann, interview with the author, Jerome, Arizona, May 16, 1982; Potter, *Many Lives,* p. 53; Helen Evans Brown et al., *The Virginia City Cook*

Book, (Los Angeles: Ward Ritchie Press, 1953), p. 56; Patricia K. Ourada, "The Chinese in Colorado," *Colorado Magazine* 29 (October 1952), pp. 280–81.

35. Mark Twain, *Roughing It,* II, p. 24; Church, "Reminiscence," vol. 4, p. 70, SCP Library; Trull, "Chinese in Idaho," pp. 30, 56, 60; Young, *Black Powder,* p. 45; Alice Curnow, "The Journey With Tom," typescript, p. 29, Small Collections, AHS; Sister M. Alfreda Elsensohn, *Idaho Chinese Lore* (Cottonwood: Idaho Corporation of Benedictine Sisters, 1971), p. 110.

36. Church, "Reminiscences," vol. 4, p. 44.

37. Jones, "Cathay of the Coast," p. 46; Jack Chen, *The Chinese of America* (New York: Harper and Row, 1980), p. 58.

38. Greever, *Bonanza,* pp. 37, 254; Chen, *Chinese,* p. 57; *Bishop's Directory,* pp. 587–88; Mathews, *Ten Years,* p. 165; Elsensohn, *Idaho Chinese,* pp. 105, 109; *New Mexico State and El Paso, Texas Business Directory* (Albuquerque: Gazetteer Publishing Company, 1915), pp. 645, 652.

39. Russell Wahmann, May 16, 1982; Jones, "Cathay of the Coast," p. 97; Chen, *Chinese,* p. 57.

40. Claire Jones, *The Chinese in America* (New York: Lerner, 1972), p. 36. James Beard, *American Cookery* (Boston: Little, Brown & Co., 1972), p. 5.

41. E. N. Anderson and Marja L. Anderson, "Modern China: South," in K. C. Chang, *Food in Chinese Culture: Anthropological and Historical Perspectives* (New Haven: Yale University Press, 1980), p. 356; Li Shu-Fan, *Hong Kong Surgeon* (New York: Dutton, 1964).

42. William Kelly, *A Stroll Through the Diggings of California* (London: Bonwit, 1852), p. 180.

43. Shaw quoted in Chen, *Chinese,* p. 57.

44. Albert D. Richardson, *Beyond the Mississippi* (Chicago: Eaton, 1869), p. 493.

45. In collaboration with Harvey Levenstein, the author is presently exploring the subject of Italian-American diet and foodways, in *Mangiar' Bene: Food, Foodways, Ethnicity and Assimilation Among Italian Immigrants to North America,* forthcoming 1986.

SOURCES

ARCHIVES   Research in manuscripts on such an amorphous topic as food and foodways is not a task that can be undertaken systematically. Entering an unfamiliar repository was in a way like climbing to the top of a desert butte in the Southwest and trying to decide where the gold was. Like the hapless tenderfoot, I depended on the almost always astonishing knowledge of librarians and archivists for their help in locating the treasure in their care. It was they who did what I surely could not have done on my own: determined through sheer force of memory which collections included material that bore on the subject of this book. Archives in which "I discovered" ore and the guides who led me to the sites of the strikes are, listed by state:

In California: Richard McGaugh of the California Parks Department and Bob Allen, Chief Ranger at the Shasta State Historical Park, and his "Greenthumb" assistant who guided me through the Litsch Papers, Mrs. Dorothy Holt; Grace E. Baker at the Society of California Pioneers in San Francisco; Richard H. Limbaugh and John Bloom of the Holt-Atherton Center for Western Studies in Stockton; John F. Burns, Chief of Archives in Sacramento: Konrad F. Schreier of the Los Angeles Natural History Museum; Kenneth J. Carpenter, Chairman of the Nutrition Department, University of California, Berkeley; Julia G. Kostello of the Archeology Department, University of California, Santa Barbara; David Beesley of the Anthropology Department, Sierra College, Rocklyn; and from county historical societies Cervera Ingraham of Placer County, Mary Etta Segerstrom and Mary Grace Paquette of Tuolumne County, and Thelma H. Hadley of Mariposa County. I am indebted to a student at California State University, Chico, Clayton B. Rice, who uncovered several interesting facts about the role of the Chinese in forming western eating customs. Finally, at those treasure troves of western history and pleasure domes of research, the Bancroft and Huntington Libraries: at the Bancroft, William M. Roberts and Marie Byrne; at the Huntington, Carey S. Bliss, Britta F. Mack, Virginia Renner, Mary L. Robertson, Virginia Rust, and Leona Schonfeld.

In Arizona: Russell Wahmann, curator of the Jerome Historical Society; Susan H. Abbey of the Sharlott Hall Historical Society in Prescott; Janet Michaelieu of the Central Arizona Historical Society, Phoenix; George A. Teague of the Western Archeological Center, Tucson; Lori Davisson and Lori Metzger of the Arizona Historical Society, also in Tucson; Cora Thorp of the Bisbee Council on the Arts and Humanities; Hollis N. Cook, Tombstone Courthouse State Historical Park; and that resident of California who is, of course, the soul of Tombstone, Carl Chafin.

In New Mexico: Orlando Romero of the Southwest Room at the New Mexico State Historical Society in Santa Fe; Donald R. Lavash of the State Archives; Marcia Muth Miller of the Museum of New Mexico; and in Albuquerque in the Special Collections Room at the University of New Mexico Library, Donald Farren and Jan Barnhart. Professor Darlis Miller of New Mexico State University kindly let me see her work on army supply problems in the Southwest before it was ready for publication.

In Nevada: Guy Louis Rocha, then Curator of Manuscripts at the Nevada Historical Society, now State Archivist, and Dorothy Paulsen of the Nevada State Museum in Carson. Professor of History Emeritus Russell R. Elliott shared personal experiences as well as his knowledge of sources.

In Idaho: at the State Historical Society in Boise, Merle W. Wells, Karin E. Ford, Jim Davis, and most of all, resourceful and indefatigable Judith Austin.

In Oregon: Kenneth W. Duckett of the University of Oregon's Special Collections; Gordon Manning of the Oregon Historical Socie-

230

ty; and Margaret N. Haines of the Southern Oregon Historical Society in Jacksonville.

In Colorado: Rachel Homer and Catherine F. Engel of the Colorado Historical Society; Eleanor M. Gehres of the Denver Public Library Western History Department; Rosemary Hetzler of the Pioneer Museum, Colorado Springs; and from the county historical societies, Deedee Decker of Ouray County, Beverly Rich of San Juan County, and Agnes Gates of Gilpin County.

From Wyoming, where my travels did not take me: Gene M. Gressley and Emmett D. Chisum of the Western History Research Center provided me with information and advice; likewise Paula West, Tim Cochrane, and Marion Huseas of the Wyoming State Archives.

In Montana: Robert M. Clark, Dave Walter, and Rebecca Kohl of the Montana Historical Society in Helena; Minnie Paugh of the Montana State University Library, Bozeman; and June Sampson of the Yellowstone County Western History Center.

In Canada: John Stewart of the Kamloops Museum, British Columbia, and Lynette Walton of the Glenbow Museum in Calgary both provided photographs and documents.

Finally, *in Alaska:* Phyllis DeMuth of the Alaska Historical Library in Juneau; John Grainger of Ketchikan; Allene Rohlf of the Trail of '98 Museum, and Ranger Yvonne Menard of the Klondike gold rush National Historical Park, both in Skagway; M. Dianne Brenner of the Anchorage Historical and Fine Arts Museum; and William Schneider of the Rasmuson Library, Fairbanks.

BOOKS, ARTICLES, DISSERTATIONS, THESES

Rather than duplicate the footnotes here, I have not listed those books, magazine and newspaper articles, and other sources that I have drawn on in the narrative only once or a few times. Readers interested in a specific subject will already have checked the notes. The following list of titles includes those books and shorter works that I repeatedly quoted and those that, while not in the footnotes, were useful to me throughout the project.

Allen, James B. *The Company Town in the American West.* Norman: University of Oklahoma Press, 1966.

Arnold, Emmett L. *Gold Camp Drifter, 1906–1910*. Reno: University of Nevada Press, 1973.

Balch, William Ralston, comp. *The Mines, Miners, and Mining Interests of the United States in 1882*. Philadelphia: Mining Industrial Publishing House, 1882.

Baldwin, Roger S., Jr. "Tarrying in Nicaragua: Pleasures and Perils of the California Trip in 1849." *Century,* October 1891.

Barth, Gunther. *Bitter Strength*. Cambridge: Harvard University Press, 1964.

Baur, John E. "The Health Factor in the Gold Rush." *Pacific Historical Review* (1949).

Bean, Edwin F., comp. *Bean's History and Directory of Nevada County, California*. Nevada City: Daily Gazette Book and Job Office, 1867.

Berton, Pierre. *The Klondike Fever*. New York: Knopf, 1958.

Bird, Isabella L. *A Lady's Life in the Rocky Mountains*. Norman: University of Oklahoma Press, 1960.

Bishop, D. M., comp. *Bishop's Directory of Virginia City, Gold Hill, Silver City, Carson City, and Reno*. San Francisco: B. C. Vandall, 1879.

Borthwick, J. D. *Three Years in California*. Oakland: Biobooks, 1948.

Boyce, Violet, and Mabel Harmer. *Upstairs to a Mine*. Logan: Utah State University Press, 1976.

Brown, Helen Evans et al. *The Virginia City Cook Book*. Los Angeles: Ward Ritchie Press, 1953.

Brown, Mrs. Hugh. *Lady in Boomtown: Mining and Manners on the Nevada Frontier*. Palo Alto, Calif.: American West, 1968.

Brown, Ronald C. *Hard-Rock Miners: The Intermountain West 1860–1920*. College Station, Tex.: Texas A & M University Press, 1979.

Buffum, Edward Gould. *Six Months in the Gold Mines*. Philadelphia: Lea and Blanchard, 1850.

Carpenter, Kenneth J. *A History of Scurvy and Vitamin C*. New York: Cambridge University Press, 1986.

Cather, Helen C. "The History of San Francisco Chinatown." Master's thesis, University of California, Berkeley, 1932.

Caughey, John W., ed. *Rushing for Gold.* Berkeley: University of California Press, 1949.

___. *Gold is the Cornerstone.* Berkeley: University of California Press, 1975.

Chen, Jack. *The Chinese in America.* New York: Harper and Row, 1980.

Child, Andrew. *Overland Route to California: Description of the Route, . . . 1852.* Reprint. Los Angeles: N. A. Kovach, 1946.

Chinn, Thomas W., ed. *A History of the Chinese in California.* San Francisco: Chinese Historical Society of America, 1969.

Chisholm, Joe. *Brewery Gulch: Frontier Days of Old Arizona.* San Antonio: Naylor, 1949.

Clappe, Louise Amelia Knapp Smith. *The Shirley Letters from California Mines in 1851–1852.* San Francisco: Thomas C. Russell, 1922.

Complete Business Directory of New Mexico and Gazetteer for the Territory for 1882. Santa Fe: New Mexican Printing and Publishing Company, 1882.

Cookbook of the Women's Art and Industrial Association of Nevada. Carson City: Appeal Steam Print, 1887.

Currie, B. W. "Housekeeping in Alkali Land." *Good Housekeeping,* August 1909.

Dallas, Sandra. *Yesterday's Denver.* Miami: E. A. Seamann Publishing, Inc., 1974.

Dana, Julian. *The Sacramento: River of Gold.* New York: Farrar and Rinehart, 1939.

Dane, George Ezra. *Ghost Town.* New York: Alfred A. Knopf, 1941.

De Quille, Dan [William Wright]. *The Big Bonanza.* New York: Alfred A. Knopf, 1947.

Delano, Alonzo. *Life on the Plains and Among the Diggings.* 1854. Reprint. Ann Arbor, Mich.: University Microfilms, 1966.

DeVoe, Thomas F. *The Market Assistant.* New York: Hurd and Houghton, 1867.

Downie, William. *Hunting for Gold: Reminiscences of Personal Experience and Research in the Early Days of the Pacific Coast*. San Francisco: California Publishing Company, 1893.

Ellis, Anne. *The Life of an Ordinary Woman*. 1929. Reprint. Lincoln: University of Nebraska Press, 1980.

Elsensohn, Sister M. Alfreda. *Idaho Chinese Lore*. Cottonwood, Idaho: Idaho Corporation of Benedictine Sisters, 1971.

Ericson, Robert E. "Touring Entertainment in Nevada During the Peak Years of the Mining Boom, 1876–1878." Ph.D. diss., University of Nevada, 1970.

Erdoes, Richard. *Saloons of the Old West*. New York: Alfred A. Knopf, 1979.

Faragher, John Mack. *Women and Men on the Overland Trail*. New Haven, Conn.: Yale University Press, 1979.

Farb, Peter and George Armelagos. *Consuming Passions: The Anthropology of Eating*. Boston: Houghton Mifflin, 1980.

Fisher, Vardis, and Opal Laurel Holmes. *Gold Rushes and Mining Camps of the Early American West*. Caldwell, Idaho: Caxton Printers, 1968.

Frémont, John C. *Report of the Exploring Expedition to the Rocky Mountains in the Year 1842 and to Oregon and North California in the Years 1843–44*. Washington: Gates and Seaton, 1845.

Greever, William S. *The Bonanza West: The Story of the Western Mining Rushes 1848–1900*. Norman: University of Oklahoma Press, 1963.

Groh, George W. *Gold Fever*. New York: William Morrow, 1966.

Gudde, Edwin G. *California Gold Camps: A Geographical and Historical Dictionary*. Berkeley: University of California Press, 1975.

Harris, Henry. *California's Medical Story*. San Francisco: J. W. Stacey, 1932.

Hess, Alfred F. *Scurvy Past and Present*. Philadelphia: Lippincott, 1920.

234

Historical Descriptive and Commercial Directory of Owyhee County, Idaho. Silver City: Press of the Owyhee Avalanche, 1898.

Holliday, J. S. *The World Rushed In: The California Gold Rush Experience*. New York: Simon and Schuster, 1981.

Hooker, Richard J. *A History of Food and Drink in America*. Indianapolis: Bobbs-Merrill, 1981.

Howe, Octavius Thorndike. *Argonauts of '49: History and Adventures of the Emigrant Companies from Massachusetts, 1849–1850*. Cambridge: Harvard University Press, 1923.

Hunt, William R. *North of 53*. New York: Macmillan, 1974.

Jackson, W. Turrentine. *Treasure Hill: Portrait of a Silver Mining Camp*. Tucson: University of Arizona Press, 1963.

Kinnersley, Thomas H. "Virginia, Nevada, 1859–1890: A Study of Police, Water, and Fire Problems." Ph.D. diss., University of California, Los Angeles, 1974.

Kung, S. W. *The Chinese in American Life*. Seattle: University of Washington Press, 1962.

Lewis, Marvin, ed. *The Mining Frontier: Contemporary Accounts from the American West in the Nineteenth Century*. Norman: University of Oklahoma Press, 1967.

Lewis, Oscar. *Sea Routes to the Gold Fields: The Migration By Water to California in 1849–1852*. New York: Alfred A. Knopf, 1949.

Lingenfelter, Richard E. *The Hard Rock Miners: A History of the Mining Labor Movement in the American West, 1863–1893*. Berkeley: University of California Press, 1974.

Lord, Eliot. *Comstock Mining and Miners*. Washington: Government Printing Office, 1883.

Madsen, Brigham D. *Gold Rush Sojourners in Great Salt Lake City, 1849 and 1850*. Salt Lake City: University of Utah Press, 1983.

Magnuson, Richard G. *Coeur D'Alene Diary: The First Ten Years of Hardrock Mining in North Idaho*. Portland, Ore.: Metropolitan Press, 1960.

Mann, Ralph. *After the Gold Rush: Society in Grass Valley and Nevada City, California, 1849–1870.* Palo Alto, Calif.: Stanford University Press, 1982.

Margo, Joan. "The Food Supply Problem of the California Gold Miners, 1848–1855." Master's thesis, University of California, n.d.

Marryat, Francis Samuel. *Mountains and Molehills; or, Recollections of a Burnt Journal.* (London: 1855) Palo Alto, Calif.: Stanford University Press, 1952.

Martin, Douglas. *Tombstone's Epitaph.* Albuquerque: University of New Mexico Press, 1951.

Mathews, M. M. *Ten Years in Nevada: or, Life on the Pacific Coast.* Buffalo, N.Y.: Baker, Jones, & Co., 1880.

McIntosh, Clarence. "The Chico and Red Bluff Route: Stage Lines From Southern Idaho to the Sacramento Valley, 1865–1867." *Idaho Yesterdays* 6 (Fall 1962).

Mattes, Merrill J. *The Great Platte River Road.* Lincoln: Nebraska State Historical Society, 1969.

Morris, Henry C. *Desert Gold and Total Prospecting.* Washington: privately published, 1955.

Myres, Sandra L., ed. *Ho for California!: Women's Overland Diaries from the Huntington Library.* San Marino, Calif.: Huntington Library, 1980.

Noel, Thomas J. *The City and the Saloon, Denver 1858–1916.* Lincoln: University of Nebraska Press, 1982.

Ogilvie, William. *The Klondike Official Guide.* Buffalo, N.Y.: Matthews-Northrup Co., 1898.

Overstreet, Daphne. *Arizona Territory Cookbook 1864–1912.* Globe: Pineria Press, 1975.

Packman, Ana Bégué de. *Early California Hospitality: the Cookery Customs of Spanish California, with Authentic Recipes and Menus of the Period.* Glendale, Calif.: Arthur H. Clark, 1938.

Paul, Rodman. *California Gold: The Beginning of Mining in the Far West.* Lincoln: University of Nebraska Press, 1947.

Pickard, Madge E., and R. Carlyle Buley. *The Midwest Pioneer: His Ills, Cures, and Doctors.* New York: Henry Schuman, 1946.

Ping, Chen. *Chinese Labor in California.* Madison: University of Wisconsin Press, 1966.

Placer Mining: A Handbook for Klondike and Other Miners and Prospectors. Scranton, Pa.: Engineer Co., 1897.

Potter, Alvina N. *The Many Lives of the Lynx: A Century of Mining on Lynx Creek between 1863 and 1963.* Prescott, Ariz.: privately published, 1964.

Reps, John W. *Cities of the American West: A History of Frontier Urban Planning.* Princeton, N.J.: Princeton University Press, 1979.

Richey, Don. *Forty Miles a Day on Beans and Hay.* Norman: University of Oklahoma Press, 1977.

Rogers, Franklin R. *The Pattern for Mark Twain's Roughing It: Letter from Nevada by Samuel and Orion Clemens.* Berkeley: University of California Press, 1961.

Rohe, Randall E. "After the Gold Rush: Chinese Mining in the West, 1850–1890." *Montana, The Magazine of History* (August 1982).

Root, Waverley, and Richard de Rochemont. *Eating in America: A History.* New York: William Morrow, 1976.

Schneider, Gretchen Adel. "Pigeon Wings and Polkas: The Dance of the California Miners." *Dance Perspectives* 39 (Winter 1969).

Shinn, Charles H. *Mining Camps: A Study in American Frontier Government.* New York: Alfred A. Knopf, 1948.

___. *The Story of the Mine, As Illustrated by the Great Comstock Lode of Nevada.* New York: Appleton, 1896. Reprint, Reno: University of Nevada Press, 1979.

Shippey, Lee. *It's an Old California Custom.* New York: Vanguard Press, 1948.

Smith, Duane A. " 'At This High Altitude One Gets Weary Very Soon': James D. Hague and the Tomboy Mine." *Huntington Library Quarterly* 46 (Summer 1981).

___. *Rocky Mountain Mining Camps: The Urban Frontier.* Bloomington: Indiana University Press, 1967.

Soule, Frank, John H. Gihon, and James Nisbet. *The Annals of San Francisco*. New York: Appleton, 1855.

Strahorn, Robert E. *The Resources and Attractions of Idaho Territory: Facts Regarding Climate, Soil, Minerals, Agricultural and Grazing Lands, Forests, Scenery, Game and Fish, and Reliable Information on other Topics Applicable to the Wants of the Homeseeker, Capitalist and Tourist*. Boise: Idaho Legislature, 1881.

Sung, B. L. *Mountain of Gold*. New York: Macmillan, 1967.

Taylor, Bayard. *Eldorado; or, Adventures in the Path of Empire*. New York: Alfred A. Knopf, 1949.

Taylor, William. *California Life Illustrated*. New York: Carlton and Porter, 1861.

Teeter, Charles Nelson. "Four Years of My Life or Adventures in the Far West." Typescript, Idaho State Historical Society Library.

Trull, Fern Cable. "The History of the Chinese People in Idaho from 1864 to 1910." Master's thesis, University of Oregon, 1946.

Ubbelhode, Carl, Maxine Benson, and Duane A. Smith. *A Colorado History*. Boulder: University of Colorado Press, 1972.

Van Orman, Richard A. *A Room for the Night: Hotels of the Old West*. Bloomington: Indiana University Press, 1966.

Villard, Henry. *The Past and Present of the Pike's Peak Gold Regions*. 1860. Reprint. New York: Da Capo Press, 1972.

Waldorf, John Taylor. *A Kid on the Comstock*. Berkeley, Calif.: Friends of the Bancroft Library, 1968.

Watkins, T. H. *Gold and Silver in the West*. New York: Bonanza Books, 1971.

Wells, Merle W. "Rush to Idaho." *Idaho Historical Bulletin 19*. Boise: State Historical Society of Idaho, 1963.

West, Elliott. *The Saloon on the Rocky Mountain Mining Frontier*. Lincoln: University of Nebraska Press, 1979.

White, Helen McCann, ed. *Ho! For the Gold Fields: Northern Overland Wagon Trains of the 1860s*. St. Paul: Minnesota Historical Society, 1966.

Willison, George. *Here They Dug the Gold*. New York: Reynal and Hitchcock, 1946.

Windham, Joey S. "Grand Encampment Mining District: A Case Study of a Typical Western Frontier Mining District." Ph.D. diss., Ball State University, 1981.

Williams, Stephen. "The Chinese in the California Mines." Master's thesis, Stanford University, 1930.

Woods, Daniel B. *Sixteen Months at the Gold Diggings*. New York: Harper and Brothers, 1851.

Writer's Program, Works Progress Administration. *Copper Camp: Stories of the World's Greatest Mining Town, Butte Montana*. New York: State Department of Agriculture, Labor, and Industry, 1943.

Wyman, Mark. *Hard Rock Epic: Western Miners and the Industrial Revolution*. Berkeley: University of California Press, 1979.

Young, Otis E. *Black Powder and Hard Steel: Miners and Machines on the Old Western Frontier*. Norman: University of Oklahoma Press, 1976.

INDEX

California Hotel, Panama City, 57
Callao, Chile, 84
Campbell, Thomas E., 152
Camper, Henry Wax, 36
Can-Can Restaurant, Bisbee, 146, 148
Can-Can Restaurant, Tombstone, 146, 176, 189
Canton (vessel), 65
Cape Ann Pioneers, 60
Capioma, Kansas Terr., 24
Capitol (vessel), 66
Capitol Chop House, Reno, 119
Carlyle, Thomas, 21
Carpenter, Helen, overland journey account, 17, 32, 35, 37, 44, 45, 47–48
Carson, William, 101
Carson Valley, Nev., 50, 103
Cary House, Placerville, 140, 192
Cashman, Nellie, 156, 159
Castle Rock, Colo., 158
Caswell, Ben, 132
Caughey, John W., 4, 162, 185
Ceavich, Louis, 146, 148
Central America, 54, 81, 82
Central City, Colo., 109, 143, 144
Chagres, Panama, 54, 56
Charpiot's, Denver, 144
Charlotte (brig), 87–88
Chenery (Panama traveler), 56
Chever, Edward E., 61
Chile, 58, 92
Chilkoot Pass, 88
China, 92
Chinese: influence on foods and cookery, 182, 187–93; in western gold rush, 186–87, 194
Chisholm, Joe, 134, 173
Cholera, 37, 54, 76
Church, Andrew Smith, 115, 140, 190
Citizens' Protective League, Bisbee, 152
City Bakery, Denver, 162
Civilian (schooner), 59
Clampitt, John, 187
Clarence House, Butte, 145
Clarendon Hotel, Leadville, 150
Cleveland, Charles Dexter, 50, 77
Clipper Restaurant, Silver City, Ida., 144
Clyman, James, 45

Cochituate Mining Company, 60
Coeur d'Alene, Ida., 150
Coffee, Alvin, 92
Cogswell, James L., 113
Coloma, Calif., 91, 107, 138, 163; described in 1849, 167–68
Colorado, 144; food shortages at mines, 99–100, 102
Colorado tick fever, 73
Colton, Walter, 3–4
Columbia, Calif., 96
Columbia (vessel), 93
Columbus, Christopher, 72
Comstock Lode, 4, 99, 124, 132, 145; illnesses, 134; miners, 127, 149–50, 159–60; prices, 103, 109, 172; ratio of women, 155; restaurants, 150–52
Consolidated Virginia mine, 152
Cookery: American in 19th century, 17; ethnic, 180–82; French, 122–24, 134, 168, 180, 186; Mexican, 183–86; mining camps, 113, 115, 133–34, 153–55, 162–63; on overland trail, 41–42, 44–49; on shipboard, 61–62
Cooper, J. W., 25
Cooper, James Fenimore, 11
Copper Queen Hotel, Bisbee, 121, 146
Copper Queen Mining Company, 146
Costello, Julia G., 181
Council Bar, Butte, 178
Council Bluffs, Iowa, 22
Couts, Cave J., 49
Cowboys, 41
Crescent City (steamship), 56
Cripple Creek, Colo., 150, 158
Crumpton, Hezekiah, 49
Curaçao, 72
Curnow, Alice, 115, 120, 132–33

Dairy products, 33, 34, 50
Dead Horse Trail, 88
DeCosta, William, 83
Delano, Alonzo, 98
Delmar, Alexander, 134
Denver, Colo., 143–44
de Packman, Ana Bégué, 37
DeQuille, Dan (William Wright), 159, 174
de Rochemont, Richard, 9, 10, 15

Dick, Av, 190
Diet: American in mid-19th century, 6, 8–10, 197–98; American in mid-20th century, 137–38, 194–95; digestive ailments, 134–35; western loggers, 129, 133, 170–71; western miners, 108–9, 111–17, 133–34, 168. *See also* Scurvy
Dinkel, William, 91
Dolan, B. F., 133
Donner party, 25–26, 138
Dowdle Company, 26, 28
Downieville Restaurant, Virginia City, 142
Dupuy, George, 144, 195

Eating establishments, 159–62, 165, 169–70, 172, 181–82; average gold rush era menu, 112, 138, 140–42, 152–53; Chinese, 187, 189–90, 192–94; female proprietors of, 155–59, 173; Isthmus of Panama, 56–57; specialty menus, 118–22, 130, 132–33, 148
Edward Everett (vessel), 60, 61, 64, 83
Elder, William, 163
El Dorado Hotel, Placerville, 140
Elizabeth (ship), 64
Elmore County News, Ida., 106
Elvira (bark), 84
Enterprise Restaurant, Juneau, 162
Epitaph, Tombstone, 121
Eureka, Calif., 101
Eureka House, Panama City, 57
Evans, G. W., 73
Exchange Hotel, Albuquerque, 162

Fairbanks, Alaska, 157
Fairview, Nev., 169–70
Famine: in Europe, 9; in western mines, 98–102, 134
Faragher, John Mack, 41; evaluation of overland journey diet, 29–31, 74, 198; 19th-century American diet, 8
Farb, Peter, x, 11
Ferguson, Charles D., 34, 90, 91
Fisk, Andrew J., 156
Florence, Ida., 99, 100, 107, 109
Florence Hotel, Butte, 145, 169
Foreign Miner Tax of 1850, 186

243

INDEX